Anarchist by Design

Mark Seely

Anarchist by Design
Technology and Human Nature

Anarchist by Design: Technology and Human Nature
by Mark R. Seely

2013 OldDog Books

ISBN 978-0-9892337-1-2

Cover art: "Life Support," mixed media sculpture by Corey Crum

Photography by Corey Crum and Juan Carlos Rodriguez

OldDog

To Toby

CONTENTS

PROLOG

Seven or eight thousand years ago, early agriculturalists living in the fertile drainage valleys of the Tigris and Euphrates rivers were struggling with a climate crisis. The spring rains that they depended on to kick-start their crops were coming later and later every year. In some years they didn't come at all. Many folks were abandoning the farming lifestyle altogether, reclaiming their birthright as members of a nomadic foraging species, and moving to where antelope and nut trees and other sources of food were still prevalent and more predictable. Out of ingenuity or out of sheer desperation—or both—some of those who stayed behind began to reroute local runoff streams and to scratch channels into the clay to bring water from the river to quench their sunbaked fields.

It worked.

But the devil included something sinister in the bargain. The use of irrigation to coordinate, direct, and control the flow of water requires a corresponding ability to coordinate, direct, and control the flow of human labor power necessary to dig the ditches and man the floodgates. And a brand new technology was born, a kind of social technology that was inconceivable just a few centuries before: hierarchically organized systems of authority and power.

Human history since then has been a protracted tale of the proliferation, repurposing, innovative expansion, and brutal application of these technologies of social control.

WORKING ASSUMPTIONS

Derrick Jensen began his two volume ecological call to arms, *Endgame*, by listing twenty premises. His first premise is that civilization, especially industrial civilization, is not sustainable. Premise seven is that the longer we wait to do something about our situation, the worse things will be. In a direct way, what I have to say in this book is predicated on these two premises, with the important caveat that industrial civilization is merely a symptom; the real problem is the asymmetric distribution of power and the intentional shaping of social relations that underwrites all civilization, industrial or otherwise. In addition, I will be operating from a base of five working assumptions in the chapters that follow. I am calling them working assumptions rather than premises because, although they serve as the foundation for what I have to say, their function is essentially rhetorical: their primary purpose is to establish a framework for discussion. They are assumptions that seem reasonable to me and serve as a point of departure. Although I will be providing plenty of supportive evidence, my main objective does not depend critically on the degree to which they are accepted as unassailable truths.

Stating foundational assumptions explicitly at the beginning may be a particularly useful device when the issues to be addressed have a high potential to elicit incendiary defensive reactions. I am a firm believer in transparency (for reasons that will soon become obvious), and readers need to know up-front what they will be getting themselves into if they continue. Below is a briefly annotated list of my working assumptions. They are not listed in any particular order of importance. Readers are free to agree, disagree, or adopt any posture whatever with respect to each of them individually or collectively. In fact, it is an abiding concern for that very freedom that undergirds my motivation for writing this book.

Assumption 1: All creatures, humans included, are better off living in ways that are congruent with their evolved predispositions.

Assumption 2: There is a dramatic mismatch between our evolutionary preparation as a species and life in post-industrial civilization. Humans possess physical and psychological needs, emotional tendencies, and behavioral predilections that reflect our evolutionary past as social primates, and more proximally as hunter-gatherers. The lifestyles we are forced to adopt to accommodate the demands of the technological order of modern global civilization are so far removed from our evolutionary preparation that many of our authentic human needs are not being met, or are being met in increasingly deficient ways.

Assumption 3: Individual autonomy—the freedom to engage in self-regulation—is an authentic human need that is not being adequately met due to the mismatch between our evolved predilections for egalitarian society and the oppressive requirements of the technological order of modern civilization.

Assumption 4: The technological order of civilization is an artificial construction. As a mode of social organization, civilization does not reflect an emergent property of the human animal. It is an artifact of history, and not an inevitable manifestation of the cognitive or social development of the human species.

Assumption 5: The technological order of civilization includes technologies specifically directed at the manipulation and control of human behavior. Innovation within these systems has rendered civilization increasingly corrosive of individual freedom and autonomy.

In addition to listing these assumptions, I feel compelled to provide some initial hints about how I will be using them. If it is not obvious from the use of the term *anarchist* in the title, my primary purpose here is a subversive one. But the target of my subversion is not a person, a political party, or an ideology. The target is the technological order of civilization. Complex technology, and the artificial authority relations it entails, is at the root of all of our most pressing problems. It is important to note that I am not a Luddite—at least I am not fundamentally anti-technology. I am not motivated by fear of "technology out of control." Nor am I motivated by fear of the dangers of specific technologies (e.g., nuclear energy) or concern about the direction that specific kinds of technological development are taking (e.g., nanotechnology, genetic engineering). The dangers are real; as is our complete lack of control. But I am not here to heap scorn upon mass society or promote any anti-tech conspiracy theories. I am not anti-technology per se, I am anti-authority. Autonomy-annihilating distributions of artificial power and authority are my primary concern. It just so happens that technology is the medium through which authority operates. And our reflexive reactions tend only to make things worse: the reflexive response to any problem with technology is to create more technology, to sacrifice even more of our freedom to feed the machine. To have any chance of escape from the oppressive grip of the technological order, we have to first understand what technology really is and how it works—or at the very least understand that more of what is killing us is not a cure. And then, just maybe, we can start to direct our attention to Jensen's premise number seven, and get on with the business of dismantling civilization and rediscovering our humanity.

INTRODUCTION

A confession

Hello. My name is Mark, and I'm an anarchist.

I don't walk around carrying homemade explosive devices. I have never been arrested for destroying property or disturbing the peace. I don't have tattoos or body piercings or black leather jewelry or t-shirts emblazoned with profanity. My head is bald, but as a result of my age, gender, and ancestry, not as a political statement. I live in a peaceful working-class neighborhood, own my own home, grow vegetables in my back yard, and ride my bicycle to a respectable job. I have a wife, children, a grandchild, and two dogs. I am soft spoken, play the mandolin, and tend toward the obsessive-compulsive end of the spectrum when it comes to my ability to tolerate disorder and chaos. In fact, there is very little about me consistent with the media caricature of an anarchist as an unruly, nonconforming, violent, destructive, Molotov-cocktail-lobbing thug in a black ski mask.

Yet, I am most definitely an anarchist. I am an anarchist to the very core of my being. I don't just call myself an anarchist as a way of getting attention, generating debate, or sparking controversy, or as a way of expressing my disaffection with a system that has done me wrong. My anarchism is not an intellectual fashion statement or a manifestation of sour grapes. I did not *choose* to be an anarchist.

I am an anarchist because, just like you, I was born that way.

Anarchy means, literally, no-hierarchy. The hierarchy that is being negated in this case is that associated with social arrangements that impose a steeply asymmetric distribution of power and authority. Hierarchical systems of power and authority are technological creations, and, as with all technologies, they have a capricious historical genesis and development. In other words, they are artificial; they are not a natural part of our evolved human design. Anarchy—society comprised of organic and direct relations with others, unmediated by artificial systems of power—is the natural social condition for human beings, and has been so for more than 99% of our species' tenure. So, in some sense, I am an anarchist because I am human and value my humanity. But, perhaps more than that, I am an anarchist because I also value my autonomy. Anarchy is a social-political condition in which no one has legitimate power over anyone else. Anarchy is a social-political condition in which each person has maximum autonomy with respect to his or her goals, choices, decisions, and actions, and is unencumbered by requirements to serve the goals, choices, decisions, and actions of any other person or group of people. All other social-political conditions, historical or imagined, incorporate a reduction of personal autonomy as an essential feature of their operative design. The more closely our social-political conditions approximate anarchy, the greater our personal autonomy: we are free precisely to the extent to which we are not entangled in oppressive power relationships with other people and things.

I have much more to say about the antagonism between autonomy and artificially structured power relationships later on. For now, simply note that autonomy is a matter of degree, and that it is possible to increase or decrease personal autonomy by decreasing or increasing the degree of entanglement with oppressive power relationships, respectively. Also note, to anticipate a common misconception, an individual's personal autonomy is not an automatic function of his or her level within artificial power hierarchies. Although power can create the illusion of freedom, and those in positions of power often enjoy greater freedom of movement and greater access to physical comforts and other "privileges of rank," those at the top of an oppressive power structure are in most cases just as bound by the structure as are those at the bottom.

Notice also that I refer to anarchy as the *natural* human social condition. Humans, as social primates, are predisposed to accommodate shifting patterns of social status in the form of relations of dominance and submission, and to that extent our species is no stranger to the presence of power hierarchies in the social world. But the social dominance relations that form naturally among chimpanzees, or bonobos, or humans living in small foraging bands, have no connection whatever to the coercively structured and violently enforced power hierarchies foisted on you and me. The former are a product of primate group dynamics, based on naturally occurring individual differences in talent, temperament, and physicality, and, as we will see a bit later, usually have little or no sustainable impact on the autonomy of individual group members. The latter are technologies of behavior control that severely limit the expression of individuality and seek to diminish or eliminate voluntary forms of self-regulation.

But wait, don't we need hierarchy? Isn't a vertical configuration of power necessary for human society to function? According to popular myth, the uneven distribution of power in society is necessary to prevent chaos and the concomitant suffering that would result if people were left to their own devices. Without civil order provided by the hierarchical structuring of power within society, life would be, as Hobbes proclaimed, a war of all against all. People simply can't be trusted, and without powerful controlling systems of authority—involving other people armed with lethal weapons and sanctioned to kill or incarcerate anyone who gets out of line—there would be nothing to prevent people from engaging in wanton rape and theft and murder. I will be evaluating this myth in terms of its underlying Hobbesian premise at later points in our discussion. But for now, consider Crispin Sartwell's response, in his book *Against the State*.[1] Sartwell notes that those who offer the people-can't-be-trusted line of justification for oppressive systems of authority and control are unlikely to claim that *they themselves* would run out and commit wanton rape and theft and murder if these systems were suddenly removed. That is, oppressive systems of control are invariably necessary to keep *other* people in line. No one ever claims that a massive corpus of laws and policies, an equally massive system of prisons and internment camps, and groups of highly trained and lethally armed "authorities" sanctioned to use deadly force are necessary to keep his or her own personal rapaciousness, covetousness, or homicidal tendencies in check. In addition, Sartwell points out that the people who operate systems of authority designed ostensibly to keep our natural human tendencies from wreaking havoc on the world are humans themselves; and he wonders what it is that prevents the people who staff these systems—the ones with the weapons and the license to express their will upon others through the use of overwhelming force—from acting on their own self-serving drives for rape, theft, and murder. The answer, according to any given day's headlines, appears to be nothing whatsoever. The fact that wanton rape and theft and murder occur even in the presence of powerful and penetrating systems of authority is reflexively interpreted as meaning that the systems aren't powerful or penetrating enough. There is a much more reasonable alternative interpretation, however: perhaps the proliferation of corruption, crime, and paranoia of "evil others" is a bi-product of the operation of these powerful and penetrating systems of authority themselves, with their power-addictive and autonomy-destroying effects. If this alternative interpretation has even partial validity, then expanding and intensifying systems of power and authority is not the appropriate response. Increasing the dosage of the poison that is (quite literally) killing us is not a good approach to treatment.

In addition to the Hobbesian justification, according to popular myth the regimentation of human action through division of labor and coordinated by systems of power and authority allows for the achievement of goals and accomplishments that could scarcely even be conceived without such regimentation. A civilization that is capable of building the Great Pyramid or of sending someone to the moon and back requires a fine-grained division of labor and an extensively asymmetric distribution of power and authority. What popular myth leaves out is just whose goals are being achieved and what exactly it is that is being accomplished in the process: who benefits and who suffers, and to what end. The spectacle of the moon landing, for instance, was launched from the backs of an uncountable number

of individual people who were forced to give their lives over to gru-
eling labor in mines and factories, and made possible only by divert-
ing money and resources away from social services and programs
that could actually have had a beneficial impact on people's lives. It
made for very potent cold war propaganda, and served as a much
needed distraction from public challenges to the ongoing slaughter of
innocent Vietnamese at the time. But the number of people who ben-
efited directly—"benefit" being defined loosely as a demonstrable
improvement of personal life conditions—was infinitesimal, and the
degree of benefit even for this elite minority was negligible when
couched in terms of the actual monetary cost of the venture (not to
mention the role that it played in the proliferation of nuclear bombs
and the technology for their delivery). According to popular myth, it
is an abstract "us" who reaps the benefits of the vertical distribution
of power and authority, a reified "we" whose goals are being serviced by the imposition of hierarchy. But despite the production of
larger-than-life spectacles and gleaming monuments, civilization is
not the kind of thing that can formulate purposes and pursue goals,
and the goals of those working the quarries and hauling the stones
are invariably underrepresented.

Anarchism, like its close cousin in the spiritual world, atheism, is
frequently (mis)taken as a purely negative or contrarian position. An
atheist is someone who is *against* the notion of god, anti-god. Similarly, an anarchist is against the established system, anti-
establishment. Both the anarchist and the atheist are often defined
entirely in terms of their opposition: the thing to be negated serves as
a point of reference and its negation is the defining feature of their
position. To be anti-god, the possibility—or at least the idea of the
possibility—of the existence of god has to be there first. To be anti-
system, some kind of system has first to exist as a point of contention. However, the fact that we have a specific label suggests that
there might be something more to anarchism (and atheism) than simple denial or the refusal to endorse a particular perspective. Notice
that we haven't found it necessary to come up with specific terms to
designate people who refuse to believe in invisible dragons or who

are virulently against the use of yellow as a color for automobile up-holstery.

This view of anarchism in the negative, as a contrarian position, is at once a simplification and an unnecessary complication. It has something in common with the popular practice of advertising the ingredients that are *not* included in a commercial food product (e.g., gluten free) in bold on the package label while presenting the actual contents in microscopic code on the bottom of the box. Producers of processed food products often don't want consumers to look too closely at the actual ingredients. In a similar vein, promoters of es-tablished power arrangements don't want their subordinates to ques-tion the legitimacy of those arrangements. Reducing anarchism to simple "rejection of the system" prevents its consideration as a po-tentially viable alternative. Historical thinkers, activists, and political figures who adopted (or were later saddled with) the anarchist label, were not simply (negatively) against the existing social or economic structure, they were (positively) in favor of a different kind of struc-ture, one in which power was distributed more equitably and access to resources was shared more collectively, for example. Far from being a simple negation of contemporary conditions, their political anarchism was a positive statement of more desirable conditions; the views they expressed were attempts at establishing concrete frame-works for social improvement. Likewise, the anti-authoritarianism expressed in this book is meant not simply as a negation of the legit-imacy of authority and its role in our lives. It reflects an attempt to provide a direction, a trajectory, perhaps even a concrete framework for positive change in our individual and collective circumstances.

Anarchism is a loaded term, with a checkered history and an am-biguous (one might even say chaotic) present. To avoid both the con-trarian entailments and the historical baggage associated with the word anarchism, I could choose another term for the perspective be-ing offered here, perhaps. "Anti-authoritarian" is a bit too general. Maybe "radical-egalitarianism," or "radical-individualism." But these are both misleading. The first might also apply to extremely oppressive systems in which the system ensures that oppression is equally dispersed among all participants (this may in fact be where mass technology is ultimately taking us, as we will explore later). My primary concern is with the complete elimination of artificial systems of control, not merely the equitable distribution of power. The second, although probably closer to the mark, conveys a libertarian, or even Hobbesian, sense of "everyone for themselves" that risks missing the point entirely. The absence of artificial hierarchies of authority does not preclude the existence of interpersonal interdependency and the cultivation of mutually beneficial cooperative— perhaps even hierarchical—*voluntary* relationships with others. The view of anarchism that provides the foundation for what follows takes anarchy in something closer to its etymological sense—the lack of artificial hierarchies of authority—as the natural condition of our species, as a necessary condition for autonomy and the free expression of individuality, and as a decidedly positive alternative to the smothering and lethal oppression of our current situation.

A return to the primitive

The notion that civilization adds something detrimental to the human condition and that we would benefit from a return to social circumstances more consonant with those of the distant past appears again and again in the chapters that follow. This, and the fact that I ground much of my discussion in terms of what we know about human evolution and our evolution-derived social and psychological tendencies for hunter-gatherer lifestyles, qualifies the anarchism I promote here as a variation of a perspective that has been given the unwieldy title, *anarcho-primitivism*. Some varieties of anarcho-primitivism focus more on primitivism, and emphasize the negative impact of industrial technology and the positive benefits of a return to a technological state better aligned with our evolutionary roots. Some focus more on anarchism and the need to extract ourselves from lethally oppressive systems of power and control that actively prevent the free expression of our innate human nature. Some focus on the natural world and the need to establish ecologically-sensitive lifestyles and harmonious relationships with the biosphere (a.k.a.

green anarchism). Although I fully embrace the anarcho-primitivist label, and I have a strong affinity toward all three of the anarcho-primitivist foci listed above, I tend to see the two-term compound as redundant. Anarchism, at its core, is a rejection of the legitimacy of hierarchical power relationships. Primitivism, at its core, is the desire for physical and social conditions more conducive to an authentic human existence. These two things are not merely compatible, they are, at least to some degree, mutually dependent. A lifestyle embedded in industrial mass technology is not possible without coercive systems of control. An authentic human existence is not possible within the mechanical schematic of hierarchically organized authority. Anarchy implies a return to the primitive and vice versa. Thus, if forced to condense my perspective down to a single term, I will refer to myself simply as an anarchist.

I want to be clear up front that by "a return to the primitive" I am not suggesting that a wholesale return to the Pleistocene is the solution to our problems. For one thing, the world has been so altered by the effects of planet-destroying technology that many of the life-ways of our Paleolithic ancestors are no longer truly viable options. The future of the human species, if there can be one, lies in the future, not the past. However, a primitivist perspective has much to offer by directing our attention to the dramatic mismatch between our evolved expectations and our current circumstances. As an approach to anarchism, it compels the intentional removal of technologies of authority, not merely to provide relief from their freedom-obliterating impact, and not to be replaced by something else, but in order to allow our natural modes of social organization, mediated through evolved psychological systems that continue to limp along beneath the surface, deformed, repressed, and misdirected, to have healthy and unfettered expression.

If anarchy is taken as a description of active and tangible conditions, conditions that reflect not merely a default or fallback state but the natural social state for humans, the unfettered expression of an active set of evolution-derived social tendencies rather than the mere absence of artificial systems of power, then a number of questions arise. Where did presently-existing systems of power and authority come from? How did they develop historically? What (and whose) purposes do these systems serve? How do they function—more specifically, how are they able to gain psychological purchase: why do we acquiesce to an artificial authority? What impact do they have on our physical and psychological wellbeing? Why have they been allowed to persist? I explore each of these questions in detail in the sections and chapters that follow.

My beef with hierarchy is limited to its oppressive application in the social arena. As a general organizing principle, as a means of facilitating memory or comprehension for example, hierarchy can be an extremely useful device.[2] Thus, this book is structured according to a fairly typical hierarchical arrangement, with parts, subsections, end notes, etc. In Part 1, I address some of the major roadblocks to clear thinking about our situation, specifically in terms of the presumed legitimacy of systems of authority. I suggest that Hobbes was essentially right, that anarchism represents the default human social situation: humans in a state of nature. And although he was utterly wrong about the "red-in-tooth-and-claw" details, he was right about using life in a state of nature, that is, life in the absence of systemic social coercion, as the default with which to gage alternative possibilities. There is substantive evidence, both logical and empirical, that there has never been an organized state or system of government, whether historical or theoretical, that, on the whole, was an improvement upon the general circumstances of human life prior to the agricultural revolution. To the contrary, every historical state or system of government that has ever existed has involved a precipitous deterioration of most or all of the general conditions present in the default natural state. And that's not because life in a state of nature was all peaches and cream—I do not subscribe to any golden-age or garden-of-Eden illusions about Paleolithic lifestyles—but, rather, because historical state systems have included such tremendous amounts of misery, grief, anguish, distress, pain, death, torment, and suffering. Also in Part 1, and in numerous other places throughout the book, I take on the pernicious delusion that civilization represents a mode of human progress. The idea of progress as something more than mere accumulation, accretion, extension, and expansion does not describe anything real about our situation. Next I present systems of authority as a kind of technology, a technology of social control that emerges from within the larger technological ordering of society. Then I highlight the close connection between authority and knowledge, and note that the frequent confounding of these terms has its source in their mutual interdependence within complex hierarchically structured social systems. After an examination of individual autonomy as seen through the lens of power, I end Part 1 with an anarchist challenge to the legitimacy of exiting forms of social organization.

In Part 2, I address the historical emergence of technologies of power and authority. Much of what I have to say in this part is underwritten by the insights of Lewis Mumford regarding the development of the first large-scale technologies of social control in Sumer and ancient Egypt, mechanical systems of authority and control over human labor power that Mumford referred to collectively as the megamachine. I suggest that the systematic manipulation of human activity through hierarchical systems of power and authority has its primal beginnings in a dramatic reorientation toward the natural world that occurred as a result of life-ways based on farming, first adopted some 9000 years ago by a small minority of humans living in a unique geographical region known as the fertile crescent. Data provided by anthropologists and archaeologists show that, allowing for wide differences among individual groups, community life prior to the agricultural revolution was a largely egalitarian affair. The sedentary life-ways of late stone-age farming people not only changed how the natural world was perceived, it also removed several of the primary drivers of egalitarianism, including the ability to simply pick up and move away from any would-be oppressor. In addition, the subsequent domestication of animals provided a conceptual framework for applying hierarchical power relations in the human world. Prior to domestication, humans and other animals were seen as members of separate but equivalent societies. Hierarchical relations between humans and animals emerged with domestication, as animals became inferior and subordinate creatures to be manipulated for human ends. Even so, it appears that steeply hierarchical relations among humans didn't become widespread until the development of large-scale irrigation, a technology that required the division of labor and a sizeable specialized workforce. Additional factors included the development of organized religion, a transition to domestic as opposed to communal modes of food storage, and the emergence of kinship-based social stratification.

As for purpose, technologies of control have historically served the purposes of those at the top of the power hierarchy. However, the complexity and scope of these systems, as with that of many of our other technologies, have long ago exceeded the point at which they can be directed, channeled, or even meaningfully understood by any single person or group of people. The complexity of modern technologies, and the intricacy of interrelations among them, renders their totality outside of human understanding and control. Systems of authority and control are woven throughout the fabric of the larger technological order of society. The larger technological order depends on the continual operative presence of these systems. In other words, technology lies at the heart of the issue. Authority is inseparable from the technological process itself. The more that our lives are embedded in technology, the more our lives are enmeshed within restrictive hierarchical systems of organization and control—and the more limited our autonomy. According to popular myth, technology serves us—it is after all "our" technology; the technological order is merely a collection of tools for pursuing human purposes. It turns out that popular myth in this case is not merely false, but a complete inversion of reality. Our most complex technologies (e.g., transnational corporations, global financial institutions, government bureaucracies—to the extent that there are meaningful differences among these) no longer serve any human purposes. At this point, the continued promotion and expansion of the systems themselves is the only purpose being served. In Part 3, I explore the technological order of modern civilization, the modern power complex, and the intimate relationship between authority and complex technology. I pay particular attention to how our lives are directed to accommodate the needs of our technologies, how we are becoming increasingly dependent on their efficient and penetrating operation, and how our authentic human need for personal autonomy is regularly sacrificed in the name of technical efficiency.

Other biological and psychological needs are being sacrificed as well. The technological order of modern civilization, with its subsidiary systems of authority and control staffed by lethally armed personnel licensed to meet resistance with overwhelming violence, profoundly impacts our physical and psychological health in both direct and indirect ways: directly, by neutralizing autonomy and by promoting and enforcing lifestyles and social conditions that are inconsistent with our evolved human design; indirectly, through the destruction of the natural world and the proliferation of toxic environmental conditions. Our most pressing medical concerns, vascular disease, diabetes, cancer, and pandemic infections, have no meaningful precedent in our Paleolithic past. And there is considerable evidence that the same is true for our most prevalent psychological maladies as well. Our foraging Pleistocene relatives no doubt had their share of problems with injuries, infections, and parasites. But they had little problem with metabolic syndrome or viral epidemics or bedbugs or rats or lawyers or tax collectors or power-intoxicated cops or any of the other common post-Neolithic symbiotic pests. And depression, general anxiety, ADHD, and erectile disorder were nonissues.

Part 4 examines the fundamental medium, the social-psychological substrate, through which authority operates. Authority can function only by tapping into our evolved social predilections and psychological tendencies, predilections and tendencies that we inherited from our egalitarian Pleistocene ancestors. In this part, I explore our continued acquiescence in terms of the nature of our psychological fetters. One of the most potent ways in which our submission is encouraged is through the arresting and deformation of our natural psychological development. The incomplete development and malformation of evolved psychological systems leaves us dependent, in a chronic state of psychological need, and eager to form infantile attachments to the teats of power. In addition, omnipresent surveillance, a legal system grounded in coercive violence and threat, and a psychiatric community that treats resistance to authority as pathology all serve to keep the stanchions of power in place. Another reason we continue to acquiesce is because we are perpetually placated with entertaining distractions—a highly addictive diet of high-tech bread and circuses. Continually under observation, psychologically immature, and perpetually distracted, most of us are simply not aware of viable alternatives to the status quo. Consumer mass society organized by the technological order and shaped around arbitrary power and authority is simply the way of the world. Part of it also has to do with the fact that those of us who have the time and resources to engage in any critical examination of our situation tend to occupy the middle and upper ends of the power hierarchy. Things seem pretty good when your head is stuffed in the front end of the consumer feeding trough. A fourteen-year-old Congolese boy working in a coltan mine in central Africa has little opportunity to contemplate alternative social possibilities—let alone write a book about it. It is enough for him to dream of a day when he has enough money—maybe in a couple of years—to buy a pair of shoes. And his suburban American counterpart is too mesmerized by the images and text streaming across the screen of his coltan-dependent phone for any activity even remotely approximating contemplation to ever grace the neural tissue in his sugar-drenched brain.

Gaining some understanding of both the enormity of the questions and the true precariousness of our situation is only the first step. In Part 5 I attempt to bring it all together and discuss how we might approach our liberation from technologies of oppression, how we might go about reclaiming our personal autonomy, how we might arrive at potential answers to the most pressing question of all: how do we set ourselves free? One word of caution. I offer what I feel to be a reasoned approach throughout this book, and one that is supported by evidence and based on objective facts where it can be. In exploring the nature of our situation we need to be suspicious of reductive, over-simplistic, one-factor explanations—and many of the ideas I explore might be construed as leaning in this reductive direction. Rather than deny this, I want to highlight this limitation upfront. It is important to bear in mind that the actual fabric of the human condition is far more complex than the weave of human thought. All explanations, regardless of how elegant or intuitively appealing, will always be simplifying stories. And, as it turns out for our purposes here, specific answers to questions concerning the function, purpose, and historical development of oppressive systems of power and authority, questions as to their physical and psychological impact, and questions as to their scope and penetrating presence are really only of secondary concern. Answers to these questions are useful only inasmuch as they offer clues to potential solutions to the real problem: the real problem is the continued existence of these oppressive systems. Ultimately this book is motivated by a set of far more essential questions, questions that are far more pressing and immediate: How can these technologies of control be reduced, reversed, removed, dismantled, or destroyed? How can we wrest ourselves loose from their stifling, dehumanizing, autonomy-annihilating grip? Or, to apply a more positive, active frame: How can we begin to pursue more authentically human forms of life? The chapters in this final part are geared toward exploring where potential answers to these questions might be found.

Yes, I am an anarchist. I give full and open confession. I am an anarchist because I value my humanity. I am an anarchist because I am a unique individual human being and I wish to preserve what is left of my individuality and my personal autonomy. I am an anarchist because I recognize the homogenizing and dehumanizing potential of mass society. But, mostly, I am an anarchist because I do not recognize the legitimacy of hierarchical arrangements of social power and authority. The oppressive structures of power and control in modern civilization do not reflect a natural extension of primate society or an emergent property of human evolution. And, contrary to popular myth, these systems of control are a primary source of human suffering. Simply put, there is no compelling moral force behind the artificial systems of power and authority within which you and I are forced to configure our lives, their presence is counter to human freedom and dignity, and their only purpose is the annihilation of autonomy.

And our continued acquiescence to these systems is insupportable.

PART 1: AGAINST AUTHORITY

The delusion of progress

From earliest childhood we have been metabolized into the techno-logical order with its systems of coercive authority—to the point where questions regarding the legitimacy or validity of these systems may seem nonsensical at first. The perspective from within the tech-nological order is cluttered with distortions. Some of these distor-tions are intentional creations of formal education and the scientifi-cally-crafted propaganda of corporate media, and some are incidental framing effects of everyday experience in post-industrial society. A few of these distortions are severe enough to warrant corrective con-ceptual lenses. Chief among these is a set of pervasive misconcep-tions about civilization as a mode of human progress.

The idea of progress is a salient feature of the highly textured mythological fabric of civilization. Human society, and specifically, Western society, has been engaged in a process of relentless and progressive development, barring minor historical setbacks (the mid-dle ages, for example), since the very beginning of time. Civilization is the embodiment of human progress, and modern global mass soci-ety represents progress' leading edge. According to myth, people in past ages were primitive and undeveloped, and the lifestyles of pres-ently existing people in non-Westernized countries are horribly un-derdeveloped relative to those of their first world contemporaries.

The idea that civilization reflects an unfolding moment in the course of human progress across time strongly invokes the metaphor of a journey. The problem with this conception of progress is that it isn't true. Civilization isn't going anywhere. It is true that Western society has changed over time. All societies change. And it is possible to discern a variety of historical patterns of progression within these changes. But these progressions are not directed toward some future goal. Progression is not the same as progress. Logically, progress requires a goal; a journey requires, at the very least, a direction. What is the goal to which we are being led? The terms "forward" and "upward" and "onward" are frequently used in conjunction with progress. Forward to what? Upward how? Onward to where? Is there some utopian state of perfection toward which society is moving? If so, who decides what it is? What is its nature and form? We need to know this in order to gage whether we are in fact making progress toward its eventual achievement or moving in some other direction entirely. All civilization generates change, and our modern globalizing world is in the midst of very dramatic and accelerating change. But *change* by itself is not sufficient criteria for progress, even if the change is occurring at an accelerating rate. Accumulation is not progress, even if it occurs at a progressively increasing rate. Landfills accumulate. Atmospheric CO_2 accumulates. Mercury traces in brain tissue accumulate. Radiation exposure, stress, and ingestion of trans fats have cumulative effects. Progress, if it is to be something more than simple accumulation, requires an end, a goal, a direction, a trajectory, some way to tell if the change of state is to count as progress or its opposite.

Belief in civilization as a mode of human progress is not just the belief that civilization involves a progression of changes, it is the belief that human society improves, that the changes are in an overall positive and desirable direction. Belief in progress has almost universal popular appeal. But the belief that history reflects the progressive improvement of the human situation is based on a narrow reading of history that ignores entire domains of objective fact that, when taken collectively, show that this belief is completely unwarranted. In fact, the belief in human progress meets all the criteria of a delusion: it is a demonstrably false belief that persists despite mountains of direct and compelling evidence to the contrary.

Technology plays a central role in perpetuating this delusion. The human condition is improving through our ever-expanding technology and our ever-increasing ability to manipulate and exploit nature. Through advances in technology, we are in the process of bringing about a better world. This feature of the delusion is a product of modernity, a purely Western view that emerged with the industrial revolution in Europe; and it is reinforced by a common misunderstanding of the process of technological innovation: technological development—some call it technological evolution—has an accumulative quality and encourages an isolation of focus on specific technical problems, both of which feed a powerful illusion of purpose and direction. Technology is an ambiguous term. And I will attempt to reduce some of that ambiguity below. For the present discussion, consider technology simply as the collection of methods and systems we have available for manipulating various naturally occurring phenomena.[1] If we compare the present technological circumstances to those of past times, we can see that there has been an accumulation of both the quantity and sophistication (complexity) of the available technology. We can harness more and more phenomena as time goes on, and our power to direct and control phenomena has increased in both scope and subtlety. In this sense, technology "advances" in that it is progressively accumulative. But how is the accumulative change in the capacity to manipulate nature progress? Where is this change leading us? Again, accumulative progression is not the same as progress. More does not necessarily mean better.

One might argue that the accumulation and expansion of technology, the increase in our ability to manipulate and control phenomena, has led to a general improvement in the human condition, and that we can call this general improvement a kind of progress. We are no longer afflicted with many of the torments of times past. We can communicate and travel with speed that would have been unthinkable just a few generations ago. We can force an acre of land to yield far more calories than we could in the past. But improvement is never general. Things have not gotten generically better; they have gotten better in very specific ways. And each specific improvement has come at a cost which ensures that we are, in general, no better off. We have eradicated small pox, but in the process we've created entirely new diseases such as metabolic syndrome and several varieties of cancer; and the risk of pandemic infection has steadily increased as viruses mutate, incubate, and spread through ever more densely populated and globally connected cities. Automobile and air travel are several thousand orders of magnitude more environmentally corrosive than travel by horse or by foot; and the levels of anxiety and stress that attach to urban commuter lifestyles neutralize any potential psychological benefits such lifestyles might offer. The increase in agricultural productivity that accompanied the green revolution has led to a concomitant increase in population and, paradoxically, an increase in the prevalence of hunger and the risk of starvation. In addition, reliance on industrial farming has made us only that much more dependent on our finite reserves of fossil fuel. Broad cost-benefit analyses show that technology is a zero sum game. For every clear benefit that a specific technology provides, there are benefit-destroying costs in terms of undesirable side-effects and diffuse negative consequences. Each technological solution generates additional problems, the combination of which leaves us no better off in the big picture, but more deeply enmeshed in dehumanizing, technology-dependent lifestyles. Technology is a treadmill where each innovation increases the angle and forces us to jettison additional fragments of our humanity just so that we can keep the pace.

The illusion that new technology leads to improvement over existing conditions is due in part to the way that our focus is naturally limited by the operation of technology itself. Any critical assessment of a specific technology is naturally directed toward the specific set of problems that the technology was designed to address. New technology involves the creation of additional problems, but these problems frequently involve conditions that are external to the set of problems for which the new technology was designed, and so don't end up in the cost-benefit calculus. By restricting the focus to the specific set of problems the technology was created to solve, or to superficialities such as the speed and efficiency with which it solves them, it appears that the incorporation of the new technology has led to an overall improvement when in fact no such overall improvement has occurred—and in many cases, from a more general perspective, we are worse off than we were prior to the adoption of the technology. Example cases where innovations actually exacerbate the exact problems they were designed to address are easy to find. Not too long ago, a study was presented at the American Diabetes Association showing that drinking diet soda actually made people fatter (a 70% larger waist as compared to sugary soda drinkers), and that the artificial sweeteners used in diet beverages raised blood sugar in diabetic-prone mice. Not only does diet soda *not* do what it was specifically designed to do, it creates additional problems.

In most situations, the zero sum nature of technology is not as blatant as it is with diet soda, and emerges only after looking at the broader context. Consider the case of modern wind turbines. In the last two decades there has been a dramatic upsurge in interest in harvesting wind energy as an environmentally friendly way of reducing dependence on fossil fuels. However, upon examination of the broader context, wind energy turns out not to produce any net benefit, and may actually lead to an overall deterioration of general environmental conditions on par with fossil fuel. Modern wind turbines are consumers of electricity themselves (e.g., for controlling the blades' pitch, direction, and speed, deicing in winter, internal operating systems, etc.), so much so that for periods of time a wind turbine may actually draw more electricity from the grid than it produces. Also, a typical modern wind turbine weighs just under 170 tons (although some are much heavier), and most of that weight is in the form of steel—much of which is manufactured and shipped from China. So not only is there the fossil energy and raw materials required to produce the steel, but there is the energy involved in transportation and construction to consider. And since wind turbines only last 20 to 25 years, the net benefit in terms of the value of electricity produced over cost reflects only a fraction of the life of a wind turbine. Consider also the amount of power line needed to accommodate the fact that wind farms are typically located some distance from the urban centers where their electricity is used. Consider in addition that the generator inside the nacelle of the wind turbine incorporates neodymium, a radioactive rare earth metal, the mining and refinement of which cause serious ecological damage. So much for being environmentally friendly. In terms of negative environmental impact, wind turbines also kill both birds and migratory bats. Bird deaths are not all that extensive—inner-city skyscrapers and cell phone towers (to say nothing of automobiles and domestic cats) kill far more birds than do wind turbines. Bat deaths may be far more considerable. Birds are killed by flying directly into the towers or by being blindsided by the spinning blades, but bats are killed by merely flying near the blades. The pockets of low pressure created by the blades' sweep damages the bats fragile lung tissue. The problem with killing bats (and birds) is that bats (and birds) eat insects, and wind turbines are typically sited in agricultural areas where insects are a threat to crops. One estimate places the value of bats to the agricultural industry at close to 23 billion dollars a year in pesticide savings alone (bat guano is a potent fertilizer, but I am unaware of any studies quantifying its effects in monetary terms). Modern pesticides are made from petroleum, so wind turbines increase the need for fossil fuel directly through their manufacture, construction, and their own use of electric power and indirectly through reducing the bat population. So much for being an alternative to fossil fuel. And as if all this were not enough, wind turbines have a negative impact on the heath of humans who live nearby: the so-called wind turbine syndrome. But none of these decidedly negative features of wind turbines have a prominent place in an evaluation of the benefits of wind turbines as a technology for producing electricity; the cost of construction and the capacity for offsetting that cost through the generation of energy is all that counts. I have much more to say about this bias in our orientation to technology in Part 3.

Progress is a "product" of the industrial revolution: speed and efficiency are its primary metrics. But progress is often also measured by an increase in power. It makes no sense at all to consider an increase in power—in and of itself—as anything other than simple accumulation. Despite this, an increase in power is progress. This is one of the more disturbing corollaries of the delusion of progress. The more powerful our technologies, the greater their ability to exploit natural phenomena; and the greater the ability to exploit natural phenomena, the greater the potential for damage and destruction. It is only by equating increased power with progress that a thermonuclear bomb could possibly represent progress with respect to one made of conventional explosives, or the capacity to vaporize suspected terrorists with a drone aircraft piloted remotely halfway around the world could be progress with respect to face-to-face confrontation between equally armed rivals.

Perhaps more disturbing than the general accumulation of ever more sophisticated and ever more penetrating methods for exploiting natural phenomena, there has been an equally significant accumulation of sophisticated and penetrating technologies of coercion designed specifically to manipulate human thought and behavior (both human thought and behavior are, of course, natural phenomena as well). What was once only accomplished through direct violence, through the liberal application of whip and mace and sword and musket, is now being effected through highly refined methods of social engineering, through propaganda under the guise of "education," psycho-pharmaceutical reprogramming, universal surveillance, and exceedingly effective forms of economic coercion. In addition to the overt tools of violence, the massively over-armed military and the licensed-to-kill police, hierarchical systems of power and authority are propped up by an ever-expanding array of less visible dehumanizing support systems.

According to the delusion of progress, oppressive hierarchical systems of power and authority are themselves evidence of laudable human achievement. The sophisticated mechanical bureaucracies that envelop our globalizing world are concrete proof of just how far society has progressed since our days as ignorant and isolated bands of egalitarian foragers. There are a few facts associated with these bureaucracies, however, that are not entirely consistent with any reasonable interpretation of the idea of progress, the fact that they are maintained through violence and the threat of violence, the fact that they operate by restricting individual autonomy, the fact that they cause immeasurable human suffering, the fact that they have very likely damaged the biosphere beyond the point of return, the fact that their existence is directly responsible for war and overpopulation and pandemic disease and nuclear meltdowns and predator drones and oil spills and planet-wide deforestation and the giant plastic vortex in the Pacific Ocean, for instance.

Progress is a delusion, a persuasive mirage that keeps us stumbling in circles from one technological remedy to another; our problems escalate exponentially as our technology advances, and all the while our authentic human needs remain unquenched.

The technology of authority

We live in a technologically advanced civilization. This much is not delusion, but demonstrable fact. But, then, every civilization that has ever existed could make the exact same boast. The ancient Sumerians with their cuneiform, the Phoenicians with their ships and their alphabet, the Mayans with their sophisticated astronomy, the Romans with their highways and aqueducts, each in their own time reflected unrivaled technological achievement. Yet there seems to be something qualitatively different about the technology of our time, something about its omnipresence, something about its sheer volume, magnitude, and diversity, something about the degree to which it penetrates our daily lives; our post-industrial, information-dense, nuclear-charged, fossil-powered, computer-mediated global civilization is somehow more fundamentally "technological" than civilizations of the past. In some sense, we "live our technology" in a way that makes our time unique relative to times past.

The real difference between our modern techno-culture and civilizations of the past, however, is not simply that we have more sophisticated gadgets or that we have the power to transform our world in more diverse and extensive ways. The real difference has to do with the functional architecture of our civilization itself. Civilization is itself a kind of technology. Perhaps it would be more accurate to say that civilization is a collection of technologies: technologies designed specifically for organizing and directing—and redirecting—human activity. Modern civilization differs from past versions in terms of the variety and potency of the ways it accomplishes its prime function. What is truly "advanced" about our civilization relative to previous iterations is its capacity for controlling human behavior.

To call civilization a collection of technologies of behavior control is not an oversimplification. We live in an exceedingly complex world. But the complexity of modern civilization is with the details, not with the essence of its overall purpose or function. The complexity lies within the technologies of control themselves, perhaps an overwhelming level of complexity. It is not my intention here to attempt a comprehensive survey of the details of the many systems of control that direct our lives. My goals are considerably more modest. Actually, my goals are two-fold. First, I want to frame the problem of authority as essentially a technological problem. "Social scientists, politicians, bureaucrats, corporate managers, radical students, as well as natural scientists and engineers, are now united in the conclusion that something we call 'technology' lies at the core of what is most troublesome in the condition of our world . . . . Technology is, according to this view, a source of domination that effectively rules all forms of modern thought and activity. Whether by an inherent property or by an incidental set of circumstances, technology looms as an oppressive force that poses a direct threat to human freedom."[2] The enemy of freedom is not a person, or a group of powerful elites, or even an ideology, but a collection of technological systems, what I am calling the technological order.[3] Second, I want to outline just enough of the overall nature and structure of this collection of systems to expose potentially exploitable points of weakness in its design, if any such exist.

The first step in framing the problem is to decide what, exactly, we mean by "technology." Elsewhere I made a distinction between *technology* and *tools* intended to highlight differences in their potential to impact personal autonomy.[4] Tools are entirely transparent in their operation, and have the potential to enhance personal autonomy by extending the sensorimotor capacities of the individual operator in ways that are consistent with personally chosen goals or purposes. Technology involves isolation of knowledge and division of labor, tends to be opaque in terms of the totality of its functions, and serves ends that are not necessarily those of its operators. This distinction between tools and technology has intuitive appeal, but is largely one of rhetorical convenience; it is not meant as a logically defensible statement of concise taxonomic categories. For our purposes here, tools might simply be considered a relatively benign subset of technology.

Above, I considered technology in general terms as methods and systems that allow us to control, manipulate, and exploit natural phenomena. Here I want to be a bit more specific. Probably the simplest way of conceptualizing technology is in terms of the application of an intentionally organized structure. "The first function of any technology—and the immediate condition of its utility—is to give a definite, artificial form to a set of materials or to a specific human activity. To put it differently, it provides a structure for the primary medium to which it is applied."[5] Langdon Winner partitions technology into four categories organized generally according to the type of medium being structured: apparatus, technique, organizations, and networks. Although they are to some extent arbitrary, and the boundaries are somewhat blurry, Winner's categories have an intuitive appeal. Apparatus includes instruments, appliances, gadgets, and machines—physical devices that include objects we normally think of as tools. Technique includes procedures, methods, skills, routines—structured ways of doing things. We share these first two general technological capacities with other animals. Other primates, and even some bird species, manufacture and use tools. And perhaps all creatures are capable of learning structured routines. Human tool and technique development far outpaces anything seen with other species, however. For instance, humans appear to be the only creatures that use tools to make other tools. Humans are also unique in their abilities to combine apparatus with technique to yield what are commonly called crafts: weaving, metallurgy, etc. Winner's third category, organizations, includes bureaucracies, schools, armies, corporations—technical social arrangements. And finally, networks are systems that combine people and apparatus linked across distance: highway systems, telephone networks, the internet, etc.

Technologies designed specifically to control human behavior cut across category lines (and, to some degree, all categories of technology involve behavior control), but fit most centrally within the "organizations" and "networks" categories; although technologies of authority and control may have had their primordial beginnings as technique: the structuring of human activity to accomplish a limited purpose or goal, for example digging an irrigation system or erecting a pyramid. It is informative to note the relationship between systems of authority and Winner's "networks" category. No organization of power can function without some way of linking and coordinating the activity of people not in physical proximity. Networks of communication, for example, are as necessary for building a pyramid as they are for running a multinational corporation. The close relationship between organizations of power and networks leads me to think that, just as "craft" emerges from a combination of *apparatus* and *technique,* truly oppressive systems of authority emerge from a combination of *organization* and *network.* Right away, this suggests that potentially exploitable points of weakness might exist at the network level—but I am getting ahead of myself.

Power hierarchies are vertically organized networks. There are other possible network structures. Some versions of anarchism advocate the development of horizontal networks of interdependent nodes in which each participant or group represents a distinct node and power is dispersed through the network in a way that doesn't give any one node predominance (the metaphor of a rhizome is a popular one). This idea has intuitive appeal. However, as will become clear within the discussion of the relationship between knowledge and authority below, the distribution of functions in a network leads to an isolation of constituent elements that, like the isolation of knowledge within specific individuals, invariably creates the potential for domination and exploitation. The idea of a perfectly balanced horizontal network might be possible in theory, but it would never work in practice in the social-political world. Also, there are additional problems with networks composed of interdependent nodes that make this form of organization dangerous and unpredictable when relations among people are involved. "A completely interdependent technological society would be one without hierarchy or class. But the distinction between dependence and interdependence points to a hierarchical arrangement of the segments of the technological order, an arrangement that includes social components. *Within each functioning system some parts are more crucial than others.*"[6] A critical

feature of true egalitarian societies is the complete absence of systemic networks of interdependency, horizontally arranged or otherwise, and egalitarianism in any meaningful form is only possible in
societies with very limited technologies. Technological society and
hierarchical society are synonymous. "Large man-machine networks
require hierarchical structure as a normal operating condition."[7]

Although we are concerned here specifically with authority and
technologies of behavior control, all large-scale technologies have
the artificial (and hierarchical) structuring of activity as a central feature of their operation. "A technical organization is an assemblage of
human beings and apparatus in structured relationships designed to
produce certain specified results. A technical operation, to the extent
that one engages in it, determines what one does. If the operation is
successful, we may say that the technology determined the result.
This does not mean that either the technology or its result are totally
rigid or inflexible. What it does indicate is that technology succeeds
through the conquest of disorder and the imposition of form."[8] This
applies as much to the use of a hammer as it does to the operation of
a government bureaucracy.

Winner lists several characteristic features of technological society. The most salient or obvious is "artificiality." Western civilization
is actively engaged in the reconstruction and modification of the natural world, and the continual reworking of the human social world as
well. More and more of our experience in mass society is contrived,
resynthesized, and "manmade" (Arthur claims that the exploitation
of nature and natural phenomena is the basic function of all technology).[9] A second trait is "rationality," which refers to the logical ordering of structure and organization. Things are made to "fit together" and flow in a logical fashion. The impetus toward standardization
and homogenization is one result of the rationality inherent in technological society. "Size and concentration" refers to the tendency
toward central accumulation of power and the proliferation of massive-scale high-energy projects and operations. Modern technology
is larger than life and exploits the rationality associated with "economies of scale." Localized production and distribution, of food, energy, or of any consumable product, is deemed wasteful and irrational. "Division" refers to the focus on components and constituents.

The world is composed of parts that can be taken apart and reassembled in different ways. "Complex interconnection" of the constituents is another feature, with a tendency toward ever-increasing complexity. "Dependence and interdependence" are a function of complexity. In addition, modern technological society involves the potential for something Winner calls "apraxia," a term he borrows from medicine. "If a significant link in the technical system ceases to function, the whole system stops or is thrown into chaos."[10] This latter feature of technological society has obvious relevance as a potentially exploitable weakness, one that we will explore in the final part of this book.

W. Brian Arthur provides an insightful contemporary view of technology in his book, *The Nature of Technology*. Arthur argues that specific technologies, regardless of their purpose, scope, or contents, all involve an inherent internal logic, and can be analyzed in terms of a hierarchically organized, recursive, and modular internal structure. All new technology consists in the creative recombination of preexisting component technologies. And the purpose of all technology is to "capture" naturally occurring phenomena and direct them toward human purposes. Arthur makes a distinction between technologies that exploit natural phenomena (e.g., the way that obsidian cleaves into sharp edges, the expansion properties of gasses, the way that high frequency radio waves reflect off of metal surfaces) and those that exploit human behavioral tendencies. Although he reluctantly admits that the latter are technologies—they involve the combination and repurposing of modular components—the fact that they do not involve natural phenomena makes them different, makes them "artificial" in a way that other technologies aren't. He calls them "purposive systems" to distinguish them from "natural" technologies. There is apparently something different about human behavior; human psychology does not involve natural phenomena. Legal systems, economies, corporations, government agencies, and the like, are different from military aircraft and computer software, according to Arthur.

I reexamine Arthur's insights about the internal logic of technology in some depth in Part 3. His ideas about hierarchically integrated modular subsystems may prove especially useful, as well as his description of how technology evolves. However, I cannot support his distinction between technology that exploits natural phenomena and "purposive systems" that operate on human psychological tendencies. Human psychological tendencies are as much natural phenomena as are the chemical combinatorial predilections of nucleic acids. In both Part 3 and Part 4 I explore the idea of dependency in more depth. Mass society's dependence on technology goes a long way toward explaining our continued acquiescence to authority. In addition, maintaining and enforcing our acquiescence is what several of these purposive systems have been specifically designed to do. And, thanks in part to the findings of modern science, they are becoming increasingly efficient. The mechanisms by which they encourage our acquiescence have become increasingly subtle and increasingly irresistible.

In terms of technology, our oppression has two major overlapping sources, one general and one more specifically focused. The general source is our technology-embedded lifestyles. Modern globalizing civilization is an expansive array of technological systems, each designed to organize and direct human activity toward some collection of purposes. The purposes have long ceased to be authentic human purposes; most are entirely incoherent from any authentically human perspective. They are the purposes of the technologies themselves, yet we are coerced into adopting them as our own. The totality of these technologies and "purposive systems" has been called by several names: the "technological collective," the "technostructure," the "technium," the "megamachine," the "power complex." I will continue simply to refer to the aggregate of technology as the technological order, with the caveat that this aggregate of technology is not a unitary or coherent assemblage such as the use of the term "order" might suggest. In addition to the technological order, the existence and relentless operation of which serves as the major source of oppression, our freedom and autonomy are constrained by the presence of unique technologies of authority and control designed specifically to ensure that human beings are not allowed to interfere with the efficient operation of the systems of the technological order. I will return to this in Part 3.

Next, I want to pick up the thread dealing with one of the auton-omy-limiting side-effects of finely-grained division of labor, a requi-site feature of technological society: the establishment of expertise and the isolation and restriction of knowledge. The isolation of knowledge is a characteristic of the modular nature of technology, and is especially salient in technologies of authority and control. The restriction of knowledge is a primary way that technologies of con-trol are able to "capture" human behavior. Authority implies a verti-cal division and separation of power. And the power associated with authority is a direct function of the partitioning and asymmetric dis-tribution of knowledge.

Authority and knowledge

According to Arthur, new technologies, instruments, methods that uncover new phenomena to be exploited, and new ways of exploiting previously known phenomena are tied to knowledge in a direct and rather straightforward way: "These technologies help build yet fur-ther knowledge and understanding and help uncover yet further phe-nomena. Knowledge and technology in this way cumulate togeth-er."[11] But the connection between knowledge and authority is more complex than commonsense notions about the relationships among knowledge, authority, and technology suggest. This complexity be-comes especially apparent when we examine authority's role in tech-nologies of social control.

Authority is a central feature of technologies of social control, and the primary psychological mechanism through which these tech-nologies operate. Authority as a concept, however, is complex and multilayered. To begin with, there appear to be two distinct ways in which the word authority is commonly used. First, authorities are people in positions of power over us, people who occupy a superor-dinate position in a power hierarchy: a parent, a school vice princi-pal, a boss, a police officer, a government official. But an authority can also be someone with privileged or specialized knowledge: an expert in a particular domain. We trust these authorities to tell us

how much mercury is safe to consume, how high our blood choles-
terol levels should be, how often to change batteries in our smoke
detectors, what proportion of our daily diet should consist of whole
grains, which drugs are safe and what dosage is appropriate, whether
the economy is improving, and what to do during a tornado. So an
authority can be someone who has the power to control our behavior
or someone who has knowledge that we lack.[12] A moment's reflec-
tion, however, shows that these two applications of the term authority are not so different after all. The pronouncements of a person in
possession of knowledge we lack can affect our behavior just as
surely as can the commands of a direct superior. Knowledge is power. Or, more precisely, a sanctioned *claim* to knowledge is power.

Forgive the didactic tenor of what follows, but it is important to
delve briefly into the realm of epistemology, the study of knowledge,
to look at where our knowledge comes from in order to get a better
idea of how the possession of privileged information can generate
authority, and how the isolation of knowledge serves as a major pillar supporting hierarchical technologies of power and control regardless of the validity or accuracy of the knowledge in question. How is
it, exactly, that (putative) knowledge becomes power?

Let's start with a deceptively simple question: How do you
know? This simple question can end political careers and ruin the
sleep of philosophy undergraduates. Not *what* do you know, but *how*
is it that you have come to possess this knowledge that you claim to
possess? (The idea that knowledge can be a possession is informative
and illustrative of the relationship between the intentional isolation
of knowledge and the distribution of power—but I digress.) In an
argument, you can weaken any claim your opponent makes using
only this question coupled in an alternating fashion with variations
on the question: What do you mean? In addition to putting your opponent on the defensive, any attempt she makes to clarify her point
while answering "What do you mean?" will expose additional targets
for "How do you know?" Eventually she will be forced to concede
that her claim is based, ultimately, on personal belief, ideologically-
based opinion, or on ultimately unsupportable assumptions.

Turn of the twentieth century philosopher of science, Charles
Sanders Peirce, pointed out that there are in fact only four ways of

knowing anything about the world, four pathways to understanding, four methods for "fixing belief."[13] Peirce was not talking about the more direct or fundamental knowledge associated with the activity of our perceptual and cognitive systems, mechanisms that we have acquired through evolution that configure our experience in ways that were adaptive for our ancestors. We frame our immediate experience in ways that reflect our biological nature: humans know a different sort of world than do birds, for example. What Peirce was talking about was belief, or how it is that we decide what is and is not true when it comes to potential facts about the world, the kind of knowledge that can inform our decisions and enter into our conscious deliberations about how we should act in concrete situations, the kind of knowledge that can be used to justify continued acquiescence to hierarchical systems of authority and control, for example.

The first and least reliable method for fixing belief Peirce called the method of tenacity. Using this method, people cling to the familiar simply because it is familiar. There is comfort in the status quo. When presented with ideas that contradict preexisting belief, people will cling stubbornly to what they already believe simply for the peace of mind it offers, and to avoid the discomfort caused by making even minor changes to their world view. Consider the following example. My oldest daughter came bounding into the room one day when she was five years old and asked, "Santa Clause is not real, right? It's really just you and mommy." Being an honest father, I confirmed her suspicions that Santa was in fact just a make-believe fairytale, and she went on her way, entirely satisfied with my response. But just a few minutes later she stormed back into the room and declared in a stern and indignant voice, "I don't care what you say, I still think Santa Claus is real!" She was not ready to let go of her Santa Clause belief because of its emotional power; it was of too central importance to her world view, and to eliminate Santa meant restructuring her understanding of holiday events in a way that she was not yet ready to do. The belief perseverance seen in the method of tenacity reflects a more general cognitive tendency to grant unwarranted priority to existing conditions just because of their familiarity.

Peirce's second method he called the method of authority. Using this method, we hold things to be true because people in positions of authority tell us so. Here we again run into the dual nature of authority: the idea of the expert, the person who knows details about a domain with which we are less familiar, and the person who has power over us. Parents, adults in general, are, for us, the first authorities—in both senses. And many if not most of our early beliefs about the world are provided for us directly by the adults in our lives. The majority of beliefs associated with organized religion are of this sort as well. I recall a refrain from a song I learned as a child in my protestant Sunday school: "Jesus loves me this I know, for the Bible tells me so." Written texts, religious and legal documents, textbooks, reference books such as dictionaries and encyclopedias, and, more recently, reference websites such as Wikipedia, are repositories for authority-based knowledge. The method of authority is somewhat superior to the method of tenacity because oftentimes the experts actually know what they are talking about, and, perhaps considerably less often, what those in positions of power tell us is really for our own good. The problem with using authority as a mode of understanding the world is that, for any given belief, there is no way to tell whether that is the case. The method of authority requires us to take it on faith that the authorities know what they are talking about and that they are not trying to deceive us. Consider the USDA's diet recommendations, historically reflected in the food pyramid and more recently replaced by a plate-shaped pie chart, that a sizeable proportion of our daily food intake should be based on dairy, legumes, and whole-grain. This, despite an increasing accumulation of evidence that regular consumption of these foods—foods not reflected in our genetically-encoded ancestral eating habits—lead to a wide variety of serious health problems. Whether the USDA's erroneous recommendations are a result of simple ignorance or signify specific pressure from corporate food interests is not the issue so much as that it presents itself as a knowledgeable authority that we are encouraged to take seriously. In many cases, we are given no choice but to trust the experts and those in positions of power. The idea of faith applies here. Faith has been used as a manipulative tool historically, especially within the Judeo-Christian-Muslim religious traditions. More recently faith has found a new role in the public consumption of science and scientific findings. We are expected to have faith in the pronouncements of scientists, despite the fact that these pronouncements seem to change with each passing news cycle. Reliance on authority increases with the complexity of the domain in question, in the same way that the general proliferation of authorities within a society increases with an increased division of labor and partitioning of knowledge. As a general rule, increasing complexity leads to increased reliance on authority-based knowledge. And in our hyper-complex postindustrial world, the method of authority is, by necessity, a primary source of knowledge, with obvious application for maintaining and enhancing the control exercised by artificial power hierarchies.

Peirce called the third method the a priori method. It is also sometimes referred to as the rational method. The a priori method uses logical reasoning based on knowledge of cause and effect to make decisions about truth. This is the method for which Sherlock Holmes was famous. It is superior to the method of authority because it doesn't leave us entirely at the mercy of the authorities. It provides a way to screen an authority's claim through the sieve of reason and logic. This method, unfortunately, does not guarantee that the person employing it will arrive at the correct conclusion. Consider another example of a situation involving my daughter when she was young. It was a summer when the local electric company was having a number of problems with the local power grid, and segments of the town would suddenly lose power, sometimes for just a few minutes and sometimes for a few hours. I came home one afternoon and the alarm clock on my bed stand was flashing. Right away, using a priori reasoning about cause and effect, I concluded that the power had been off at some point while I was gone. And, further, because the clock was flashing 3:05am, and that particular kind of clock was designed to zero-out the time at 12:00am when it lost power, I knew that the power had come back on exactly three hours and five minutes prior to my arrival. What I didn't know was how long the power had been off. So when I saw my daughter, who had been home all day, I asked her. She looked at me a bit sheepishly, and then confessed that the power had not been off at all that day, but rather that she had been roughhousing with the dog in my bedroom and the dog had unplugged the clock, and she did not know how to reset the time. The main problem with Peirce's third method is that, because it requires establishing assumptions about unknown—and in many cases, unknowable—variables, there is no guarantee that any two people applying it will come away with the same understanding of the truth. Another way of saying this is that there are, theoretically, an infinite number of potential causes for any given event, and logic alone is not sufficient for deciding which are valid. Additionally, this method presupposes prior understanding of causal relationships, much of which might well be a product of authority-based knowledge.

This leads us to the fourth method Peirce identified, the scientific method. The scientific method is essentially the a priori method, with one critical additional feature. Like the a priori method, our understanding is founded upon questions that correspond to logical cause and effect relationships. The scientific method is different in that the questions are constructed in such a way as to let the world itself provide the answers. This empirical approach solves some of the problems with deciding which potential causes are valid. Unfortunately, even using the scientific method, we are not guaranteed to arrive at unassailable truth. The "truths" of science are limited both by the specific questions we choose to ask and how we choose to ask them. Science is good at ruling out competing possibilities, but it is entirely unable to ascertain whether the possibilities that have not been ruled out today will still be viable possibilities tomorrow. And it is entirely mute about possibilities that no one has thought about. Science can potentially arrive at the truth only if the truth is among the possibilities that have actually been conceived. Also, and more important for our present discussion, the scientific method and the method of authority have become close bedfellows in postindustrial technoculture. Despite its serious limitations, science has been granted a position of power and authority comparable to that awarded to the priests and god-kings of ancient Egypt and Mesopotamia. We will be exploring some consequences of this unholy alliance later on. In addition, we will be exploring the ways that our tendencies to rely on tenacity and authority are being enhanced to keep us servile, how our ability to think critically and employ logical reasoning are being curtailed, and how both our personal access to the methods of science and our ability to interpret the results of scientific inquiry have been systematically degraded.

Before we leave our brief excursion into the realm of epistemology, there is an additional feature of knowledge that needs to be addressed: the distinction between empirical and conventional understanding. Long before Peirce divined his four paths to fixing belief, David Hume made a potent distinction between different kinds of truth.[14] Hume's fork, as it is sometimes called, splits truth along two tines. One tine spears what we might call conventional truth, or truth that deals with accepted practices or agreed-upon definitions. It is true that a triangle has three sides and that a bachelor is an unmarried male, for example. These truths derive from the definitions of triangle and bachelor, and lose their truth-value the moment there is any substantial change in definition. Truth along the conventional tine of Hume's fork is bound to cultural context. The second tine stabs at what we might call empirical truth, truth about the world that is a matter of observable and testable fact, that water boils at 100 degrees Celsius at sea level, for example, or that bachelors have less sex than do married men. This second type of truth is not subject to the whims of culture, or tradition, or arbitrary definition in the same way as is the first. We might, for example, measure temperature using a different scale or reverse the definitions of "bachelor" and "married man," but the underlying truth previously referenced by "water boils at 100 degrees Celsius" or "bachelors have less sex than married men" remains what it is, we will just be using different words to describe it. Whereas in the first case, with conventional truth, changing the definition of bachelor negates entirely the truth as it was originally designated.

Hume's fork is a useful utensil for examining the relationship between authority and specialized knowledge. On the surface it would appear that conventional truth has more of an affinity with Peirce's methods of tenacity and authority, whereas empirical truth has more of connection with logic and science. However, the practical distinction between conventional and empirical knowledge disappears if you are unable to engage in critical thought or do not have access to the tools of empirical observation. How much mercury is safe to ingest is not an empirical question if you lack either the physical means to observe or the conceptual tools to interpret your observations. You have little choice but to rely on the proclamations of the "experts." Specialization and the fine partitioning of domains of expertise increase the extent to which all knowledge is, practically speaking, of the conventional sort, to be defined and disseminated by authorities—authorities whose very power comes from the fact that they possess knowledge that is not in general circulation.

Thus the two ostensibly distinct applications of the word authority, authority as possessor of power and authority as possessor of privileged knowledge, are closely related, both tied ultimately to the division of labor and specialization that attend the stratification of roles within hierarchically-organized systems of social power. For a hierarchical system of social power to function efficiently, knowledge has to be channeled vertically such that critical information flows upward unheeded, but is severely restricted in the downward direction. The unidirectional flow of information ensures the unidirectional flow of power in the opposite direction. The restriction of knowledge helps to maintain the hierarchical power structure by establishing vertically-directed relationships that attach subordinates like textured hooks of Velcro to their superiors in clingy bonds of dependency. In this context it is interesting to note that much of the global political unrest we have witnessed in the last decade can be traced to the dramatic change in access to information that has accompanied the proliferation of the internet. Those in positions of power no longer have the same ability to restrict access to certain types of knowledge, and the legitimacy of their authority has suffered as a result. Unfortunately, as we will see, the system's ability to manipulate and control is actually greatly enhanced by the information collected and asymmetrically disseminated through interactive mass media and social networking technology.

Power and autonomy

Knowledge is power. The isolation and asymmetric distribution of knowledge is one way that authority is established and maintained. But authority and power are not the same thing. "Authority is the right to command, and correlatively, the right to be obeyed. It must be distinguished from power, which is the ability to compel compliance, either through the use or threat of force."[15] The relationship between authority and power involves layers of complexity in addition to those that attend the asymmetric distribution of knowledge. For example, a person can be in a position of authority and yet have little or no power. And, conversely, a person can have considerable power and yet not occupy a position of authority. "To claim authority is to claim the right to be obeyed. To *have* authority is then— what? It may mean to have that right, or it may mean to have one's claim acknowledged and accepted by those at whom it is directed."[16] It is one thing to claim to have authority, another to have that claim accepted as legitimate, and yet another to be able to elicit obedience.

The water gets even murkier when we dissect reasons for obedience. The connection between authority and obedience is not necessarily a straightforward relationship. "Obedience is not a matter of doing what someone tells you to do. It is a matter of doing what he tells you to do *because he tells you to do it.*"[17] A given act of obedience might be supported by a sense of duty to obey, a desire to please your superior, the pursuit of reward, the fear of punishment or some other negative consequence, blind habit, or some combination of factors. "Domination ('authority') in this sense may be based on the most diverse motives of compliance: all the way from simple habituation to the most purely rational calculation of advantage. Hence every genuine form of domination implies a minimum of voluntary compliance, that is, an *interest* (based on ulterior motives or genuine acceptance) in obedience."[18] This fact, that compliance is ultimately directed at self-interest of those who comply, will prove to be important later on in Part 5, in our discussion of potential ways to dismantle artificial systems of authority and control.

But how does authority attain its legitimacy? In mundane everyday situations, the legitimacy of authority is not usually questioned. "In everyday life these [authority-based] relationships, like others, are governed by custom and material calculation of advantage. But custom, personal advantage, purely affectual or ideal motives of solidarity, do not form a sufficiently reliable basis for a given domination. In addition, there is normally a further element, the belief in legitimacy."[19] According to one of the foundational thinkers in the field of sociology, Max Weber, there are both subjective and objective sources of legitimacy as it applies to authority. The legitimacy of an authority can be purely subjective, based on an emotional response, based on rational or value-based belief, or based on religious beliefs that obedience to the order is necessary to ensure salvation. But legitimacy can also be based on more objective beliefs about interests, and the consequences that a lack of obedience would entail. Weber sorts this latter source into *convention* and *law,* both of which have the power to punish deviation: convention, through the psychological coercion of social approbation, and law, though physical force. A good portion of an authority's ability to maintain power over an individual, at least with respect to trivial or day-to-day matters, is normative, and derives from perceived and actual social and psychological pressures imposed by fellow targets of the authority's power: *some of our most enduring chains are the ones forged by our fellow slaves.*

Weber identified three "pure types" of authority, three sources of validity for claims of legitimate domination: rational grounds, traditional grounds, and charismatic grounds.[20] Validity based on rational grounds involves belief in the "rights" of those in power to command authority as a legal matter, as a function of the rules of the system. When engaged in large-scale projects, building a pyramid, running a business, fighting a war, maintaining the integrity of a global commercial infrastructure, the legitimacy of authority is tied to an overarching goal or purpose. The question then becomes whether the goal or purpose is valid or legitimate—and, more specifically, for whom? In the vast majority of cases, the goal or purpose being pursued is not originally that of the individual who is the target authority. Despite this, the targets of authority typically come to adopt the goal or purpose as their own—even in cases where the goal is directly opposed to their own self interests. The corporate bureaucrat acquires feelings of loyalty for the company, the factory worker comes to identify with the product, in much the same way, perhaps, as kidnapping victims are thought to identify with their captors (the supposed Stockholm syndrome).

Validity based on traditional grounds centers on respect for the status quo and belief in the sanctity of tradition. Both respect for the status quo and belief in the sanctity of tradition tend to be default modes. "Most men . . . feel so strongly the force of tradition or bureaucracy that they accept unthinkingly the claims to authority which are made by their nominal rulers. It is the rare individual in history of the race who rises even to the level of questioning the right of his masters to command and the duty of himself and his fellows to obey."[21] Validity based on tradition shares much in common with Peirce's method of tenacity. As a child, many of us were taught to obey authority figures simply because obedience is the only valid response to authority; the source of the command is its only necessary validation. Later we will review some of the research on children's responses to authority and their understanding of legitimacy. Legitimacy may in part be determined by tradition, but children's capacity to assess an authority figure's legitimacy relative to specific contexts appears to follow a predictable developmental progression.

Validity based on charismatic grounds rests on attachment to an individual person, on beliefs about his or her character or religious mandate, for example. Great leaders are those who have the ability to generate followers through the power of charisma alone. Their beliefs, ideas, or goals are in some sense secondary to the influence of their personality and charisma. History is filled with both famous and infamous examples. This source of validity plays less of a role in the present global system than it did in the more provincial past, perhaps; or maybe it's that personality and charisma operate somewhat differently in mass society. The system itself, through its penetration into all facets of life, its shear omnipresence, is becoming more and more its own source of validation simply through the elimination of alternative possibility.

Legitimacy is ultimately a matter of belief. And while it might be easier for a system of authority to function if the targets of authority believe the system is legitimate, the system's actual power to affect behavior is not simply a matter of establishing and maintaining legitimacy. History traces uncountable situations in which an initially illegitimate system comes to be seen as legitimate once established. Violence, not legitimacy, is the central driver of authority. All obedience to authority, even that associated with norms and social approbation, is ultimately underwritten by violence. Violence is the frame with which hierarchy is constructed, and violence and the threat of violence is the force that keeps power hierarchies from collapsing under their own oppressive weight. Violence floats across the surface of every command and each act of compliance, whether or not the authority is seen as legitimate.

To comply with the commands of authority, irrespective of whether the authority is seen as legitimate, and irrespective of whether the compliance is voluntary, is to relinquish autonomy. Robert Paul Wolff, in his 1970 landmark essay, *In Defense of Anarchism,* traced the inverse relationship between obedience to authority and autonomy in convincing detail. Wolff came to the conclusion that individuals have a duty to be true to themselves, to act in accordance with their own conscience, and that this duty is incompatible with obedience to the commands of authority. Simply put, we have a moral duty to act autonomously, to make our own decisions about what is right and what is wrong in any concrete situation and then act accordingly, and obedience to authority reflects an abandonment of our primary duty to personal autonomy.

There are many forms and degrees of forfeiture of autonomy. A man can give up his independence of judgment with regard to a single question, or in respect of a single type of question. For example, when I place myself in the hands of my doctor, I commit myself to whatever course or treatment he prescribes, but only in regard to my health. I do not make him my legal counselor as well. A man may forfeit autonomy on some or all questions for a specific period of time, or during his entire life. He may submit himself to all commands, whatever they may be, save for some specified acts (such as killing) which he refuses to perform. From the example of the doctor, it is obvious that there are at least some situations in which it is reasonable to give up one's autonomy. Indeed, we may wonder whether, in a complex world of technical expertise, it is ever reasonable *not* to do so![22]

Consider the last sentence in the above quote in light of our discussion of the role that knowledge plays in maintaining authority. The partitioning of knowledge into isolated pockets of expertise leads by necessity to a reduction of autonomy. "The paradox of man's condition in the modern world is that the more fully he recognizes his right and duty to be his own master, the more completely he becomes the passive object of a technology and bureaucracy whose complexities he cannot hope to understand."[23]

Wolff's anarchism is based on the inverse relationship between autonomy and authority, and the assumption that autonomy is the primary duty of each person. For Wolff, "legitimate authority" is an oxymoron, and anarchism is the only means of preserving autonomy:

The defining mark of the state is authority, the right to rule. The primary obligation of man [sic] is autonomy, the refusal to be ruled. It would seem, then, that there can be no resolution of the conflict between the autonomy of the individual and the putative authority of the state. Insofar as man fulfills his obligation to make himself the author of his decisions, he will resist the state's claim to have authority over him. That is to say, he will deny that he has a duty to obey the laws of the state *simply because they are the laws*. In that sense, it would seem that anarchism is the only political doctrine consistent with the virtue of autonomy.

Now, of course, an anarchist may grant the necessity of complying with the law under certain circumstances or for the time being. He may even doubt that there is any real prospect of eliminating the state as a human institution. But he will never view the commands of the state as *legitimate,* as having a binding moral force.[24]

The explicit commands of the state, its written laws and policies, are not the only—not even the primary—source of oppression. Michel Foucault mapped out the historical trend toward the reduction of autonomy as a matter of the progressive and implicit infiltration of the power of authority into the minutia of our daily lives:

> But in thinking of the mechanisms of power, I am thinking rather of its capillary form of existence, the point where power reaches into the very grain of individuals, touches their bodies and inserts itself into their actions and attitudes, their discourses, learning processes and everyday lives. The eighteenth century invented, so to speak, a synaptic regime of power, a regime of its exercise *within* the social body rather than *from above* it.[25]

The power of authority is only truly effective when it reaches this "capillary form," when it penetrates the weave of the fibers of our daily activities, when it becomes inseparable from the activities themselves. Foucault traces this "synaptic" form of power to the economic changes that occurred in Europe in the 1700s. "[T]he economic changes of the eighteenth century made it necessary to ensure the circulation of the effects of power through progressively finer channels, gaining access to individuals themselves, to their bodies, their gestures and all their daily actions. By such means power, even when faced with ruling a multiplicity of men, could be as efficacious as if it were being exercised over a single one."[26] The industrial revolution introduced mechanical modes of social control that paralleled the mechanization of production in the factory. The flow of power became increasingly a matter of the structure of the machine of society, increasingly a matter of the social-political architecture, and decreasingly associated with specific powerful individuals. "One doesn't have here a power which is wholly in the hands of one person who can exercise it alone and totally over the others. It's a machine in which everyone is caught, those who exercise power just as much as those over whom it is exercised. . . . . Power is no longer substantially identified with an individual who exercises it by right of birth; it becomes a machinery that no one owns."[27]

The significance of this transition of power from being a matter of birthright to being relative to a position within a mechanical system cannot be overstated. The ultimate source of power, and by extension, the ultimate source of authority, lies not with any specific agent, but with the structure of the system itself, a mechanical system that, like all complex technologies, came into being slowly and in piecemeal fashion with no conscious intent and no attention to its ultimate direction or design.

> On the other hand, if power is arranged as a machine working by a complex system of cogs and gears, where it is the place of the person which is determining, not his nature, no reliance can be placed on a single individual. If the machine were such that someone could stand outside it and assume sole responsibility for managing it, power would be identified with that one man and we would be back with a monarchical type of power. . . . A distinction needs to be made here. It's obvious that in an apparatus like an army or a factory, or some other such type of institution, the system of power takes a pyramidical form. Hence there is an apex. But even so, even in such a simple case, this summit doesn't form the 'source' or 'principle' from which all power derives as though from a luminous focus (the image by which monarchy represents itself). The summit and the lower elements of the hierarchy stand in a relationship of mutual support and conditioning, a mutual 'hold' (power as mutual and indefinite "blackmail"). But if you ask me "Does this new technology of power take its historical origin from an identifiable individual or group of individuals who decide to implement it so as to further their interests or facilitate their utilization of the social body?' then I would say 'No'. These tactics were invented and organized from the starting points of local conditions and particular needs. They took shape in

piecemeal fashion, prior to any class strategy designed to weld them into vast, coherent ensembles.[28]

This piecemeal process is reflected in the development and impact of virtually all technological instruments and processes, not merely those associated with social control. The components and capacities for the production and assembly of all complex technology develop and accumulate long before the technology itself is even conceived. I have much more to say about this later. I will also address how participation in the public sphere has increasingly required the use of technology and the capacity to navigate complex technical bureaucracies, and that this technological mediation and the mandatory submission to monitoring and the requisite relinquishment of privacy that it demands, along with the increasing mechanization of social interaction, place additional, perhaps catastrophic, restrictions on our autonomy.

One of the most profound areas of technological development with respect to systemic power and control is that associated with surveillance. According to Foucault, there was a central historical moment in terms of the nature of repression in civilization in which "it became understood that it was more efficient and profitable in terms of the economy of power to place people under surveillance than to subject them to some exemplary penalty."[29] Rather than punish deviants in public spectacles as examples to cow the masses into submission through fear, it is far more effective just to place everyone under continuous scrutiny, where a cautious, irrepressible introspection replaces occasional fear with obsessive (perhaps largely unconscious) self-monitoring and chronic low-level anxiety. "In contrast to that [violent forms of power maintained through spectacular public punishment such as public executions] you have a system of surveillance, which on the contrary involves very little expense. There is no need for arms, physical violence, material constraints. Just a gaze. An inspecting gaze, a gaze which each individual under its weight will end by interiorizing to the point that he is his own overseer, each individual thus exercising this surveillance over, and against, himself."[30]

We will address the technology of surveillance in some detail in Part 4. The watchful electronic eye, in conjunction with powerful computerized data management capacities, has rendered virtually all aspects of our lives, public and private, transparent and open to corporate (and police) inspection. And the information being collected about us is being used to make us into more efficient (and compliant) consumers.

That power should flow vertically is only common sense—it has its source in our most basic experience with gravity. We will explore evidence in Part 4 of a peculiar asymmetry that emerges as a function of our metaphoric mapping of the vertical dimension of our physical experience to our social experience of power and authority. The will to power is a basic feature of all life, a fundamental aspect of a world with potentially limited resources. But this sense of the word "power" is not readily transferrable to technologies of control, and has virtually no relation to the deeply oppressive circumstances in post-industrial society. In physics, power refers to the rate at which energy is transferred, used, or transformed. In everyday parlance, power is frequently used as a synonym for strength, or as the capacity to act, or as a force of control. To have power is to be able to affect the world around you in an intentional way. To be on the receiving end of power is to be affected against your will. Hierarchically organized power is power dispersed according to an artificial and quite often arbitrary schematic.

Being embedded in this schematic, we are not free. Freedom and autonomy are roughly synonymous from a psychological perspective. To be free is to be an autonomous agent. Freedom and autonomy are matters of degree. You can be more or less free; you can have more or less autonomy. Freedom and autonomy are both situation-dependent and context-bound. Submission to authority and personal autonomy are mutually incompatible. At one extreme, the completely autonomous person is one whose moment by moment activity is directed entirely at the pursuit of freely chosen goals and subject only to the authority of his or her own conscience. At the other extreme is the shackled slave. Most of us occupy a position along this continuum that is far closer to shackled slave that we realize. The vast majority, if not the entirety, of our moment by moment activity is directed at the pursuit of goals that we have been coerced to adopt—goals that serve interests that are not ultimately in our own best interests and that are entirely removed from any meaningful considerations of conscience.

To be authentically human requires maximal autonomy. Note here that the truly autonomous person is not someone who is flitting from one thing to the other as the mood strikes. Autonomy is not simply the freedom to pursue the whims of the moment. In fact, to be subject to the whims of the moment is in a very real sense the opposite of autonomy: it is to be a prisoner of fleeting emotion or transient desire. As with anarchy, definitions of autonomy suffer from the tendency to be deformed and simplified. Anarchists are frequently reduced to violent, hedonistically-focused, anti-authoritarian narcissists by the protectors of the status quo. True, some persons who identify as anarchists probably fit this definition, but we need to be on guard for the tendency to simplify and otherwise warp sophisticated ideas so that they can be dismissed as something they are not. The method of tenacity and the method of authority can be very close in terms of their underlying psychological motivations.

I will be returning again and again to the psychological underpinnings of authority's power. Our evolved psychology, and more specifically the mismatch between our evolved expectations and our present circumstances, can provide a potent framework for thinking about our situation; and specific nodal points of mismatch can serve as targetable lynchpins, potential keys to our disengagement from the power machine. But before we get there, we have some considerable preliminary ground to cover. My purpose in the next several parts is to expand on—and provide some concrete frame for—Wolff's contention that there is no such thing as *legitimate* authority, that all authority is based on the illegitimate restriction of personal autonomy, that no one has a moral right to assume a position of power and control over someone else, and that, because of this, our hierarchically-structured civilization itself has no claim to legitimacy.

The anarchist challenge

The fact that every political state that has ever existed has been hugely oppressive and violently antagonistic to personal freedom is not in itself proof that a non-oppressive state is impossible. Just because every swan that has ever been seen is white doesn't mean that there can't be a black swan hiding in the bushes somewhere (or in Australia, as the actual case turned out to be). But the case for anarchism doesn't depend on divining a thoroughgoing proof that all possible governments are anti-human by definition (a task for which I am neither intellectually nor dispositionally equipped). Neither is it necessary to show that anarchy itself is without problems. The transition from a massively controlling state to the statelessness of anarchy involves a number of tradeoffs in which certain benefits are exchanged for others. There are, no doubt, several extremely desirable features of modern life that would be lost in such a transition. And it is also likely that statelessness would include several undesirable features that are not currently part of modern life. Perhaps all that is required for the case for anarchism is to show that the benefits provided by the presence of an oppressive state are not worth the sacrifices required in terms of freedom, autonomy, and actual human lives.

This is not as straightforward as it might seem, however. It is not a simple cost-benefit analysis. It is not a matter of simply providing evidence that, in the balance, anarchy provides a net benefit, or that the benefits of statelessness outweigh the benefits of the state. For one thing, I'm not sure how such evidence could be provided. Immediately we run into a problem to the extent that things such as autonomy, security, comfort, or any other dimension of human experience, are incommensurate. There is no metric by which we can translate between a gain in security and a loss of autonomy, for instance. Security and autonomy are unique and independently valuable qualities. In addition, each individual person weighs these qualities differently in terms of his or her own unique set of personal priorities and dispositions. Some people would be willing to sacrifice most if not all of their autonomy for a small amount of security (and indeed many have done so), whereas others would be willing to risk their lives to protect what little autonomy they still happen to possess (and indeed many have done this as well). Also, to speak in generalities about these things, to say for instance that "the human condition" is generally improved under the state, is to speak nonsense. There is no overarching human condition, and things never generally improve; they improve in specific ways and for specific people. You don't get air conditioning without coal miners.

Thus the first step in making a case for anarchism is to clarify the question. The question is not: "Why should anarchy be preferred over the state?" If, as I have suggested in the introduction, anarchy is the natural condition of human society, then, logically, the onus should be on the non-anarchists to show how their system (or any system) can represent an improvement upon anarchy. Hobbes apparently recognized this, and started with "man in a state of nature" and pointed toward the improvement in the human condition that was brought into existence by the state. The challenge, then, is not to show that anarchy is superior to any other social-political situation— current, historical, or imagined—but, rather, just the opposite. If anarchy is taken as the default social state of humans, the state to which our genes—and the epigenetic developmental programs that give our genes their collective expression—have been fine-tuned by evolution to expect, the challenge is for any other possibility to demonstrate that it gives us something better—not "us" in some abstract, "humanity" or "society" sense, but us in the sense of you and me (and all seven billion other you's and me's) as unique individual persons. The question should be configured: "Why should the state be preferred over anarchy and who is it that should express this preference?"

Stating the question this way might seem a bit awkward for some folks; even intuitively wrong. There are at least two related psychological reasons for this. One has to do with something called the naturalistic fallacy. The naturalistic fallacy is a logical error in which "is" is equated with "should," the erroneous belief that because a certain state of affairs exists, it was meant to exist. The fact that the state with all of its oppressive machinery exists gives it a latent moral advantage over any presently nonexistent situation; and the mere existence of a situation is perceived as serving as evidence in its own favor. Even a single counter example is sufficient to show that mere existence is not validation of "ought-ness." Consider the Nazi regime in this light. This error in reasoning is driven in part from two related cognitive biases that distort our decisions and choices: the existence bias and the status quo bias. With the existence bias, an existing circumstance has value, just because it exists, over conditions that don't exist or no longer exist. Studies have shown that merely telling someone that a certain set of circumstances is true (regardless of whether they are in fact true) is sufficient to increase the degree to which the person will evaluate those circumstances positively.[31] The status quo bias refers to the tendency to be willing to invest more energy in maintaining the status quo than we would have been willing to invest to bring the conditions that represent the status quo about in the first place. Post-industrial mass society is the proper form of social organization (naturalistic fallacy), has obvious value over previous social conditions (existence bias), and needs to be fortified against attempts by anarchists to undermine its operations (status quo bias).

Grounding our situation in terms of our evolved predispositions for small-group hunter-gatherer lifestyles—and taking something maximally approximating anarchy as reflecting the default social-political expectation for humans—provides a way of framing the question that puts the onus on promoters of the state to demonstrate that it offers us something better than we had before the state came along and relieved us of the burden of autonomy. The anarchist challenge is essentially this: is there a social-political design of any kind that can improve upon the evolution-supported default for the human species? If "the human condition" is recognized as an abstraction, a conceptual place-holder for the condition of numerous unique individual persons, then logically, the answer has to be "no." There is no design that can improve upon the human condition as it relates to the expression of individuality and individual autonomy because autonomy is at a maximum under anarchy, and any systematizing of human relations necessarily involves a reduction in autonomy for someone.

The case for anarchism that provides the conceptual cloth of the sections and chapters to follow is stitched along three separate but interwoven patterns. The most general pattern derives from anarcho-primitivism and is based in the intuition that certain forms of life are more authentically human than are others. Two prominent assumptions feature in this part of the argument:

(1) Anarchy is the default social state of humans.
(2) Anarchy is a state of maximum autonomy.

A subsidiary motif latent in the weave of the argument derives from considerations of legitimacy, and, allowing that legitimacy is a matter of degree, involves straightforward logic:

(1) To be legitimate, a social-political system (government, state) has to be recognized as such by the persons whose lives are affected by its operation.
(2) Since there is no social-political situation, historical or theoretical, that has ever existed that was recognized as legitimate by all people involved, there has never been a *completely* legitimate social political situation.
(3) Anarchy, being the absence of systematic social-political organization, is the only social situation that is immune from considerations of legitimacy. In other words, there can be no completely legitimate social-political condition (government, state), and anarchy is the only condition that is not (at least partially) illegitimate.

The most highly textured feature of the pattern, the feature that will take up a preponderance of the ink in the pages that follow, is the role of technology. When we deal with hierarchical systems of authority, we are dealing with a kind of social technology. As it turns out, the two, authority and technology, are intimately related—so much so that neither one can exist without the other. I see this feature of our situation as the one that may prove to be the most useful in practical terms, providing physical handles, as it were, for us to take hold of authority:

(1) Oppressive systems of authority are technologies of social control. As with any technology, they have a hierarchically-organized internal logic and a propensity to change over time in the direction of increased efficiency. And as with any other technology, they are open to innovation and subject to re-appropriation ("function drift") and expansion.

(2) These systems work by imposing structure on human relationships, and function through the organization and asymmetric distribution of power within and among these relationships, where some persons or groups of persons (typically a small minority) are given the means (e.g., lethal weaponry, control of bureaucratic systems of coercion, etc.) to direct, restrain, or otherwise manipulate the actions of others.

(3) These technological systems of social control emerged historically in conjunction with the emergence of large-scale technology itself. All complex technological systems, to the extent that their construction, operation, distribution, or maintenance relies on human participation, require the presence of systems of authority.

(4) The more technologically-saturated our global civilization becomes, the more we will be required to surrender our personal autonomy to pervasive and penetrating systems of authority.

The case for anarchism is not motivated by the belief that human life under conditions of anarchy will necessarily be peaceful and idyllic. Humans are not pacifists by design. We are primates prone to occasional intra-group and intergroup aggression. We are complex organisms capable of extreme violence as well as extreme compassion. The elimination of oppressive systems of authority—if it were ever to happen—would not usher in a utopic golden age. The case for anarchism is simply that life embedded in oppressive systems of power and authority—even with all of the potential advantages such a life affords for some (almost always a tiny minority of) people—is not worth the loss of autonomy and the capacity for individual expression that it entails. Second, and perhaps more to the point, even if the advantages of the state were to outweigh the costs, there is no possible way of grounding systems of authority in legitimacy. All authority, by definition, is illegitimate. As individuals, we are under no binding obligation to accommodate any system of authority and never will be. It might be practical for us to do so. It might be to our great advantage to do so. It might even be stupid—or lethal—for us not to do so in some cases. But systems of authority possess no binding moral force or claim to our acquiescence.

In Part 2, I will be addressing, among other things, the bias latent within the delusion of progress that present-day oppression is somehow an extension of natural primate dominance relations, that it reflects a progressive extension of a natural or default feature of the human condition. When scientists come across what appears to be peaceful coexistence, either in an animal or a human group, they seek to explain its source. What mechanisms does the group use to keep the potentially powerful in check? The inverse question is rarely asked of any group that is sorted into hierarchical relations based on dominance and submission. The expression of power and control is thought to be the default, a baseline expectation, and egalitarianism a deviation, an aberration to be explained. Consider this typical description of egalitarianism: "Egalitarian societies constitute a very special type of hierarchy, one in which the rank and file avoid being subordinated by vigilantly keeping alpha-type group members under their collective thumbs."[32] Hierarchy is the default condition and power is dispersed equitably only through deliberate and sustained "vigilance." This type of bias, where the exception is taken as the rule, is reminiscent of the common class inclusion error in which an ellipse is considered to be a special kind of circle: the circle is taken as the default and deviations from its perfect symmetry are exceptions (blame Plato, I suppose); whereas in reality, it is the circle that is the exception. There are infinite varieties of ellipse, the circle being a very specific and limited subtype. Likewise, human communities have expressed themselves in a large number of ways, the vast majority of which have incorporated a sizeable dose of egalitarianism. Only a very few—and then only fairly recently—have involved highly oppressive power hierarchies.

It appears obvious to many folks that the complex social power structures of civilization have their source in the simple dominance hierarchies of our primate ancestors. The idea that most animals live embedded in tooth-and-claw-and-beak-enforced systems of dominance and submission is an understanding of animal behavior derived in large part from thousands of years of observing barnyard animals, creatures whose natural social response systems have been dramatically altered by the domestication process. This barnyard lens, in combination with a healthy dose of anthropomorphism, has unfortunately also distorted the perspective of more recent scientific studies of animal social systems. Anthropologists are keenly aware of the bias that ethnographers work under, and are quick to qualify any conclusions they draw. This awareness of bias seems to feature far less in the animal scientists' data. As we will see, scientists actually speak of chimpanzees "going to war," as if there is anything remotely comparable between ape inter-band skirmishes and the highly organized mass murder and genocide associated with human warfare.

On the one hand it makes some sense that we interpret chimpanzee behavior in light of our human experience. We are essentially a species of chimpanzee ourselves, after all. Jared Diamond refers to humans as "the third chimpanzee," and backs this claim with an extremely compelling logic and a convincing array of evidence.[33] However, much of our behavior, unlike that of our closest primate relatives, is no longer produced by the operation of natural social systems. Much of our behavior, social and otherwise, is in response to the artificial machinations of a complex collection of behavior-control technologies called civilization. Academic and philosophical discussions of human nature frequently highlight the flexibility of the concept itself. Human nature is maximally malleable, ineffable, or entirely a matter of self-definition. Humans are the one creature with the capacity to determine their own nature. Such proclamations fail to recognize the true source of what is mistakenly called human nature is not human at all, but a potent assemblage of human-generated technologies. They fail to distinguish the part of our behavior that is a natural response to our genetic plan as humans designed for small-group social existence from the part that is a response to the artificial strictures of the global industrial machine. Part of the putative benefits of studying other animals is that it gives us a better window into our true human nature, that part of us that is not a forced deformation, that part of us that is not a reaction to the artificial demands of the machine of civilization. And, if approached carefully, comparative psychology might help us to delineate more clearly the distinction between our human nature and our machine nature. But first it is necessary to acknowledge the distinction.

One of the side-effects of the failure to make this distinction is that science serves only to rationalize and justify the oppressive power hierarchies of the modern world: birds, do it, bees do it, even gorillas and chimpanzees do it. So that fact that humans do it too—and far more extensively and effectively—is to be expected. But the truth is that what the birds and bees and chimpanzees are doing is something qualitatively different from what is being forced upon civilized humans. And to say that the modern police state has its roots in the natural stratification found in primate society is like saying the plastic components of the keyboard I'm presently typing on have their roots in the decayed bodies of prehistoric plankton. While it is true at a certain trivial level of analysis, it leaves out all of the meaningfully relevant intermediary features of the connection.

PART 2: DOMESTICATION AND THE POWER COMPLEX

The pecking order

Much of our understanding of animal behavior—both in terms of popular cultural beliefs and scientific theory—is grounded in the observation of domestic animals. The problem with this is that weird things happen in the barnyard that would never happen naturally in the wild. Many of the animals themselves have been genetically altered to the point that they bear little resemblance to their undomesticated counterparts. Most modern food animals are unable to survive without continual human intervention; many have experienced so much cumulative genetic modification that they have no naturally occurring counterparts, and teasing out what part of their behavior is due to the animal's natural proclivities and what part reflects side-effects of domestication technology may be impossible: the animals' "natural" proclivities are themselves the intentional products of domestication. Zoos and captive research colonies might provide a slightly clearer window, especially when data obtained through naturalistic observation in the wild is included. Nevertheless, much of what we know about the lives of other animals is grounded in the aberrant behavior of despoiled captives and genetic Frankenstein beasts.

The same, of course, might be said of our understanding of human behavior. It is likely that weird things happen with humans forced into a barnyard-dependent lifestyle that would never happen in the wild. With very few exceptions, almost all of our empirical knowledge of humans is based on the study and observation of *do-*

mestic humans. Attempts to get at something closer to what humans would be like in their authentic natural habitat—if such still existed—ethnographic studies of indigenous foraging peoples, for example, are unlikely to give an accurate picture because of the extreme environments that the remaining present-day hunter-gatherers inhabit (African desert, South American tropical rainforest, arctic tundra), and because in all but a select few cases they have been sullied by millennia of contact with their non-foraging neighbors (and several generations worth of contact by anthropologists). Archaeological data provide a lens into our evolutionary past and the kinds of human lifestyles that our DNA-coded developmental programs are designed to accommodate, but, as with the results of all scientific investigations, these data are subject to a wide variety of potential interpretations, each of which is limited and biased by contemporary circumstances. Recall our discussion of Peirce in Part 1: knowledge acquired through the use of the scientific method of inquiry is ultimately limited by the types of questions that are pursued and how they are formulated. It is quite likely that there are important questions that our "civilized" minds simply would never think to ask.

In addition, the delusion of progress casts an obscuring veil across any question that our civilized minds might be tempted to ask about authentic human nature. For example, according to the notion of progress, there are no *authentically* human habitats because humans make their own habitat. What may have been true for our prehistoric ancestors is no longer true for us because humans have progressed since that time. Human nature has been changed. Mass society is now our authentic habitat. Or, perhaps, as a post-modernist might say, there is no such thing as either an authentic nature or an authentic habitat, that the narrative of authenticity can be superimposed as a template on any sort of concrete circumstances—but that's just a more obscure way of saying that humans make their own habitat. In Part 3, we will explore in some depth how humans are in fact perpetually involved in the alteration of their concrete circumstances, but that these circumstances incorporate less and less of anything that might be considered authentically human. The habitats that the vast majority of us are forced to occupy today are historically-contingent artificial creations of technology, and have only the most tenuous connection to the kinds of physical and social environments that comprised the bulk of our evolutionary preparation. What we can safely surmise about natural human existence outside of the grip of civilization and prior to domestication is limited to broad generalities: it generally involved nomadic or seminomadic foraging in small, close knit, mostly peaceful, spiritually and emotionally satisfying, largely egalitarian multigenerational groups. Even these broad generalities, however, are sufficient to bring into sharp relief the dramatic contrast between present conditions and the kind of lifestyles for which we are genetically prepared. And the degree of authenticity of any human lifestyle is a direct function of its congruence with our genetic preparation.

It would be wrong to subject a genetically-altered domesticated animal, a modern dairy-cow, for example, to the harsh conditions of life outside the controlled feedlot. It would be unethical to release an inbred Yorkshire terrier into the forest to fend for itself—although the dog would probably stand a better chance of long-term survival than would the cow. There is at least one major difference between modern humans and their domestic counterparts in the animal world, however. Thousands of years of artificial selection have generated in some cases massive genetic differences between contemporary domestic animals and their wild or prehistoric counterparts. The same has not occurred with Humans. Human domestication has not yet led to the meaningful genetic alteration of the human species.[1] Our chromosomes are packing Pleistocene contents. Nine thousand years of conquest, genocidal pogroms, and the development and deadly application of oppressive technologies of power may have eliminated much of the human genetic variability that existed previously, but we have yet, as a species, been physically altered in a way that precludes our readopting social conditions more consistent with our evolutionary past. Another way of saying that is that our evolutionary preparation for life as hunting-gathering foragers in small, close knit, mostly peaceful, spiritually and emotionally satisfying, largely egalitarian multigenerational groups is virtually intact and operational, and reflects the genetic present of every newborn human infant.

There are two important facts about the relationship between hierarchy and our evolutionary preparation that need to be kept in the forefront as we proceed. The first is that modern systems of power and authority are technologies of control that have emerged extremely recently in terms of our species tenure on the planet, and as such they are not themselves meaningfully reflected in our natural developmental programs or evolved behavioral predilections. From the perspective our genes, hierarchical authority is something brand new. The second is that these modern systems of power and authority can function only by employing and directing our natural developmental programs and evolved behavioral predilections. In other words, although oppressive hierarchy is not part of our human design, it gets its traction only by exploiting processes and tendencies that are. This latter fact will prove to be of critical importance to the issues discussed in Part 4.

Back to the barnyard. "The pecking order" is a common expression typically used to refer to the hierarchical regimentation of power and authority within an institution or social group. The term entered popular vernacular following a series of articles in the early 1920s by a German researcher, Thorleif Schjelderup-Ebbe, about the social dominance relations that occur among chickens in hen houses. As direct evidence that weird things happen as a result of the artificial environment of the barnyard that would probably never happen in the wild, if there is no rooster around, one of the henhouse hens will spontaneously stop laying eggs, take on a rooster-like watchdog role, and begin to dominate the other hens. Complex hierarchical patterns of dominance and submission emerge as a result, a literal pecking order.

Birds have been a favorite object of scientific study of dominance ever since Schjelderup-Ebbe's pecking order articles. The presence of sophisticated social hierarchies implies a concomitant level of cognitive sophistication. For example, to know your place in a social hierarchy without constantly testing yourself against everyone else in your group—and ruffling a lot of feathers—it is necessary to have at least a rudimentary ability to engage in transitive reasoning: if X is above me and Y is above X, then Y is above me too. Without this ability, you would have to test yourself against both X and Y (and everyone else in the group). In a small group, this would be possible. And if the social structure is fairly simple, then it might be unnecessary to understand the detailed interrelations among the various members. It might be enough simply to know who is above you and who is below. But as the social situation becomes more complex, the ability to employ at least rudimentary forms of logical reasoning becomes more important. As it turns out, some wild bird species demonstrate the capacity for this kind of transitive reasoning: Pinyon jays, for example, have been found to use transitive inference to sort out the hierarchical structure of their social environment.[2] An interesting thing that Schjelderup-Ebbe found in his hen-house observations was that occasionally there were "triangular" relations that formed that violated this transitive logic: X would be dominant relative to Y, Y would be dominant relative to Z, but Z would be dominant relative to X, suggesting either the absence of true hierarchy, or, perhaps, a context-sensitive system with additional layers of complexity. The evidence points to the latter.

Humans are not birds, however. And the symbolic grounding of our social structure makes it considerably more complex than that seen with any other species. This claim is not an expression of anthropocentric hubris. Our use of language alone, perhaps the most salient feature of our symbolic prowess, makes our social capacities incomparably complex with respect to other primates, and even our closest cousins, chimpanzees and bonobos, may not serve as truly meaningful comparison groups in this regard. Nevertheless, observations of our knuckle-walking relatives have been extremely informative. Chimps and bonobos, and even gorillas and orangutans, as it turns out, engage in strikingly human behavior. Or, perhaps it might be more accurate to say that much of what we have traditionally considered characteristic human behavior is strikingly similar to the behavior seen in other apes. In terms of evolutionary relationship, we are equidistant from chimps and bonobos, having diverged from a common ancestor species 6 million years ago. And human social and political proclivities seem to fit snuggly between the chimpanzee's male-dominated world of threat, bluster, and king-of-the-mountain-style aggression and the bonobo's kinder, gentler, matriarch society based on networks of alliance, calculated reciprocity, sexual favors, and the occasional back-stabbing betrayal.

Those who wish to accentuate our warlike nature find easy analogs in anecdotal accounts of chimpanzee aggression. In reality, however, although chimps can be very aggressive, actual fights are not all that common. In rare cases, both in the wild and in captive situations such as zoos or research colonies where access to resources has been artificially restricted, for example, chimp dominance hierarchies can lead to lethal aggression. In the wild, chimps have been observed engaging in "war" with neighboring colonies, sometimes carrying out ambush style attacks using sticks and rocks as weapons. But the use of the term "war" is clearly an exaggeration. Chimps can direct individual aggression in a collective fashion in a way that suggests premeditation and cooperation. Chimps gang up, ambush, and murder other chimps. But to call this "war" is a clear overextension of metaphor. Lion prides gang up, ambush, and murder gazelles. So is that war too? War requires the calculated elimination of the autonomy of the participants. Soldiers become mindless mechanical constituents functioning under a central locus of command. Individual humans don't engage in war; tribes, clans, armies, states, and nations do. There is every indication that the chimps engaged in mass acts of violence directed at other chimps are at all times acting as autonomous individuals. To see the difference highlighted, compare the emotional state of an ape engaged in an aggressive act of protecting territory or renegotiating his social status and the emotional state of a soldier in battle following arbitrary and unquestionable orders from a superior—or better yet, with the calm focused precision of a "soldier" with the joystick of a deadly drone aircraft in her hands. War is not possible in the absence of artificial technologies of power and authority. The presence of territorial aggression in primates—regardless of the level of premeditation, cooperation, or lethal violence involved—is not comparable to human war even as a loose analogy. "Those who attempt to impute war to man's biological nature, treating it as a manifestation of the ravenous 'struggle for existence,' or as a carry-over of instinctive animal aggression, show little insight into the difference between the fantastic ritualized massacres of war and other less-organized varieties of hostility, conflict, and potentially murderous antagonism. Pugnacity and rapacity and slaughter for food are biological traits, at least among carnivores: but war is a cultural institution."[3]

Humans are the only creatures capable of actual war; and only then after they have been stripped of their autonomy and reduced to servomechanisms, converted to subservient mechanical components of an artificial power hierarchy.[4] War, true war, is a byproduct of technologies of authority, and was impossible—entirely inconceivable—prior to Neolithic domestication. Humans are not pacifist by nature. And there were probably a lot of situations prior to the Neolithic in which conflict over hunting territory—or just plain xenophobia—led to deadly aggression between neighboring bands. But Pleistocene hunter-gatherers lacked two things that prevent me from calling this kind of inter-band conflict war. First, and the archeological record is pretty clear on this, they didn't have weapons. They had all kinds of potentially deadly tools, spears, knives, poison arrows, etc. But they didn't have any tools *specifically* designed for use against other humans. Spears, knives, and poison arrows were no doubt used to kill people on occasion (just like hammers and box cutters are today), but they were designed for aurochs and antelope. You don't start to see things like battle axes and maces in the archeological record until you get domestication and agriculture. And second, even more important than the lack of specifically designated weapons, as we will see in the next chapter the social structure of hunter-gatherer bands lacks the hierarchical systems of power and authority necessary for assembling and coordinating the deadly labor-power required for warfare. The division of labor that occurs with agriculture sets the stage for the hierarchical ordering of power-relations necessary to organize and carryout military operations.

Although war is an example of an activity that is unique to modern humans, there is much of what we think of as characteristically human that is more accurately considered characteristically primate. Primatologist Frans de Waal has written extensively about the connection between human behavior and that of our closest primate relatives. It is clear from the research observations he reports that much of what we consider human behavior is not unique to humans. It is also clear that humans are highly aware of dominance in the social world, and that we act in ways that reveal our primate nature.

> Consciously or unconsciously, social dominance is always on our minds. We display typical primate facial expressions, such as retracting our lips to expose our teeth and gums when we need to clarify our social position. The human smile derives from an appeasement signal, which is why women generally smile more than men. In myriad ways our behavior, even at its friendliest, hints at the possibility of aggression. We bring flowers or a bottle of wine when invading other peoples' territories, and we greet each other by waving and open hand, a gesture thought to originate from showing the absence of weapons. We formalize our hierarchies—through body postures and tone of voice—to the point that an experienced observer can tell in only a few minutes who is high or low on the totem pole.[5]

According to de Waal, hierarchy has a paradoxically stabilizing function for primate social groups—a function that serves the oppressive technologies of authority and control found in modern society as well, perhaps, but we'll get to that in a moment.

> This brings me to the greatest paradox, which is that although positions within a hierarchy are born from contest, the hierarchical structure itself, once established, eliminates the need for further conflict. Obviously, those lower on the scale would have preferred to be higher, but they settle for the next best thing, which is to be left in peace. The frequent exchange of status signals reassures bosses [sic] that there is no need for them to underline their position by force. Even those who believe that humans are more egalitarian than chimpanzees will have to admit that our societies could not possibly function without an acknowledged order.[6]

The last part of de Waal's statement above needs serious qualification: "our societies could not function without an acknowledged order" is a trivial tautology if he is referring to modern post-industrial society. If he is referring to all human societies, he is simply wrong. There are ways of being human that involve an acknowledged order in only a general "this is the way people are expected to act" way. He is making the common error of equating the oppressive and artificial hierarchies of civilization with the natural expression of evolved tendencies toward social dominance seen with primates and other animals. The fact that we obey the commands of our overbearing supervisor at work to keep from being fired or that we promptly comply with the TSA agent's request to remove our shoes in order to avoid being detained, interrogated, and strip-searched or that we allow the police officer with a search warrant and a revolver to enter our home does not reflect the simple elaboration of evolved tendencies toward dominance and submission in the social world. It is true that our society could not function without oppressive hierarchies. And it is true that our evolved proclivities for social dominance and submission serve as a psychological substrate for these hierarchies. But it is a mistake to think that these oppressive systems of authority are just a natural extension and elaboration of chimpanzee behavior.

Chimpanzees, bonobos, and humans share a common ancestor. Because of this, chimps and bonobos provide windows into our recent evolutionary past. The problem with this window is that it is made with two-way glass: humans might just as easily serve as a window into the evolutionary past of chimps and bonobos. Modern day chimps and bonobos are just as far removed from our common ape ancestor as are we. So any insights we glean from observation of our closest genetic relatives need to be tempered with the caveat that we are not looking at more primitive versions of ourselves. Consider in this vein what de Waal says about the relationship between the evolved hierarchy of primates and modern political ideology:

Was democracy truly achieved via a hierarchical past? There is an influential school of thought which believes that we started out in a state of nature that was harsh and chaotic, ruled by the "law of the jungle." We escaped this by agreeing on rules and delegating enforcement of these rules to a higher authority. It is the usual justification of top-down government. But what if it was entirely the other way around? What if the higher authority came first and attempts at equality later? This is what primate evolution seems to suggest. There never was chaos: we started out with crystal clear hierarchical order and then found ways of leveling it.[7]

If by "we started out" he is referring on the one hand to all primates, or to the common ape ancestor of chimps, bonobos, and humans, and the idea that "we" learned to level the hierarchical order means on the other hand that humans as a species acquired social proclivities that subverted the strict and oppressive dominance relations maintained by chimps, and to a far lesser degree also by bonobos, then he is correct. It is clear that that is not what he is saying, though. He suggests instead a kind of inside-out Hobbesian account of the role of civilized order as that of countering the oppressive dog-eat-dog, top-dog kind of animal domination that ruled before we (humans) developed sophisticated political methods of power dispersion. He is also clearly conflating the unnatural power hierarchies of civilization with natural evolved proclivities toward forming dominance hierarchies that humans might possess as a primate species. The former provide a template for *increasing and expanding* the capacity for dominance of those already in power, not for leveling the playing field for the little guy. De Waal has deep understanding of the social world of bonobos and chimps. He appears woefully uninformed, however, about the third primate in the group. And he is not alone in this.

A common error is to assume that a more egalitarian society requires that we ignore or downplay our natural human tendencies toward social control and domination. It is also an error to consider these tendencies as unnatural. Anthropologists examining the power relationships within hunter gatherer groups have found that they take the opposite tact. They are acutely aware of our human nature and are actively on guard for the problems that can result. De Waal, himself, points this out: "Egalitarianism is *not* based on mutual love and even less on passivity. It's an actively maintained condition that recognizes the universal desire to control and dominate. Instead of denying the will to power, egalitarians know it all too well. They deal with it every day."[8] The egalitarians de Waal is referring to are present-day hunter-gatherers. Although there are and have been non egalitarian hunting and gathering societies, some of which involved extreme inequality, and there are and have been simple pastoral and agrarian societies that were largely egalitarian, hunting-gathering societies are the only type that can support an extreme emphasis on equality among members, and perhaps the only kind of society in which true egalitarianism can exist.[9]

Actively egalitarian

Humans appear to be hardwired for collaboration in ways that other primates are not. Studies comparing human children to adult chimpanzees find that human children show a strong preference for working together to obtain food while chimps tend to prefer more solitary foraging activities.[10] Human children are also more likely than chimpanzees to share the spoils of a cooperative venture, and to be concerned with the equitable distribution of resources among peers.[11] Researchers have found adult patterns of cooperative behavior in children less than 4 years old,[12] and children as young as 14 months demonstrate the ability to cooperate in shared goal-pursuit and to altruistically help other people achieve their goals.[13] In short, human children demonstrate egalitarian social tendencies early on, and in ways that suggest that these tendencies are inborn, a byproduct of human evolution.

Human societies that qualify as egalitarian, that is, societies of near-equals in which everyone has more or less equal access to resources and more or less equal power in terms of community decision-making, are found only among certain groups of hunter-gatherers. Egalitarianism is not a passive condition in these societies, but something that is actively asserted and zealously maintained.[14] In addition to the presence of sometimes very elaborate and intentional social leveling mechanisms designed to guard against domination by specific individuals or groups, there are several characteristic features of a foraging lifestyle that naturally limit the concentration of power and authority. All of these characteristics involve the preservation of personal autonomy and the lack of mediation between the individual and his or her access to life's necessities.

Anthropologist James Woodburn distinguishes between two categories of society in terms of the relationship between personal labor and access to life's necessities: immediate-return societies and delayed-return societies.[15] Immediate-return systems are the only type that can support true egalitarianism. In immediate-return systems, there is a direct and immediate return on labor investment. People hunt or gather food and then eat the food they obtain either immediately that day or later on at their leisure. There is little or no processing involved, and no need for storage. Social groupings in egalitarian immediate-return systems are flexible, freely chosen, and involve mutual sharing and exchange, and acquiring life's necessities does not depend on the formation of binding relationships or the cooperation of specific other people. In other words, there are no intermediaries between a person and the targets of his or her needs and there is a complete lack of any specifically acknowledged hierarchical social order.

Physical and social mobility is a fundamental and necessary feature of egalitarian immediate-return societies, and serves as a primary leveling mechanism.[16] The easiest way to deal with conflict is to simply move away from the person or persons with whom you are in conflict. This is a preferred mode of diffusing conflict in small nomadic bands with flexible and ever-changing social groups, where an individual or a group of individuals can simply move to a different camp whenever the mood strikes, and without any restriction in the access to resources to satisfy their physical or social needs. "Most important of all for the present discussion is the way that such arrangements are subversive for the development of authority. Individuals are not bound to fixed areas, to fixed assets or to fixed resources. They are able to move away without difficulty and at a moment's notice from constraint which others may seek to impose on them and such possibility of movement is a powerful leveling mechanism, positively valued like all other leveling mechanisms in these societies."[17]

In addition to a high degree of physical and social mobility, the lack of dependence on specific other people for life's necessities is also a critical precondition for egalitarianism. The highly flexible nature of association along with reciprocal exchange and ritualized sharing of food ensures that even persons with physical or mental limitations are not forced into dependency relationships with specific others. Shared access to potential means of coercion, access to tools that might be used as deadly weapons, for instance, means that threats or attempts to dominate through coercion run a serious risk of yielding lethal repercussions. If everyone is packing poison arrows, for example, it becomes extremely important to avoid being the target of envy and to settle grievances before they escalate. "In normal circumstances the possession of all men, however physically weak, cowardly, unskilled or socially inept, of the means to kill secretly anyone perceived as a threat to their own well-being not only limits predation and exploitation; it also acts directly as a powerful leveling mechanism."[18]

Woodburn ties egalitarianism directly to the lack of mediation in immediate-return societies: "What we have here is direct and immediate access to social control, access which is not mediated through formal institutions or through relationships with other people. It is directly analogous to, and matched by, the direct and immediate access, again not normally mediated through formal institutions or through relationships with other people, which people have to food and other resources."[19] If there as one defining social feature of our modern techno-culture, it is mediation. Virtually all of our access to the physical, social, and psychological necessities for life is institutionally mediated. The recent explosion in the realm of internet-based social networking has pushed mediation in the social world to a hypoxic level. Although Westerners have become increasingly nomadic in recent decades, neither our decisions to move nor our options with respect to location are freely chosen, and our physical ability to move requires the mediation of numerous technologies, the cooperation of multiple persons, and the navigation of numerous institutions. We clearly live in a delayed-return society.

Delayed-return societies are characterized by a temporal or social disconnect between a person's labor and his or her claim to assets obtained through labor. For example, the food obtained might have involved the use of elaborate and labor-intensive tools, long-term storage or elaborate processing, the accumulation of labor across time, or the pooling of labor in a way that requires binding commitments and reciprocity arrangements with other people or institutions. Delayed-return systems are a necessary requirement for the existence of hierarchical systems of power and authority. Or, perhaps it would be more accurate to say that hierarchical systems of authority are ways of organizing and coordinating "return" in delayed-return systems. Hierarchical systems of authority would be incoherent in an immediate-return system. Mobility, complete freedom of association, equal access to potential tools of coercion, and the lack of dependency on others to satisfy basic needs means that in immediate-return systems there is no social substrate to provide authority with any traction. This is an important fact to keep in mind later on when we are exploring potential ways to disengage from the oppressive grip of our modern delayed-return power complex.

Immediate-return systems were the only systems in existence for the bulk of our species' evolutionary history, which means that egalitarianism was likely very common, and perhaps the norm, for most of human existence. The advent of domestication in the Neolithic was contemporaneous with the emergence of delayed-return systems. The social changes associated with delayed-return were one factor in the development of hierarchically structured systems of authority. The advent of domestication, however, was associated with the appearance of additional hierarchy-promoting conditions as well. For one thing, domestication alters the perceived relationship between humans and the natural world. The natural world emerges as the *other*, as a force to be coaxed and coopted, and, ideally, commanded.

The idea of nature

It's two o'clock on a warm Saturday in early June. One of the residents of the large yellow house kitty-corner from mine emerges from her garage with her lawnmower in tow. It's an oversized self-propelled job with an engine that sounds like a small Harley Davidson. She mows first in a horizontal pattern across the front of the house, and then goes over the entire front lawn again on a diagonal to give the yard the look of a major league outfield. She stops every few passes to empty the grass catcher into a pile in the street. Although the yard is small and almost treeless, it nonetheless takes over an hour for this first step to be completed. The mower is silent for a few moments before the next phase begins with the high-pitched nerve-grating drone of a gas-powered weed-whacker. She runs it along the foundation of the house, around and around the small ornamental tree recently installed in the center of the yard, then along the sidewalk and curb like an edger—and even along the gutter in the street, slapping away any stray weeds that might have sprouted in the moist crack between the asphalt and the curb. The final step involves a leaf blower, belching blue smoke and sounding like the death howl of a thousand wolves. She works the grass off the sidewalk and into the street, herds rolling green piles toward the main pile of mower-dumpings, and then spends considerable time blowing the main pile around until it forms an aesthetically appealing mound along the curb. This weekly ritual will be repeated again and again until late fall. Every couple of weeks starting in early spring, a small van emblazoned with the logo of a professional lawn care service pulls up and a man wearing knee-high rubber boots reels a hose spewing chemical fertilizer and pesticide (a potent weed-killer in this case) around the yard, ensuring a bountiful green weekend harvest throughout the summer.

An alien from another planet on an anthropological mission to Earth would be hard-pressed to explain this behavior.

The suburban American lawn makes an informative case study for highlighting our estrangement with respect to the natural world in general, a kind of dualistic separation from nature that has been called a "fundamental delusion of humankind."[20] When a colony of lowly termites builds an elaborately wrought mound, the result is considered part of the natural world. But when a colony of humans builds a skyscraper, it is evidence of human uniqueness and superiority. That we ourselves are a part of nature only applies to our physiology. The human mind is simply not natural, beyond natural, even divine. And further, because of our superior intelligence, we have the right to use the natural world in whatever ways we see fit. Who, after all, is in a better position to judge how the natural world is to be used? Nature is viewed as inert material "stuff," and when anthropomorphized, is a foreign antagonist, dumb and potentially hostile, but usually benign, something to be "overcome" and "subdued." It is our manifest destiny as a species to conquer and ultimately control the natural world. This can be seen not just in our idiotic lawn practices, but in our mass-production approach to agriculture and in the ways that we "manage" our remaining wilderness areas as well. One writer traces our desire to manipulate and control the natural world to our primate nature, and specifically to the possession of opposable thumbs: the world and all its objects become potentially graspable.[21]

Not all groups of humans, however, view the natural world this way. Ethnographic studies of hunter-gatherers suggest that, for some, the idea of nature as a distinct entity or even as a conceptual category borders on incoherent. It would be like talking about "everything" as if totality itself was a kind of object. The conceptual separation of humans from the rest of nature appears to be a view unique to agriculturalists. A similar caveat needs to be in place regarding ethnographic studies of present-day hunter-gatherers as was used to temper insights gained from observation of our closest primate relatives. But here, the caveat is not just that hunter-gatherer societies today are likely different from those of past ages, but that there is not any logical developmental relationship connecting hunter-gatherer societies with modern civilization. In other words, we need to guard against the delusion of progress. Foraging people are not undeveloped humans. The difference between existing hunter-gatherers and their civilization-dwelling contemporaries is more akin to the distinction between chimpanzees in the wild and captive chimps in zoos.

They are both equally evolved chimps, but one group is living in a system that is consistent with their evolutionary preparation, and the other is living in something artificial, contrived, and alien with respect to their DNA-coded developmental programs.

The world-views of present-day hunter-gatherers suggest that the antagonism toward the natural environment displayed by my neighbor's insane lawn-care activities is not itself part of our innate human nature. It is a historical artifact, a mindset that some have linked to Judeo-Christian notions about humankind's role in the divine order of things and the emphasis on a distinct separation between humans and the rest of the natural world, although it clearly predates Judaism. Recent elaborations of this view incorporate mechanistic, technology-based interpretations of the role of science, in which the natural world presents us with "problems" and science provides us with technological "solutions," and encourage unidirectional linear thinking with respect to material acquisition and the exploitation of natural resources. Nature-human separation is implied in virtually every aspect of our present global corporate consumer culture. In fact, in the absence of this underlying dichotomy, our current system makes little sense whatsoever. This view of separation fully endorses an economic system built on the extraction and exploitation of natural resources—that natural phenomena are "resources" is itself an idea that makes sense only from within this view—and considers the failure to exploit an available resource, an old growth forest for example, to be a foolish waste. Nature-human separation serves as a foundation for the delusion of progress. "The world that is being created by the accumulation of technical means is an artificial world and hence radically different from the natural world."[22] In addition to the sharp division between human concerns and the rest of nature, this view reduces the dizzying complexity of the natural world to simple flow-chart dichotomies based on human (read: corporate-consumer) goals. Is it a threat or benign? If a threat, can it be controlled and exploited? If it can't be controlled, destroy it. If benign, can it be manipulated and exploited? If it is neither useful nor a threat, ignore it, it might as well not exist.

Daniel Quinn, in his engaging and unique novel, *Ishmael,* makes a distinction between two general ways of being in the world, represented by two groups that he calls the *leavers* and the *takers.* The leavers are those people (and the rest of the natural world) who live according to the fundamental laws of nature, including the law that you kill only what you need to survive and the law that you don't actively prevent others from taking what they need. The leavers respect the diversity of the natural world and recognize their place as part of that diversity. The takers, as the name suggests, live by a different code entirely. They see the diversity of the natural world as a threat. They not only take more than they need, but they actively seek out and destroy their competition. Quinn equates the historical emergence of agriculture with the rise of the taker approach and the beginning of widespread displacement of leavers by takers. By its nature, a sedentary agricultural lifestyle leads to an increase in population. Additional land is necessary to feed the increasing number of mouths, which leads to an even further increase in population necessitating even more land. Eventually, the agriculturalists' need for land put them in competition with those following a subsistence lifestyle (the leavers). When this happened, the leavers were either assimilated or destroyed. Modern civilization has globalized this process. And as a society of modern-day takers, we have the full power of the industrial revolution behind us, which has greatly enhanced the speed and efficiency with which we are able to eliminate the competition. One need only look at the increasing rate of species extinction, and at what is happening to the last remaining leavers, the isolated indigenous in Africa, South America, and the arctic regions, who are being given the Hobson's choice: either assimilate or disappear.

The emergence of the idea of nature as a separate domain of substance malleable to human purposes and subservient to human goals is tied to the emergence of delayed-return systems, and more specifically to the technologies of domestication. The change in the relationship between humans and other animals that accompanies animal husbandry is informative in this regard. Hunting and gathering in immediate-return systems frequently coexists with what has been referred to as totemic culture. In totemic cultures, humans and other animals each belong to their own unique communities. There is the wolf community and the deer community, just as there are specific human communities. These communities equally participate in the world, although each may serve a different function with respect to the others. Humans in totemic culture occupy a special place in the world, but no more special than that occupied by the hawk or the opossum or the snake. Domestication changes this relationship among equals in the animal world and introduces hierarchies based on human purposes. First, it leads to an immediate distinction between those animals that are under human domestic control and those that are "wild" and uncontrolled. Hierarchy with respect to the animal kingdom emerges as domestic animals become dumb, subservient creatures, both in human thought and, through the accumulative deformation of artificial selection, in actual fact.

There is some not-so subtle irony in the fact that I am capitalizing on this very tendency to differentiate between the natural and the human-created as I write this book, by highlighting artificial—human created—systems of authority and control. These systems came into being as a means of controlling natural human behavior, a means of redirecting natural human proclivities toward behavior and activities that serve goals other than those possessed by the specific humans who are targets of the systems of authority and control. There is nothing unnatural or extra-natural—or supernatural—about the situation itself. Systems of authority and control are technologies designed to exploit our natural tendencies. And they came into being though a piecemeal, accumulative, historical process that, although not external to nature, is not itself a characteristic feature of nature or the natural world.

When it comes to modern commonsense beliefs about the nature of human nature, there are actually two levels of misunderstanding involved. The first has to do with the view of our place in the natural world as biological beings as it is filtered through the lens of the delusion of progress. Despite almost two-hundred years since Darwin, humans are still presented as the pinnacle of creation. Although chimps, bonobos, and humans are equidistant from our common ancestor, humans are nonetheless viewed as further along on the evolutionary train. The second level of misunderstanding has to do with cultural evolution. Here, the pinnacle is occupied by global mass society. And although we grudgingly acknowledge the few remaining indigenous people as human, anyone still living a subsistence lifestyle is quickly dismissed as primitive and undeveloped. There is a tendency to equate culture with technology and then to rank cultures according to their technological sophistication (the delusion of progress yet again). Cultural evolution becomes just a proxy for changes in technological complexity.

Our extensive tool use is what separates us from our ape cousins. And, truth be known, our extensive reliance on tools might have been the chink in our species behavior that provided a foothold for oppressive civilization. The manufacture and use of tools perhaps encourage certain habits of mind or tendencies of thought that serve as preconditions for a civilized world view. Tool manufacture requires that nature be modified from how it is presented in raw form. Tools also serve as mediators, separating us from direct experience with the world. And finally, tools provide a frame for interpreting the substance and phenomena of nature as exploitable resources. Domestication, however, represents a quantum leap in each of these tendencies: where nature itself becomes a tool.

We see initial seeds of domestication (so to speak) long before the agricultural revolution, with a reduction in nomadism, horticultural experimentation with fruit trees, and the gathering of wild cereals and pulses as far back as 23,000 years ago.[23] For whatever reasons, perhaps an increase in sedentary habitation reflecting local population increases, a post-glacial warming that led to a change in food sources and availability followed by rapid climate change as glacial ice melt wreaked havoc on north Atlantic ocean currents, simple spontaneous discovery, or, more likely, a combination of these things, delayed-return systems employing a variety of forms of domestication began to proliferate in the river valleys of the Near East, and perhaps a few select other places, starting some 9,000 - 10,000 years ago. Although largely sedentary lifestyles organized around the harvesting and storage of local grasses, seeds, and tree nuts (pistachios and acorns in the Near East) had existed for millennia, there is no evidence of broad-based agriculture prior to that time. According to popular myth, the spread of agriculture is a function of the superiority of agriculture-based lifestyles over hunting and gathering. When foraging people were exposed to farming, they quickly traded their spears for hoes. All evidence available runs counter to this myth, however. For example, a recent study comparing mitochondrial DNA from skeletons of the first European farmers, from skeletons of late European hunter-gatherer people, and from modern Europeans found that the first farmers in the area were not descendants of local hunter-gatherers but came from someplace else, and the hunter-gatherers in the area at the time were not absorbed into the farming culture, nor did they decide to take up farming as a result of exposure to agricultural practices.[24] The emergence of large-scale domestication was not a happy bandwagon with everyone jumping onboard. Like the emergence of civilization a few thousand years later, it was a slow moving bulldozer.

Large-scale agriculture produces exploding populations and exhausted soils, and, without a constant infusion of fossil energy and petroleum-based fertilizer and pesticides, can only survive through ever-expanding migration and conquest. Foraging people were helpless against the agriculturalist's advance because the early farmers had something that hunting-gathering people did not, something completely impossible in foraging cultures. The farmers had nascent versions of a technology that would eventually come to dominate the entire planet: systems of authority.

A tale of two societies

Anthropology and archeology are heavily biased toward material culture. There are obvious reasons for this that relate directly to the nature of the data available. But these two sciences, like all science, are grounded in our technological present, and are therefore likely to bend the data toward explanations that fit into a present-day template. For example, "production" and "consumption" play a central role in the distinction between delayed-return versus immediate-return societies discussed above. Since the industrial revolution, Western culture has become increasingly defined in terms of these two activities. As we look at past cultures, there is a tendency to judge them in terms of our present concerns. "Because we judge in modern terms, we believe that consumption and production coincided with the whole of life."[25] The fact that we are drawn to interpret other cultures in terms of material conditions of production and consumption tells us something important about our own culture.

The word "culture" is frequently used in ways that conflate three distinct kinds of thing: lifestyle (e.g., hunting and gathering, agriculture), social structure (e.g., egalitarian communities, oppressive hierarchical systems of authority), and the aggregate of traditions, customs, memes, and stories that serve to transmit the details of a group's lifestyle and social structure across generations. O'Sullivan defines culture as "the means by which humans adapt and by which they are selected," and says that at its root, culture is simply "a store of knowledge about the world, by which the group adapts to changing circumstances."[26] Changing circumstances, in turn, lead to changes in the group's store of knowledge about the world. Culture is thus a dynamic process sensitive to changes in internal and external circumstances, rather than a static collection of knowledge, beliefs, and practices. And note that "changes in circumstances" is not limited to changes in production and consumption, but applies to an open-ended range of contexts, events, and phenomena that include such disparate things as climate, geography, population density, changes in the prevalence and dispersion of local flora and fauna, accidents and natural disasters, disease, and chance asymmetries in group demographics. Despite this underlying dynamism and continual adaptive change, culture serves a stabilizing function, and provides a conduit for continuity across generations.

But we need to be careful when we say things such as "culture serves a stabilizing function, and provides a conduit for continuity across generations." A common error, and one made by social scientists who should know better, is to imbue culture with causal power. Culture is a descriptive abstraction. To say that our problems are due to the way that our culture is set up, for instance, is a kind of non-sense. It is equivalent to saying that our problems are due to our problems. It doesn't tell us anything that we don't already know. Consider the following imaginary tale of culture change involving a Paleolithic community living on the coast, whose primary source of food is mussels and ocean fish. The women spend their days collecting shellfish and making seashell jewelry while the men fish and play games of chance with notched sea-turtle shells. One year there is an algae bloom that kills most of the fish and renders the mussels inedible, so the people move inland in search of another source of food. After a while, they settle into a different pattern of life. Now the men go off for several days at a stretch in search of deer and elk while the women and children stay back and gather and process acorns. The turtle-shell game has been replaced by a different kind of gambling using sticks, and the seashell jewelry has been largely replaced by jewelry made of bits of carved antler. Because the men are gone for long stretches, the men and the women have developed noticeably different ways of interacting with each other both within and across genders. A test of hunting prowess is imposed as a rite of passage for young boys to determine when they are eligible to go on the hunt, and there are numerous other changes in daily life relative to their coast-dwelling days. Notice that during this entire description, culture was entirely absent as a causal factor in any of the changes. The changes were in response to changes in the demands and opportunities of the environment. Culture is a catch-all term for the aggregate of community practices; as an abstraction, it can play no role in changing those practices. Culture is a way of categorizing.

Social scientists typically partition human societies into three broad cultural categories based on how they obtain the necessities for life such as food. Why social scientists use physical necessities as their criteria instead of, say, spiritual sensibilities, or social activities, or any of a number of other variable features of human existence, again says something about the type of society that would come up with social science. Be that as it may, the three major categories are foraging (hunting and gathering), agriculture, and civilization. Note that these are frequently (and mistakenly) interpreted, not as incom-

mensurate but equally valid modes of livelihood, but rather in delusion-of-progress terms of a linear developmental progression from
primitive and ignorant hunter-gatherers to more sophisticated but
backward farmers to modern and enlightened denizens of civilization.

These three categories each imply a different social organization,
forms of governance, politics, and economy. Foraging involves a
band society governed by consensus and (typically) an egalitarian
politics based on open and transparent discussion and deliberation,
with an economy based on voluntary reciprocal exchange. Agriculture requires a more structured social, political, and economic fabric:
a society in the form of either a more or less egalitarian tribe or a
decidedly less egalitarian chiefdom, governed in a more or less authoritarian fashion that includes a politics of status, rank, and kinship
affiliation, and an economy based on (usually stratified) redistribution. Once we "progress" to civilization, we get our familiar complex
authoritarian state society with opaque class-based politics and an
economy based on involuntary (coerced) participation and severely
stratified redistribution.[27]

A side-effect of agriculture is surplus production. There are predictable relationships among surplus production, division of labor,
and social stratification. When you get division of labor, you get the
requirement to produce enough food to cover those people whose
labor is not directed at food production itself. The greater the specialization, the greater the stratification, that is, the greater the inequality
in a society, and the more surplus is required. Thus "the more complex the society, the more it lives beyond its (local) means."[28]

The differences among the three categories of society in terms of
per capita energy production are a nonlinear function of division of
labor and specialization. Hunting and gathering requires only about 5
Kcal per person per day, of which 3, or 60%, are directly consumed
as food. Agriculture requires between 12 and 26 Kcal per person per
day, depending on the extent to which domesticated food is augmented by hunting and wild harvesting. Once we move to industrial
agriculture, the figure jumps to 77 Kcal per person per day. And in
our post-industrial electrically-charged coal and nuclear civilization,

the number is over 230 Kcal per person per day, of which less than 5% is (over-)consumed as food.[29] To put this another way: life in post-industrial civilization requires 77 times more energy per person than it takes for a hunter gatherer to feed herself. Or to put it yet another way, the energy it takes to keep one civilized person alive for a single year is more than a hunter-gatherer can eat in a lifetime.

Of course, the biggest difference between the energy demands of civilized life and those of our prehistoric ancestors has to do with population. If everyone on the planet required the same energy input that those of us living in the heart of Western civilization use, it would take almost 270,000 times more energy to feed the human population now than the entire population of humans at any point during the Pleistocene could possibly eat. Modern civilization would not be possible if it were not for the persistence of the severely impoverished conditions in China and Angola and Somalia and Afghanistan and...

The dream of a truly globalized world is so much fairy dust.

With the adoption of a domestication-based lifestyle comes a dramatic change in social organization. But the emergence of highly oppressive systems of power and authority are not an immediate or even necessary consequence of agriculture. Although early Neolithic life involved delayed-return and a fundamental change in the perceived relationship between humans and the rest of the natural world, with humans seeing themselves in ways that placed them increasingly outside the sphere of the natural, human society remained broadly egalitarian for a time.

Marcella Frangipane distinguishes between two types of "egalitarian" society that emerged between 5000 and 6000 BCE in Mesopotamia: *horizontal egalitarian societies* and *vertical egalitarian societies*.[30] With horizontal egalitarian societies, all members were of essentially equal status and had equal participation in the decision making process. Such societies were marked by the prevalence of small, unstable villages, scattered standard dwellings, collective storage and equitable redistribution of surplus food, group cooperation, and a diffuse community government. In contrast, vertical egalitarian societies were marked by the presence of privileged status based around kinship relations, stable villages with large architecturally distinct individual dwellings, domestic rather than community storage of surplus, and competition among family groups and the presence of aristocracy. In other words, in vertical-egalitarian societies, we see the inchoate beginnings of authority. Vertical egalitarian societies do not represent a progressive development or an evolutionary change relative to their horizontal egalitarian contemporaries. "The archaeological information on the Mesopotamian earliest fully agricultural societies shows that the two contrasting systems of egalitarian societies described above are seen to be different models of social, economic, and political structures which are not in a chronological and evolutionary succession."[31] Both systems have as a major distinguishing feature the tendency to expand into new territories.[32] Population growth and soil exhaustion makes the tendency to expand to new territories a feature of virtually all agricultural societies up to the present day.

There are some notable differences between the two systems in terms of the capacity to change across time. The structure of horizontal egalitarian societies makes them extremely resistant to change. "Strictly egalitarian societies of this kind do not usually develop into more stratified societies, because . . . the society *reproduction* mechanisms, which are always powerful in every social system, which necessarily tends to reproduce and preserve itself, must maintain total social and economic equality and the horizontal distribution of powers, to avoid altering the nature of the system and avoid throwing it into crisis. The *horizontal egalitarian system,* in other words, tends to remain unchanged."[33] Vertical egalitarian systems, on the other hand tend to become more authority-based, and move over time toward "a widening gap between the population and a leadership, which was initially only ideological and kinship-based, and which subsequently acquired more social and political roles, leading to an increased capacity to centralize wealth."[34] The vertical systems of ancient Mesopotamia eventually became fully stratified societies, which set the stage for urbanization.

Unlike what occurred in the 'horizontal egalitarian societies', which need to remain unchanged to be efficient, in 'vertical egalitarian societies', based on a system of potentially competitive economic relations among households and kinship systems which contain the seeds of differences in their rules of descent, the mechanisms for reproducing the system can themselves drive the gradual widening of these differences, to the point of transforming the whole society into something radically new. The dominant relations change from being 'equal' to being 'unequal'. And the seed of inequality is terribly destabilizing and victorious, because it produces more dynamic societies, able to absorb contradictions and ready for change.[35]

The horizontal egalitarian societies associated with the emergence of agriculture in Mesopotamia were easily conquered and replaced with societies based on inequality and organized around systems of authority.

If we assume that horizontally egalitarian society is more consistent with the pre-Neolithic human design, then where did verticality come from in the first place? One of the major differences between the horizontal egalitarian and vertical egalitarian societies was that the agricultural practices of the vertical societies included the extensive use of irrigation, a technology that required the coordination of a large labor pool. This single feature, the need to assemble and coordinate a labor force around large-scale technology, might be the one critical factor, with the other differences, kinship-based power, domestic rather than communal storage and distribution of surplus, and superficial indicators of class such as dwelling size, reflecting characteristic "symptoms" of verticality rather than serving as causal factors.

Broad-based division of labor, such as that required for building and maintaining irrigation systems, brings into existence the need for a powerful organizing authority. Once such an authority structure is in place, it can then be redirected toward other sorts of projects, configuring armies for territorial conquest, for example. Horizontally egalitarian agricultural societies and the remaining local foraging populations were defenseless against their vertical-oriented contemporaries, swept into the highlands, and, other than a few trivial cultural fragments in the form of stories and mythological anecdotes, perhaps, brushed entirely out of history.

But hierarchical authority had an even more profound impact on the history of complex technology. The hierarchically ordered part-to-part relationships, the standardization and interchangeability of parts, especially those at the lower levels of the hierarchy, the laborers, brought with it the ability to conceptualize human action in terms of mechanical process, and served as the basis and prototype for all major technological development to follow. The first true machines were built entirely of human flesh and bone.

Civilization and the birth of the megamachine

The true story of the emergence of civilization will forever remain untold. The ease with which the word "emergence" seems to apply suggests an underlying assumption of inevitability. Civilization was somehow latent within the human design, destined to become manifest the moment conditions were ripe. And, further, once civilization appeared, its spread and development reflect the unfolding of an inevitable process. Consider the following description of historical events surrounding the emergence of civilization, a description that reeks of the delusion of progress, as a typical example indicative of the inevitability assumption:

> Between 3000 B.C. and the Middle Ages, human society continued to grow and evolve . . . with ever more complex technology—bronze, and then iron; mounted cavalry; powerful compound bows that greatly extended the archer's range—and larger empires: Assyria, Persia, Greece, and Rome to the west, the Han and Khmer Empires in the East, the Mauryans in India, Great Zimbabwe in Africa. Religion became more formalized, with monotheism replacing polytheism among the majority of the world's population. Two of the world's great mono-

theistic religions, Christianity and Islam, with their great zeal for conversion, spread over wide territories to dominate the world. Their adherents soon numbered in the tens of millions—a far cry from the localized ancestor cults of the early Neolithic. *But all of these events unfolded with a certain predictability, a natural outcome of what had been set in motion by the Neolithic Revolution.*[36]

The idea that, for example, the Crusades and the Spanish Inquisition—and the emergence of the Persian or Roman or Khmer Empires—collectively reflect "a natural outcome" of the adoption of agriculture-based lifestyles is ludicrous on its face. And the smelting of copper with tin and the domestication of horses is in no way "predictive" of the invention of either iron or Islam.

Evidence for the inevitability hypothesis is nonexistent. For one thing, it is a mistake to craft generalities using a sample size of one. In addition, there are limitations associated with retrospective historical analyses that ensure the tentativeness of even the most plausible theories. For example, there is a logical problem with starting with conditions at some specific point in time, conditions in the present or some known point in the past, and then trying to determine how those conditions came about. It is not unlike trying to determine the past shape of an ice cube from a puddle of water on the kitchen counter.[37] A small puddle of any shape is consistent with an infinite number of ice cubes—and an infinite number of other possible sources of water. It is impossible to start with an end result and then read causality backward into the initial stages of the process. The domestication of plants (fig trees, for example) occurred in numerous places long before the grain cultures of the Fertile Crescent appeared. And ancient clay sickles suggest the gathering of grain in the Fertile Crescent occurred long before its deliberate planting.[38] It is tempting to connect the dots to make the picture coherent and consistent with what we know eventually happened. But the outcome was far from a foregone conclusion. The invention of clay sickles to harvest wild grain does not lead inevitably to irrigation canals any more than the invention of gunpowder leads inevitably to the employment of lethal drone aircraft. We are not starting with the ice cube and then predicting the shape of the ensuing puddle—which is something that we could do with some confidence. All we have is the puddle.

The causes of civilization, as with the causes of large-scale domestication, will likely forever remain mysterious. All we have are these facts. Civilization happened. And it happened multiple times. It happened first in the agricultural centers of large river valleys in the Near East, then Africa, then India and China, then into Europe. And somehow it slipped across to the Americas while avoiding Australia. It eventually spread to the rest of the globe. We need to guard against the idea that we are dealing with a natural linear developmental progression rather than with the unpredictable and non-directional accumulation of historical events. Perhaps even more important, we need to guard against the "bandwagon" hypothesis. We have no evidence that either civilization or the agricultural-based lifestyles that preceded it, were freely chosen. On the contrary, we have considerable evidence to suggest that civilization was violently imposed on many of its participants, and maintained from the beginning by coercion and force. The vertical nature of civilized power, as with systems of authority wielded by the vertical-egalitarian farmers previously, was the driving muscle behind this "civilizing" force. "At this point [by the Third Millennium BCE], human effort moves from the limited horizontal plane of the village and the family to the vertical plane of a whole society. The new community formed a hierarchic structure, a social pyramid, which from base to pinnacle included many families, many villages, many occupations, often many regional habitats, and not the least, many gods. This political structure was the basic invention of the new age: without it, neither its monuments nor its cities could have been built, nor, one might add, would their premature destruction have so persistently taken place."[39]

Lewis Mumford provides a compelling description of the historical forces in play prior to and during the time of the first civilizations in the Near East. He begins with a gradual broadening of the separation between gathering and hunting that occurred in the Neolithic agrarian villages. Prior to the Neolithic, the herbaceous component of the community's diet was provided by females and children—the typical gatherers—while the males provided the occasional animal protein. Archeological evidence suggests that there was a protracted period of time in which communities became increasingly sedentary and the gathering became progressively tied to specific locations and to the harvesting and processing of tree nuts (almost exclusively by women) and perhaps some wild grasses.[40] Things changed with the advent of agriculture, and male labor was diverted to farming and herding with limited time for hunting. Herds and fields need protected from natural pests such as wolves and deer, however. This situation created a niche for a new kind of full-time hunter, one who could demand a share of the harvest in exchange for his protective services. Thus two different kinds of male-dominated lifestyles emerged, one tied to dominating but passive husbandry (of both animals and womenfolk) and one tied to equally dominating but more active hunting. The hunters tended to monopolize the weaponry and the skill in its application, and eventually turned this to their advantage against the passive villagers. Tribal chiefs appeared on the scene, exacting tribute in the form of cattle, grain, and women, and the villagers had little choice but to comply. The powerful among these chiefs became the first kings.

The historical veracity of Mumford's description of the emergence of kingship is not as important as the story it tells about the appearance of oppressive forms of vertically-oriented social power, a kind of social power that had no Paleolithic equivalent. Kingship might equally be explained as an inevitable result of the progression through time of the tendency of vertical-oriented kinship-based societies to extend the scope of inequality, but, again, we need to guard against reading necessary linearity and inevitable progression into historical process. Regardless of the actual historical events and processes that produced the institution of kingship, the king was the original apex of a unique kind of power hierarchy. And the most important contribution of kingship wasn't the creation of the hierarchy itself, according to Mumford, but the mechanizing of the relationships among the components of the hierarchy, a mechanization that led to the eventual assembly of the archetypal machine that "proved in fact to be the earliest working model for all later complex ma-

chines, though the emphasis slowly shifted from the human opera-
tives to the more reliable mechanical parts."[41]

"Such submission, such abject self-humiliation, never had a counterpart among the humble members of any village community until
'civilized' institutions filtered down from above. But this drill had
the effect of turning human beings into 'things,' who could be galva-
nized into a regimented kind of cooperation by royal command, to
perform the special tasks he assigned them, however stultifying to
their family life and incompatible with normal village routines."[42]
Kingship, and its requirement for unqualified obedience, provides a
social-psychological substrate for the functioning of mechanically
organized hierarchical power. "This mechanical obedience was
achieved by various symbolic and practical devices; and first, by establishing an insuperable psychological distance between the king
and all who came near him. His person was not merely inviolate,
untouchable; but those who came within his presence were commanded to prostrate themselves, as if dead, fully conscious that if
they offended the king, nothing would stand between them and
death."[43]

Mumford's study of the role religiously-grounded kingship
played in the pyramid age of ancient Egypt suggests that "[t]he
unique act of kingship was to assemble the manpower and to disci-
pline the organization that made possible the performance of work
on a scale never attempted before. As a result of this invention, huge
engineering tasks were accomplished five thousand years ago that
match the best performances in mass production, standardization,
and meticulous design."[44] The king's power may have been justified
by religion, but it was ultimately grounded in physical force. "On
earth, only one who was appointed by the gods a king could command such unconditional obedience: only one who could back such
presumptive claims with armed force, in the face of skepticism or
active dissent, could have broken down the habits of self-government
that small communities had evolved on the basis of ancestral customs and their own limited capabilities for taking counsel and exercising the common sense through prudent actions."[45]

Mumford traces the development of power in early civilization from the emergence of verticality of king-centered authority and its associated mechanical obedience, to the eventual assembly of vast hierarchically-ordered labor, military, and communication systems in which humans assumed limited and highly prescribed mechanical roles. It was the development of this mechanical order that made the difference for all succeeding generations up to and including our own. It wasn't physical technology in terms of sophisticated tools or weapons that was important—the Great Pyramid, after all, was built without the aid of the wheel or any tool more complex than the lever and the incline plane—it was the mechanical ordering of human behavior through a rigid, largely self-maintaining hierarchical system of power and authority, what Mumford called an invisible machine, invisible because the interacting parts (human beings) were physically separate.

Viewed from our present technical perspective, the passage to 'civilization' is hard to interpret. While no single technical factor marked the transition from the Neolithic economy to the typical forms of power-centered economy, abundant power was available, power sufficient to build if not to move mountains, before metals had been smelted and hard-edged metal tools had been put to work. Yet 'civilization' from the beginning was focused on the machine; and it will help us to understand what was new in the post-neolithic technics, if we place the new inventions side by side, along with the institutional controls that they demanded. We shall see how the might of an invisible machine anticipated the machine itself.[46]

Mumford referred to the coordinated totality of the hierarchically-organized mechanical systems of power and authority in the first civilizations, including the various labor machines, the military machine, and the intricate communication bureaucracies necessary to keep the parts integrated, as the *megamachine*. "Whether organized for labor or for war this new collective mechanism imposed the same kind of general regimentation, exercised the same mode of coercion and punishment, and limited the tangible rewards largely to the dominant minority who created and controlled the megamachine. Along with this, it reduced the area of communal autonomy, personal initiative, and self-regulation. Each standardized component, below the top level of command, was only part of a man, condemned to work at only part of a job and live only part of a life."[47]

It is important to note that Mumford's megemachine is not metaphor. The power structure of the first civilizations was the technological equivalent of a machine, albeit one whose sprockets, gears, and pulleys were composed of human beings rather than of metal parts. Modern civilization no longer involves kingship in any meaningful sense. But very little else has changed about the ultimate mechanical structuring of civilized life. Mumford sees the advanced technologies of authority and control that are active in the 21st century as mere variations on the "archetypal machine composed of human parts" that was assembled in the very first authoritarian civilizations of the Near East. We use different materials now, sources of power come in more varieties, are more numerous, are more dispersed, and the application of mechanical authority has become more subtle and at the same time more compelling, and mechanical authority has penetrated far more deeply into every aspect of our existence, but the differences between the first megamachines and our own reflect quantitative extensions and expanded applications resulting from technological innovation, complex variations on the same theme. The mechanization of human relations, the reliance on bureaucratic networks of authority, the fundamental top-down organization, is the same. The modern megamachine is incomparably more powerful, more omnipresent, and orders of magnitude more efficient relative to its bronze-age counterparts in Sumer and Egypt. In the late 1960s, at the onset of the information age, Mumford saw clearly the direction and the rapidity to which things were moving, and prophesied the end to which we have arrived today with the ascendancy of multinational corporations and too-big-to-fail world-wide financial institutions: "With this new 'megatechnics' the dominant minority will create a uniform, all-enveloping, super-planetary structure, designed for automatic operation. Instead of functioning actively as an autonomous personality, man [sic] will become a passive, purposeless, machine-conditioned animal whose proper functions, as technicians now interpret man's role, will either be fed into the machine or strictly limited and controlled for the benefit of de-personalized, collective organizations."[48] The term *globalization* was not in common parlance when Mumford wrote those words.

We no longer have god-kings at the top of the hierarchy. And the "dominant minority," the "one-percent" who make an easy target for the disenfranchised masses, for all of their wealth and their apparent power, are indentured functionaries in the service of the technological order. There is no king on a high throne, no dictator in his military command center, no greedy tyrant in his palatial mansion to issue directives from the top. There are no directives from the top because there is no top. There is only hierarchy, only the technological order, only the oppressive power complex of the machine itself.

The modern power complex

Mumford's description of the megamachine brings the mechanical, fundamentally technological nature of civilization into high relief. Modern civilization is a collection of organizational structures, of methods, of mechanisms and techniques, of technologies for achieving the highest possible level of efficiency in every domain of activity to which they are applied. The organizational structures of civilization are technologies, and, more specifically, they are technologies that operate through the systematizing of human behavior and the mechanizing of human relationships. But to refer to the totality of civilization's technologies of control as merely a complex kind of machine—even a megamachine—is a gross simplification. There is much more to civilization than a simple arrangement of technologies and organized mechanical relations. This is especially true of our hyper-complex modern techno-culture. Mumford himself acknowledged this, and developed the notion of *the power complex* as a way of thinking about the dizzying complexity of the megemachine of post-industrial civilization with its ubiquitous mass-technologies and unimaginably massive systems of power and control.

The power complex of post-industrial civilization reflects an expansive re-tooling and global-repurposing of the megamachine that began during the industrial revolution and brought about "a new constellation of forces, interests, and motives, which eventually resurrected the ancient megamachine, and gave it a more perfect technological structure, capable of planetary and even interplanetary extension."[49] Economist John Kenneth Galbraith coined the term "the technostructure" to refer to the loosely organized collection of interests, decision-making bodies, and individuals with specialized knowledge and experience that direct the mechanical operations and technological development in modern society.[50] Mumford's power complex is more comprehensive than Galbraith's technostructure, and includes all of the physical technology, the machines of government and industry and their coordinating corporate bureaucracies, along with the loosely organized decision-making bodies and special interests that appear on the surface to be controlling the direction and development of technology. It is the power complex, a complex that includes a massive, perpetually expanding technological infrastructure, along with the loosely coordinated activity of bureaucratic institutions, powerful individuals, and networks of organized groups, each narrowly focused on their own special interests, that assembles, continually reconfigures, coordinates, and directs the numerous visible and invisible machines of our global civilization.

No one controls the power complex. There is no single person or coalition of powerful rulers at the helm. There are no god-kings perched at the apex of the pyramids of power in the modern world. This is a critical point. The view being forwarded by Galbraith, Mumford, and others who have ventured into this area of investigation (e.g., Jacques Ellul, Langdon Winner, Neil Postman) is that the power complex is self-perpetuating. The modern technostructure is self-supporting. The technological process is in a very real sense autonomous and—perhaps most relevant for our purposes here—it achieves this autonomy only at the expense of our own. The autonomy of the power complex allows us to quickly dispel any conspiracy-theory notions that society is ultimately under the conscious control of ultra-powerful individuals or syndicates of the powerful elite. As will become evident below when we reexamine the internal logic of technology and explore phenomena associated with reverse adaptation and the technological imperative, there is no wizard behind the screen. There is no puppet master pulling the strings. The massive complex of interdependent technological systems that comprise our modern world has its own momentum and inertia. Technology itself is in control. Although human activity is critical to the technological process at a variety of levels, the car is driving itself and we are just along for the ride.

Perhaps the most valuable feature of this view is that it puts a spotlight directly on technology and the technological process as the source of the problem. Our problem is not political. It's not a conservative versus liberal, traditional versus progressive issue. These sorts of distinctions are completely irrelevant. The present historical situation is not political, it is technological. Neither is the world suffering from cumulative human moral failure. Humankind is not in the grip of an identity crisis or a failure of conscience. The problem is technology itself. The oppressive systems of power and authority in civilized society are technologies of control that are doing exactly what they are configured to do. In a somewhat broader sense, the technological process is synonymous with control: technology *is* control, the capturing and purposeful redirecting of phenomena. Power has its source in the technological system; it is generated and directed by the system; it flows from the architecture of the power complex. Authority is a feature of the technological order. The problem of oppressive authority is a technological problem, but its solution is not a matter of simply finding a patch, or tweaking the system until we get it right, or creating new technology that works like it is supposed to. The complex systems of power and control are working exactly how they were designed to work, and in some cases even better than they were originally intended. Finding a solution—if there is one—requires that we first understand the true nature of technology, and perhaps more broadly, the nature of technological development as a historical process: how technology "builds out," in

Arthur's words.[51] Finding authority's exploitable weaknesses—if any exist—is a technological issue, a systemic issue, not a moral, or an ideological, or a social-psychological one. To resist authority is to resist technology. And, as we will see, to be able to resist authority is going to require that we take a resistant posture toward *all* technology, not just that which serves as the proximal sources of oppression.

So how do we resist technology? If history is any indication, we simply don't: technology compels us to follow where it leads, technology draws our map and entrains our compass needle; technology is, in a very real sense, irresistible. It is an imperative. If that is true, if the history of technology as an unalterable inertial force is correct and predictive of our future inevitable course, then where does that leave us in terms of options? Do we have any? Are we doomed to continue as slaves to an ever-expanding technological order, destined for an ever-more oppressive future? Below I will argue that the answer to that question is a qualified "yes" where the specific nature of the qualifications holds the key to true resistance.

But first, let us check some of our assumptions. The historical account of technology as an inevitable force, for example, is not quite accurate. The story of technology's at times slow but unrelenting growth through human history is a product of the delusion of progress, and based on a "presentist" view of historical facts. For most of European history, technological change was exceedingly slow and at points regressive, as several factors conspired to keep "progress" in check. Jacques Ellul identified five factors that were necessary to eventually produce our present technologically-saturated state of affairs.[52] First, a very long and protracted incubation period was required, specifically leading to the industrial revolution—an event that was not at all inevitable, given that almost all of the necessary technology was available long before the first industrial factory was assembled. Second, there had to be a large enough population, both to provide the labor and to provide the intellectual pool from which to generate needed innovation. Third, there had to be a suitable economic infrastructure. Fourth, it was necessary to have a society that was completely "malleable and open to the propagation of technique." This fourth requirement meant overcoming the powerful sta-

tus quo-promoting forces associated with all societies, numerous social taboos in operation at the time, the conservatism of traditional
religion, and the formidable self-interests of professional guilds. The
final factor, perhaps the most important of all, was "a clear technical
intention" and a technical state of mind that included a powerful illusion of technological progress. None of these factors were present in
sufficient potency until the second half of the eighteenth century, and
none were, strictly speaking, inevitable even then. That there was a
large enough population to fuel the industrial revolution, for instance, was itself contingent on a specific configuration of an uncountable number of widely ranging variables, from global climate
to chance events of geopolitical history.

But history is past. That the present power complex did not have
to exist is a counterfactual point that is of theoretical interest only.
The absence of absolute inevitability might offer some hope for the
possibility of a less oppressive future, but it does not provide any
concrete direction. At this point, in the first quarter of the twenty-
first century, the technological order has become entirely self-
perpetuating and self-directing: a horse-drawn chariot without reigns,
an accelerating brake-less train that lays its own track. How can we
possibly free ourselves from a technology that has us so thoroughly
removed from any controlling access to its operative programs? The
question of our emancipation from the oppressive authority and control of the power complex is the single most important question we
face. Nothing less than the future of the world is at stake in the answer. When it appears that the only possible answer to a question this
important and this pressing is unacceptable—emancipation is impossible—then we are left with only two options: either we give up or
we find some way to reframe the question.

The reframing process requires that we thoroughly understand the
nature of the enemy. We need to understand what kind of a thing the
technology of power is; we need to take a closer look at the modern
machine, the power complex, and at how it organizes and directs our
activity, at how it effectively annihilates the freedom to pursue our
own ends as autonomous individuals. The ways that the first iterations of the megamachine were able to do this were straightforward,

and involved a fairly transparent conduit of direct and lethal physical force, violent coercion, and fear. Despite the dramatic similarity in their function and purpose, there are several notable differences between the ancient megamachines and their modern variant. Lethal physical force, violent coercion and fear are still present and active mechanisms of control. But the modern machine includes a large variety of far more subtle mechanisms, many of which are entirely opaque, and all of which are tied directly to innovation and the development of specific technologies.

When discussing technological innovation, it is easy to get distracted by the power and scope of modern technology. It is easy to become awestruck by its complexity, by the level of sophistication and shear intricacy and elegance of function involved. Present-day technology is nothing short of magical when compared to that of even a generation ago. It is important, to massacre an adage, to separate the devil from the details. We need to look beyond the sparkle and glitter of our high-tech gadgetry, and focus instead on the ends to which it is being applied. The delusion of progress can distort our capacity for objectivity. For all of its complexity, modern technology is relatively unimpressive when placed in an appropriate historical context. Consider that a common reaction to the accomplishments of the ancients is amazement that they were able to create such admirable monuments, the likes of the Egyptian pyramids, or Stonehenge, or even the Roman Coliseum, with such primitive technology. It is interesting that the converse amazement is rarely expressed: why, given our vastly superior and advanced technological capacities, have we not created "monuments" of comparable superiority. It's always "How were they able to do what they did with as little as they had?" and never "Why have we done comparably so little given all that we have now that they didn't?" It seems that the impressive advance in technology has not led to a comparably impressive advance the construction of "monuments." Our cities are far larger, with complex networks of energy, water, and sanitation, and our buildings are taller and made from high-tech materials, but the modern city is just a sprawling upgraded variation on the original ancient theme. The walled citadel has morphed into the central business district with a fortress of office buildings. The bazaars have become shopping malls. The merchant quarters have been converted to subdivisions, and the slave quarters, into suburban trailer parks and high-rise urban housing complexes.

There are, of course, several qualitative differences between post-industrial civilization and the civilizations of the ancient Near East. An obvious difference has to do with the shear amount of power available to feed the machine. The first civilizations were entirely biologically powered, powered by human (and animal) labor. It might be suggested that their critical dependence on the ability to move and redirect large volumes of water through dam and irrigation technology means that the first civilizations were essentially water-powered; which is why they are sometimes referred to as "hydraulic" civilizations. Our modern global techno-culture is powered almost entirely by fossil energy. The proportion of physical power derived from human labor, even with a potential global labor pool of seven billion people, is so small as to be an inconsequential fraction of the whole of our energized civilization. In terms of energy, the available whole is many orders of magnitude greater than what was available even just a couple centuries ago. And the coercive capacity to divert power toward violent force is immensely greater as well. The hydraulic societies of ancient Mesopotamia were constructed and maintained with the aid and threat of sword and whip and mace operating at an upper limit of speed equal to that at which a horse could be made to run. The modern machine has access to an arsenal of highly specialized, minutely targetable tools of coercion and weaponry that can be applied in seconds and with planet-annihilating levels of force. And, of course, it also has numerous tools of distraction— hypnotic high-tech bread and circuses—and a psychologically-informed propaganda to groom a compliant state of mind among the masses so that overt force is seldom necessary.

In the past, the physical geography of earth served to limit the machine's reach and scope. Distance and geography no longer pose a serious impediment. In addition to space, many of the impediments associated with time have been conquered as well. The mechanical clock, first created to coordinate medieval monastic life and later employed by factory industrialists to coordinate the labor of wage-slaves, has yielded the capacity for precise levels of synchronization of activities separated by vast distances of physical space. Likewise, the explosion in electronic communication technology, augmented most recently through the development of computer-mediated cellular and internet-based real-time audio-visual modes, has removed all physical and temporal obstacles to global bureaucratization that relate to physical separation and distance. The modern machine has rendered the entire planet immediately present and capable of fitting in the palm of your hand. The role that modern communication technology plays in the mechanizing and control of the masses cannot be overstated. "Both ancient and contemporary control systems are based, essentially, on one-way communication, centrally organized. In face-to-face communication even the most ignorant person can answer back, and he has various means at his command besides the word—the expression of his face, the stance of his body, even threat of bodily assault. As the channels of instantaneous communication become more elaborate, the response must be officially staged, and this means, in ordinary circumstances, externally controlled."[53] Mediation always means restriction and external control. I have more to say about this in Part 4.

Many of the qualitative differences between early megamachines and the modern power complex are a function of economies of scale. Enormity trails white-water in its wake, and the ensuing waves erode and reshape even the most distant shoreline. The corporate and economic machines of the power complex are gargantuan leviathans with tentacles wrapping around the entire planet (and soon even beyond the planet, if recent asteroid mining operations manage to get beyond the venture capital stage). Massive increase in size is accompanied by an increase in bureaucratic density, a steepening of the cliffs of hierarchy, and an increase in the pull of gravity at the centers of control. The larger the system, the smaller the contribution each individual part makes to the whole. Also, in mass-production terms, bigger means more efficient. Because of this, we see a clear historical trend from local, small-scale idiosyncrasy-infused craft to massive-scale standardized production. "In their very nature, modern technologies are large-scale, high-energy, high-resource systems requiring massive commitments of capital and technically trained manpower. Small-scale, localized arts and crafts live on, of course, primarily as vestigial remnants of a tradition of material culture that has lost its vitality. While technical organizations and apparatus of enormous size are not a totally new phenomenon in history, they are clearly more central to contemporary social existence than to any previous era."[54]

Despite the economy of scale and the massive size and scope, and despite a high degree of internal centralization of power and control within individuated and largely self-contained subsystems, the total assemblage of complex technological systems of modern society is not under any sort of centralized control. In fact, the autonomous functioning of massive technological systems makes them largely resistant to centralized authority and control. The state is in a very real sense at the beck and call of the technological systems, setting policy and crafting law in ways that ensure the technology continues to function and expand with the least amount of interference.[55] This is an important point. The police state, a proximal source of oppression, is a technological response to the need to protect and preserve technology from potentially corrosive internal and external influences. The modern state is a system designed to preserve technology, to ensure that human beings with their idiosyncrasies and their all-too human tendency to want to pursue non technological needs, are prevented from gumming up the system's smooth operation. The modern police state is a tool for enhancing efficiency. It has absolutely no other function.

This brings us to perhaps the most fundamental difference between the modern and ancient versions of the megamachine, a difference tied to the blurring of the distinction between the human and the mechanical. For all of their ability to mechanize human behavior, the first megamachines were unable to eliminate what was truly human from the equation. Humans are not machines, and the only way they can be deformed into mechanical parts is through some kind of externally-applied force. Particularly telling in this regard is a reproduction of an image from ancient Mesopotamia that Mumford includes in his book, *Technics and Human Development,* that depicts a line of "laborers" hauling a monument of a bull on a large sledge, with soldiers wielding swords and a whips positioned at intervals between the workers.[56] There were clear limits to the extent to which humans could be expected to act as cogs in the machine. And they would certainly not do so freely. Coercive force had to be applied openly and continuously in order for the machine to function. One of the major triumphs of the modern power complex is that it has largely succeeded in reducing the human to the mechanical, and as a result has greatly reduced (but not quite eliminated) the need for explicit forms of coercion. In the name of efficiency, the human element has been whittled to the bare minimum. Mumford condenses the historical transition in terms of the progressive siphoning of the human element from the labor process as follows: "manual work into machine work; machine work into paper work; paper work into electronic simulation of work, divorced progressively from any organic functions or human purposes, except those that further the power system."[57]

The gradualness of the processes (over several generations) in conjunction with the slow recalibration of human psychology and the re-socialization of the human role in the technological scheme has led to a progressive mechanization of the human self-concept. We think of ourselves in mechanical terms. We apply the rationality of efficiency to our personal lives and to our most intimate personal affairs. We "plan" our lives as if they were a business venture. The minutes and hours of our day become resources to be used productively or wasted—we "spend" time and expect a return on our investment. We assess our personal relationships in terms of a cost-benefit calculus. Self-help sections of bookstores are brimming with systems and techniques—technologies—for self-improvement: all personal problems are a failure of self-organization and are thus solvable through the appropriate application of the right self-control technology. That we see ourselves as machines is reflected in the ease with which we impute intelligence to mechanical forms of organization: concepts such as "computer intelligence" are coherent only because our own thought processes have been stripped of all but the mechanical, all but that which allows us to interface with the technology of the power complex. We have become servomechanisms.

PART 3: THE GHOST IN THE MACHINE

The engine of progress

Anyone who has been around for the last decade has first-person experience of technological change. For those of us who have been around somewhat longer, the changes have been striking. And a few have resulted in fundamental changes in the way we live our lives from day to day. My parents gave me a state-of-the-art electric typewriter as a gift shortly after I started college. By the time I graduated, the personal computer had rendered it an antique from a bygone era. By the time I completed graduate school, the internet had had a similar impact on a wide variety of appliances and activities. I am presently typing these words on an already grossly outdated laptop computer with broadband wireless access to unlimited cloud-based storage on the internet. The changes in hardware are most noticeable. The first cell phones were bulky hip-mounted contraptions that bear very little resemblance to the sleek touchscreen device I carry today. My office is still equipped with a two-piece wall-mounted telephone connected to a landline. But it is only rarely used and no one ever calls—at least no one I want to talk to. What is not so noticeable, both because human memory has higher resolution for the recent past and because behavior does not leave fossils of itself, is the extent to which our daily activity has been altered as a direct result of "upgrades" in hardware. That we accommodate changes in our technology is obvious. The fact that these accommodations alter our lives in elemental ways is somewhat more obscure. And the corollary that our lives are largely *determined* by our technology is acknowledged only unconsciously, if at all.

Technology changes, and drags us along with it. Change appears to be a fundamental feature of the technological process. There is an apparent regularity, a pattern, a developmental growth to technological change: a systemic "building out" in terms of complexity and scope that some have likened to biological evolution. There appears to be something natural and predictable about the way that technology evolves. An electric typewriter and a laptop computer appear as distinct transient stages in the natural unfolding of technological possibility. An ICBM is the remote genetic descendent of a obsidian spearhead. Appearances aside, the comparison of technological evolution with biological evolution is only metaphor; but the analogy points to some rather striking parallels. There is frequently a "survival of the fittest" quality to technological options, for example. And, as with natural selection, it is often not just a single characteristic, a single superior feature, that determines the survival of competing technological "organisms." It is how the specific technology as a whole fits into the larger social, political, and economic context. Consider the competition between alternative entertainment recording media in the mid-1970s, between cassette and 8-track audio formats, and between VHS and Betamax video formats, as prosaic examples. Each alternative had its strengths and weaknesses, but the survivors won out because they were better adapted to their niche, better able to interface with the larger consumer milieu.

Both biological evolution and technological evolution involve the modification of preexisting structure. Technological evolution differs, however, in that what emerges from the modification can be a qualitatively different "species," with different principles of operation and suitable for entirely different applications. Biological evolution takes several generations to produce a new species even when environmental pressures promoting change are at their highest. And what emerges from the process is almost always very similar to what existed before. According to an evolutionary principle known as Romer's Rule, evolutionary changes are initially conservative: adaptations that allow the organism to continue its previous way of life.

Unlike biological evolution, technological innovation can lead in a single "generation" to the sudden appearance of an array of things the likes of which never before existed. All modern computer-based technology traces back to the invention of the lowly transistor. To get a comparable event in biological evolution, an amoeba would have to become an entire set of large African mammals, an elephant, a zebra, a gazelle, a rhinoceros, a hippopotamus, and a lion, within the course of just a few cell divisions. And since each new technology becomes immediately available for modification itself or to serve as a constituent in additional innovation, technological evolution follows an exponentially expansive trajectory. The rate of technological change itself increases across time.

There are other interesting parallels between biological organisms and technologies in terms of the componential structuring of internal "organs" and the complex, hierarchically ordered external relationships that embed them in their operative niches. You will recall Arthur's insight that technology has an intrinsic logic to its internal structure. First, all technology involves an assemblage of preexisting and repurposed components. Each component is a technology in its own right, composed of previously existing and repurposed components. This process of regressive internal analysis is recursive to the extent that each level of resolution yields the assemblage of additional modular components until we arrive at some elemental component, a base metal, for example. The process of analysis can be extended in the other direction as well, as each independently functioning technological system interfaces and communicates with others as an individual component of a larger purposive system. Arthur traces the air intake of a naval fighter jet in this fashion, regressively inward down to a specific metal alloy, and progressively outward with the fighter jet a component of an aircraft carrier, the aircraft carrier embedded in a naval fleet, and the fleet just one constituent part of the US military infrastructure, an infrastructure that includes not just hardware, weaponry, communication structures, and innumerable support systems, each a self-contained, finely-structured technology in its own right, but an enormous complex of interacting organizational bureaucracies as well. He doesn't go as far as the larger

global geopolitical system, but there nothing preventing such a broad
outward extension of the hierarchical embedding involved.

An important point that Arthur makes about the logical structure
of technological systems, and one that is salient in the military example, is that they are densely or deeply hierarchical. They are not
simple pyramids of ascending and descending coordination and control, but rather they are potentially hyper-complex interconnected
tree-like structures with a main trunk, a number of major limbs, and
branches and twigs that interlace in sometimes extremely complex
patterns of looping feedback. The fractal-like recursiveness seen at
different levels is not an exact replication of form but a replication of
this general tree-like hierarchical structuring among the forms that
operate at each level. It is the modular structuring of each component
that gives the system its robustness against catastrophic failure despite the complex interdependencies involved. Arthur recounts a
classic parable related by Herbert Simon about two watchmakers:
"Each assembles watches of 1000 parts. The watchmaker named
Tempus does this from individual pieces, but if he is interrupted or
drops an unfinished watch, he must start again. Hora, by contrast,
puts his watches together from 10 assemblies, each consisting of 10
subassemblies, each consisting of 10 parts. If he pauses or is interrupted, he only loses a small part of the work."[1] Arthur points out
that an important consequence of this kind of recursive modular construction is that it allows us to separate out various components for
improvement or upgrading with more efficient replacements, and to
rapidly reconfigure the technology for application to different purposes. In Part 5 we will explore how this feature of technology can
serve as an impediment to resistance under normal circumstances,
but might also be exploited as a potential insurrectionary tool. Also,
and to anticipate the direction I will be taking this with respect to
anarchism, Arthur notes that, "all these parts and assemblies must be
orchestrated to perform together harmoniously. Combination must
necessarily be a highly disciplined process."[2]

In discussing the specific mechanisms for how technology
evolves, Arthur presents a simple yet compelling story of technological evolution as a natural byproduct of standard engineering practic-

es. Engineers are given a task, say, to design a bridge over a specific ravine, or to build an aircraft that can carry 350 passengers. In designing the bridge or the aircraft, the engineers draw heavily from preexisting "off-the-shelf" component technologies. The landing gear for a Boeing 747 can make use of the same exact component technology as does the landing gear in a 727, for instance—it is not necessary to reinvent the wheel every time a wheel is needed. In this way, new technologies come into existence as a novel combination of already existing technologies; and these new technologies, once created, are then available for entering into combination with others to serve as component parts of entirely new technologies in an ever more complex outward expansion. In addition, because specific component technologies have never been assembled in exactly this combination before, there are likely to be problems that emerge in the design process that have to be solved by making adjustments and modifications to the components themselves. Some of these changes are improvements in themselves, some provide solutions to future design problems—and some, a few, may suggest entirely new applications or lead to discoveries and extend knowledge about underlying phenomena. The specific technologies that emerge from this process do not necessarily represent the best possible solution to the problems they were designed to solve. There is a lot of room for chance and arbitrary choice. And once a choice is made, there is a "rich-gets-richer" process whereby the chosen technology becomes the standard and the alternatives fade from view. Arthur gives the example of the proliferation of light water cooling technology in nuclear reactors—there are far better, and far safer, options—as the result of a series of chance events following the Soviet Union's first atomic test and the need for the US to rapidly establish nuclear superiority. Because early designs used light water cooling, knowledge and experience with these systems increased relative to others, and light water cooling became a standard design feature. It is interesting to speculate whether the Fukushima meltdowns would have occurred if the reactors had used another cooling design. Would the reactors even have been built within tidal-wave range?

Arthur's overall point is that, despite a lack of foreknowledge with respect to what will ultimately emerge, there is a certain deliberateness attached to the process of technological evolution. Technologies evolve because they are purposely altered as solutions to standard engineering problems. Not all technology is of this type, however. Some "purposive systems" simply emerge over time as a function of historical changes in the traditional practices and conventions of society. Arthur says that this kind of "nondeliberate coming-into-being is not unusual,"[3] but his interests lie with the technologies that "evolve" as a function of the problem-solving activities of engineers, and especially with airplanes. Arthur is, like every young child, dazzled and awestruck by our complex and powerful machines. And he has drunk deeply from the delusion-of-progress Kool-Aid. At several points in his book, he makes reference to the myriad ways that technology has greatly improved the human condition—in complete denial of the present state of the world. We will pick up the thread of this denial later. But first, there is something I have left out about Arthur's story of technological evolution, something that relates directly to these purposive systems he refers to, and their not-unusual nondeliberate coming-into-being.

I think that Arthur's account of technological evolution as I have presented it so far has things backward—or, perhaps, inside out. According to the account so far, technological change is a function of novel combination of constituent technologies, leading to modification and potentially novel application. What is left out of this account is why the impetus for the novel combination and application arises in the first place. This is a natural oversight to make if you are firmly embedded in a view of history that emerges from the delusion of progress. Novel application, change, the quest for increased speed, power, and efficiency, "progress," is taken as the natural course of things rather than something to be explained itself. Why this incessant drive for efficiency? Why the quest for increased speed, power, and control? Given the delusion of progress, efficiency stands as its own explanation. The fact that worries over efficiency were either extremely minor, extremely rare, or entirely absent for over 99% of human social existence, and, until very recently for over 99% of the existing members of the human population, suggests that the idea of efficiency itself is in need of explanation. I would argue that rather than efficiency being the ground of technological evolution, it is just the inverse: it is something about the nature of technology that creates the drive for efficiency. And more specific to Arthur's theory of technological evolution, the purposive systems that lie outside of engineering proper, the ones that emerge through this "nondeliberate-coming-into-being" are the ultimate source of technology's evolutionary impetus. It is from these systems that we get "needs" for bridges over ravines and aircraft that can carry 350 passengers. Technology, we are told, is directed at human purposes; it is designed to solve problems in ways that satisfy human needs. The bridge is an engineering problem. Packing 350 passengers in a single aircraft is an engineering problem. But the *need* for a transportation system that includes bridges and gargantuan passenger planes is something else entirely. And it is not a human need!

How do such needs arise? Where do they come from? They are the product of the "purposive systems" that control and orchestrate our larger social world. They arise as a function of the technologies of authority and control; they are the "needs" of component systems in the power complex. The needs that are being serviced through technological innovation are needs that are generated by the technological order itself. We can do with the specific activity of an engineer attempting to solve a technical problem what Arthur did with the air intake of a fighter jet, and track the hierarchical embedding progressively outward to see the engineer's activity as a component of a larger organization of structured processes. The "need" being serviced by the engineering task is "human" only to the extent that the activities (and goals) of physical people have been entrained as part of the process. The specific individuals involved didn't create this "need." Their activity is purposeful, but the ultimate purposes to which it is directed are not their own. No one wakes up one day and thinks to themselves, "What I really need is a 350 passenger aircraft."

That's not to say that we are not motivated by needs. An engineer—or anyone else—has real needs. But many of the needs that direct our daily activity are externally imposed by the technological order. They are the needs of technology. They are artificial needs. They are not authentic human needs. Why does a specific engineer feel the "need" to do what she does when she directs her expertise to a given engineering task? One might answer that there are numerous reasons having to do with everything from the need for intellectual challenge or psychological fulfillment, to economic rewards (or pressures), to social rewards (or pressures). The question then becomes: why does designing a bridge or an airplane yield psychological fulfillment? Why do the economy and the social order have this kind of reward structure? And the answers, if we apply Arthur's scheme objectively, can only be that these things are a function of larger purposive systems: the technologies of authority and control that form the constituent structure of the power complex.

It is important to pause briefly, and clarify what I am not saying here. I am not saying that we are mindless passive victims of our technology. We lead active goal-directed lives. And we make important choices about which goals we pursue. But the goals we choose are severely conditioned within the context of operative technological systems, the ways we pursue our goals are tightly constrained by the requirements of these systems. In a game of chess, you are free to select your strategy, and you are free to change your strategy in response to that of your opponent. And you can freely choose your move with each turn. But your moves are bound by the rules of the game, and each piece is highly restricted in terms of how it can be moved across the board. And, of course, you cannot choose your opponent's strategy. In the same way, the purposive systems of civilization set both the rules of the game and our terms of engagement. And choosing not to play is not an option.

Biological evolution is not the only applicable metaphor for technology. Technology has also been called a language. A linguistic metaphor is particularly useful in highlighting the tree-like hierarchies and constituent structure of technology that Arthur's theory so eloquently captures. "Looked at from the outside, each technology in the collective appears to fulfill some set of purposes and not much more. If we want to measure we have surveying methods; if we want to navigate, we have global positioning systems. We can do particular things with surveying, and other particular things with GPS. But this is a limited view of what technology is about. Technology does not just offer a set of limited functions, it provides a vocabulary of elements that can be put together—in endlessly novel ways for endlessly novel purposes."[4] Technology is a "vocabulary." The question I have is whose speech are we writing? The answer is that the more technology evolves to accommodate the expanding needs of the technological order, the more that the technological order becomes self-sustaining and self-directing, the more the speech will be writing us. "The implications of self-augmentation become clearer: the individual's role is less and less important in technical evolution,"[5] and, I would argue, less human.

The comparison between technology and human language is a potentially productive one. Not only does it highlight the ways that a theoretically infinite number of novel technologies can emerge from the combination of independent, modular component technologies—in the same way that an infinite number of sentences can be constructed from a large but finite number of self-contained words—but it also directs us to gaps in our understanding about how we as humans fit into the technological order that may not have been apparent at first. The analogy between technology and language is imperfect, and the blank spaces in the comparison are at least as informative as the points of overlap. The metaphor works quite well in terms of the parallel between technology and language that involves the hierarchical structuring of modular constituents. Also, language and technology both serve as a point of interface between the individual and the larger community to which the individual belongs. Although language is generated within the individual, supported by symbolic cognitive capacities and uniquely human brain structures, language is a fundamentally social phenomenon. Technology, likewise, is fundamentally a social phenomenon supported by human cognitive capacities. But when we track technology back to the individual, the analogy disintegrates and the gap emerges. Individuals are themselves constituents in technological "expressions." The modularity that results from the division of labor and the isolation of knowledge transforms individual persons into technological constituents some-thing like the phonemes of spoken language. Language is a means for the individual to interact with the community to pursue his or her own social needs—language serves human purposes. Technology on the other hand transforms humans into component mechanical parts of artificial devices for the pursuit of its own purposes. The next two sections will explore the manner by which this mechanization of human beings occurs.

The technological imperative

According to the theory of technological evolution presented above, although human goal-directed activity is a necessary part of the pro-cess, the technological order in a very real sense creates itself. "The collective of technology builds itself from itself with the agency of human inventers and developers much as a coral reef builds itself from the activities of small organisms."[6] The analogy with a coral reef, however, fails to adequately capture the extent to which the technological order is built-out in a top-down fashion. A coral reef emerges as the historical residue of individual creatures pursuing their own biologically-programmed needs. By contrast, the techno-logical order emerges as authentic human needs are deformed, de-flected, and replaced by the needs of technology.

Langdon Winner provided an informative discussion of some-thing called "the technological imperative," which holds that *"tech-nologies are structures whose conditions of operation demand the restructuring of their environments."*[7] Winner compared this feature of technological structure to what economists call "vertical integra-tion," where one operation's output becomes the next operation's input.[8] Arthur's discussion of hierarchical embedding is directly rel-evant here as well. Because the operation of any specific technologi-cal system can serve as a necessary component process embedded in a larger system, changes in the larger system can necessitate altera-tions of the component system and vice versa. At some point in the process of "building out," complex webs of technological systems reach a critical mass in which they are perpetuated by the inertia of their own expanding presence. Once this critical mass is achieved, the individual systems must be maintained even if it is clear that they no longer serve the ends they were originally designed for, or whether they serve any desirable ends at all. Their continued presence in the technological order becomes an imperative. Another way of saying this is that the technological order serves as its own justification because any determination of whether it is justified is entirely encapsulated within the web of relationships among component systems. We must have technology because technology itself demands it.

Ultimate authority has been usurped by the technological order. Individual people in positions of "power" have no choice but to direct their own authority in ways that serve the needs of the existing configuration of the technological order. "A multiplicity of technologies, developed and applied under a very narrow range of considerations, act and interact in countless ways beyond the anticipations of any person or institution."[9] Nowhere are individual persons in control. At this point, it doesn't matter who occupies positions of power and authority, "they will be forced to take the same steps with regard to the maintenance and growth of the technological means."[10] Class or ideology or personal interests can play only a very minor role, if any at all. "The privileged position of an elite or ruling class is not proof that it steers the mechanism but only that it has a comfortable seat for the ride."[11] Class and ideology and ostensive personal interests function as little more than political red herrings, redirecting our attention and channeling potential insurrectionary energies from the true source of power in the system: the system itself. "Individuals and elites are present, but their roles and actions conform so closely to the framework established by the structures and processes of the technical system that any claim to determination by human choice becomes purely illusory."[12]

But note that although class and ideology and personal interests cannot serve as true sources of power and control, they too can be structured and arranged in ways that serve technological purposes. Class distinctions, for example, can be used as a way of structuring human relationships to better serve the needs technology. Ideology is coached by propaganda. Personal interests can be manufactured and directed. This is a crucial point that I will be returning to later. The ways that we see ourselves in relation to other people or groups have been shaped to facilitate the purposes of the technological order. The present configuration of the technological order grooms a world view that promotes its own continual expansion as a fundamental necessity and human relationships as merely one type of technological arrangement.

> It is important to notice, first of all, the conception of society which takes shape in the technological perspective. Absolutely fundamental is the view that modern technology is a way of organizing the world and that, potentially, there is no limit to the extent of this organization. In the end, literally everything within human reach can or will be rebuilt, resynthesized, reconstructed, and incorporated into the system of technical instrumentality. In this all-encompassing arrangement, human society—the total range of relationships among persons—is one segment. "Technological society" is actually a subsystem of . . . the technological order. Social relationships are merely one sort of connection. Individuals and social groups are merely one variety of component.[13]

The French sociologist, Jacques Ellul, emphasized the absence of any role for human choice in the technological process. "Technology itself . . . without indulgence or possible discussion, selects among the means to be employed. The human being is no longer in any sense the agent of choice."[14] The imperative nature of technological needs emerges, according to Ellul, in relation to the internal automation and mechanical selection among options within the technological structure—the mechanization of decision-making that strips humans of the faculty of choice.

> If a desired result is stipulated, there is no choice possible between technical means and nontechnical means based on imagination, individual qualities, or tradition. Nothing can com-

pete with the technical means. The choice is made a priori. It is not in the power of the individual or of the group to decide to follow some method other than the technical. The individual is in a dilemma: either he decides to safeguard his freedom of choice, chooses to use traditional, personal, moral, or empirical means, thereby entering into competition with a power against which he must suffer defeat; or he decides to accept technical necessity, in which case he will himself be the victor, but only by submitting irreparably to technical slavery. In effect, he has no freedom of choice.[15]

Again, technology structures the game board and sets the rules of play. As Winner tells it, despite their virtual limitless power, our technologies are "tools without handles. Often they seem to resist guidance by preconceived goals or standards. Far from being merely neutral, our technologies provide a positive content to the area of life to which they are applied, enhancing certain ends, denying or even destroying others."[16] By this account, humans are hapless servomechanisms whose activity is directed toward the needs of the machine. Yet the illusion that authentically human purposes are being served is so powerful, the illusion that technology is ultimately being steered by truly human needs is so compelling, that even the most enlightened appraisers of our technological situation frequently fall under its spell.

A hidden contradiction in Arthur's description of technological evolution provides a clear example of this tendency. Consider the blinding incongruity in Arthur's claims that "[T]echnology is a programming of nature. It is a capturing of phenomena and a harnessing of these to human purposes. An individual technology 'programs' many phenomena; it orchestrates these to achieve a particular purpose."[17] Technology "harnesses" phenomena to human ends and at the same time "programs" the very phenomena it "orchestrates" to achieve a purpose. So which is it, a human purpose or a technological purpose? In the end, Arthur is forced to admit, with Winner and Ellul, that it is ultimately technology's purpose: "And needs themselves derive more from technology itself than directly from human wants; they derive in the main from limitations encountered and problems engineered by technologies themselves. These *must* be solved by still further technologies, so that with technology need follows solution as much as solution follows need."[18] Arthur was apparently entirely oblivious to the elephant sitting on his keyboard as he wrote those words, because at the end of his book, after providing a convincing demonstration that the majority of our needs in modern society are not our own but are generated by technology, he says that we should be careful to distinguish technology that "enslaves" from technology that "extends our nature," and that "[W]e should not accept technology that deadens us; nor should we always equate what is possible with what is desirable."[19] But if our needs are being driven—no, created—by the technological order, then we have no choice. Our acceptance is irrelevant, if not guaranteed. If technology provides us with the rules of engagement, if technology configures the purposes as well as the roles we are to play in their achievement, then we have no way to distinguish enslavement from extension. Can there even be such a distinction?

The technological imperative makes questions of the legitimacy of the technological order seem nonsensical. "People are content in the knowledge that things are as they are and that they are in good working condition, and that in society everyone and everything has a certain job to do and does it. And everyone, like every thing, does not find occasion to inquire into this condition or to dispute the manner in which it structures life."[20] The technological order demands that our lives have structure and organization. That our lives must have structure and organization is an unquestionable premise; efficiency demands that we coordinate our personal aspirations with the workings of the system. And our lives become entrained to the mechanical order of our own—ostensibly, our own—creations. The lingering feeling that our lives are not really our own lurks as a weighty subconscious shadow and bubbles across the surface of our dreams.

Authority emerges from the technological order as a simple and effective mechanism for the coordination of component systems and processes in which humans play a necessary role. As we saw in the introduction, an individual's authority, their capacity to manipulate and control the activities of others, is a function of their possession of (or claim to) specialized knowledge. The fine partitioning and isolation of knowledge is demanded by the complexity of the system. And some forms of knowledge are more important than are others with respect to the priorities of the technological order. Those who are in possession of specialized knowledge essential to the continued growth and expansion of the technological order are almost always granted authority over those whose knowledge is less useful.

> Authority, like power, is in this point of view the product of knowledge and extraordinary performance. If those persons valuable or indispensable to the policy are those entitled to govern, then a society based on sophisticated technologies will tend to legitimate its scientists and technicians as rulers [note that a corporate CEO is a kind of technician]. Their expertise and accomplishment will naturally gain the esteem of the other members of society. Other sources of authority from earlier times and earlier understandings of the common good—tradition, religion, natural law, contract—must inevitably yield to this new mode of legitimation.[21]

The technological order rewards those who service its needs with positions of authority and the illusion of power, and punishes those who act in ways that are obstructive to its needs. Resisting authority is becoming more and more a technological matter. "We are today at the stage of historical evolution in which everything that is not technique is being eliminated. The challenge to a country, an individual, or a system is solely a technical challenge. Only a technical force can be opposed to a technical force."[22] The problem here lies in the contradiction that any technical solution to authority requires submission to authority. "To be commanded, technology must first be obeyed. But the opportunity to command seems forever to escape modern man."[23]

To summarize, the needs of the technological order become imperatives. The needs of technology trump authentic human needs whenever the two are in conflict. And, further, authentic human needs are overwritten by the needs of technology. This happens not through any mystical force or purposeful sinister intent on the part of the technological order, but simply as a function of the technological process itself, simply as a function of technology continually expanding into new niches of operation. "The vast majority of niches for technology are created not from human needs, but from the needs of technologies themselves. The reasons are several. For one thing, every technology by its very existence sets up an opportunity for fulfilling its purpose more cheaply or efficiently; and so for every technology there exists always an open opportunity. And for another, every technology requires supporting technologies: to manufacture it, organize it for production and distribution, maintain it, and enhance its performance. And these in turn require their own subsuporting technologies. [Additionally] Technologies often cause problems—indirectly—and this generates needs, or opportunities, for solutions."[24]

There is no ghost in the machine. Technology is not an occult force altering the human world to accommodate its own agendas. Rather, we become entrained to the purposes of the technological order through the operation of fairly straightforward principles—one might be tempted to call them "natural" principles, principles that emerge from the complex interactions between technological development and human society. One of these principles, one to which we now turn for a more in-depth look, is the process of reverse adaptation.

Reverse adaptation

On June 30th, 2012, a leap second was added to the day to make up for the gradual slowing of the planet's rotation. Another second will presumably have to be added again at some undetermined point in the future—undetermined because the rotational slowdown is not uniform or predictable because of the internal liquid wobbling of the planet. Ultra-precise atomic clocks and the earth's position relative to fixed stars is how scientists will determine when another 61 second minute will be needed. That the stars aren't really fixed and wobble unpredictably along their own path is apparently not important. The fact that a second was added to the day rather than gradually extending the standardized length of time that a second demarcates by some infinitesimal fraction to accommodate the rotational slowing demonstrates how the machine dominates all, and provides a prosaic example of why. To add a second is simply a matter of obtaining the general agreement of a handful of authorities whose job such things is. To change the duration of a second, even by a fraction measured in atomic heartbeats, would require abandoning or reconfiguring every precision timepiece on the planet. Every component clock in every interacting piece of high-tech would have to conform to the new duration. Much easier to simply tap the second hand back a notch every so often. A similar choice—although one of vastly different scale—presents itself in places that engage in the semiannual practice called "daylight saving time." It is far easier to push the hour hand of every clock back and forth twice a year to exploit changes in the duration of daylight than it would be to adjust the work schedules and operating hours associated with every business, school, hospital, government institution, etc.—and far, far easier to tweak the clock twice a year than to make day-to-day adjustments to accommodate changes in the timing of sunrise and sunset.

As discussed in the last chapter, the technological order sets and continually adjusts the parameters for our purposeful activity. Human needs are conditioned to accommodate technology, not the other way around. This is one of the most counterintuitive aspects of our situation, and one that flies in the face of the delusion of progress. Technology extends human capacities, and by all rights should therefore facilitate the achievement of human purposes. And this in fact may be how things work with simple technologies—tools whose design and operation are entirely transparent. But with the complex and opaque technologies of post-industrial mass society, the tables are turned, and our purposeful activity is shaped to fit the requirements of our technology. The use of technology has consequences that go beyond just extending our existing capacities. Technology structures our lives in ways that accommodate its own operative requirements.

Langdon Winner called the process by which this occurs "reverse adaptation." Reverse adaptation is defined as "the adjustment of human ends to match the character of the available means."[25] Technologies may start out serving specific human ends or addressing a highly circumscribed set of problems. But once they come into being, they shape human thought and activity in ways that conform to the structure and organization of the technology itself. The technological solution becomes a way of reframing the original problem, and features of the original problem that do not correspond to the technological solution are ignored or redefined.

A clear and rather straightforward example of this can be seen in the changes in public education that followed the implementation of the No Child Left Behind act, a congressional mandate that required states to adopt measurable goals with respect to the objective assessment of students' learning of basic skills in public schools. Each state was required to set high standards, develop tests to see to what degree those standards were being met, and then reward or punish specific schools according to the collective test performance of their respective students. The narrow focus on test performance, and the implied equivalence between test performance and student learning, led many schools to adopt, implicitly or explicitly, a "teach to the test" approach. Knowledge and abilities that were not being explicitly assessed by the tests were given low priority in the curriculum relative to knowledge and abilities that were being tested. Student learning became redefined in terms of the assessment technology, and the teaching process changed accordingly.

Some amount of reverse adaptation occurs following the incorporation of any new technology. Even the simplest of tools can lead to adaptations by the persons who use them. The regular use of a stone-age hand ax involves changes in arm muscle strength, neuromuscular changes relating to eye-hand coordination, and, perhaps, the formation of calluses. All new technologies have the potential to cause changes in the physical, psychological, and social environments within which they operate. The initial introduction of a hand ax to a given Paleolithic community would have likely changed a variety of features of community life. This potential for change increases with the complexity of the technology. The last few decades have seen the application of computer technology in virtually (so to speak) every domain. The ways in which our lives have become reverse-adapted to accommodate the computer are innumerable and continually increasing and expanding. The habitual ways that we think have been substantially altered and molded to fit a computer template. "Highly productive, fast-moving, intensive, precisions systems require highly productive, fast-moving, and precise human participants. The computer has been an especially powerful goad in this direction. Its capacity to do prodigious amounts of work in a very short time puts humans in the 'interface' in a frantic struggle to keep up. The virtues of slow information processing and labor done at a leisurely pace have long since been sacrificed to the norms of work appropriate to the electronic exemplar."[26] Speed, efficiency, precision measurement, and productivity, generally speaking, are not authentic human concerns. The descriptions that anthropologists have provided of the relaxed pace of daily life in many present-day hunter-gatherer communities provide convincing evidence that concern for these things does not reflect a pan human characteristic. They are priorities set by industrial technology and recently intensified by the operative capacities of the digital computer.

Technology is frequently seen as "just our tools," as neutral mechanisms for satisfying human goals and purposes. The idea of reverse adaptation, in conjunction with the notion of the technological imperative, makes the *neutral tool* view of technology completely untenable. "When one discovers that people are subtly conditioned by their apparatus, when one learns that their conduct is largely determined by preestablished function and learned technique, when one finds that important social relationships are established according to organizational rationality alone, then the idea of technology as controlled extension becomes entirely misleading."[27] Technology is designed to accommodate specific purposes, but, as we have seen, quite often the purposes themselves are changed in response to the operation of the technology. "The goals, purposes, needs, and decisions that are supposed to determine what technologies do are in important instances no longer the true source of their direction. Technical systems become severed from the ends originally set for them and, in effect, reprogram themselves and their environments to suit the special conditions of their own operation. The artificial slave gradually subverts the rule of its master."[28] Reverse adaptation is a primary mechanism by which the technological order subverts human needs to its own purposes. It also explains how many of our so-called needs arise in the first place. "Human needs are . . . created directly by individual technologies themselves. Once we possess the means to diagnose diabetes, we generate a human need—an opportunity niche—for a means to control diabetes. Once we possess rocketry, we experience a need for space exploration."[29]

Reverse adaption to complex technology is not limited to the specific domain in which the technology itself operates, but extends to domains related to the infrastructure of supportive technologies involved. The automobile is a perhaps overused example of this effect. Suburban American life is life built entirely on a foundation provided by the automobile. The presence of the suburb is a direct result of automotive technology. Because of the automobile, people are able to live at a distance from their jobs. An infrastructure of roadways and highways is needed to provide for the daily commute. Once built, the interstate highway system engenders a need for interstate commerce and tourism. Along with the enormous network of industries required for automobile construction, a gargantuan global industry has emerged to provide automobiles with fuel. Oil interests require protection, which necessitates a powerful military. The need to maintain access to oil at all cost drives political and environmental policy around the globe, and is directly responsible for numerous wars and environmental catastrophes. The automobile and the capacity to transport resources over distance allowed cities to expand far beyond what can be supported by local resources. This generates the need to import goods, which, again, necessitates a powerful military to ensure access to imported goods—it has been estimated that the typical American city has only enough food reserves to last three days. Without the automobile, half the country would be starving within a week. There are far too many economic and social ramifications of automobile technology to list here. The point is, it is not just the needs served by the specific technology that are subject to adaptation, but the needs served by all of the subsidiary technologies involved, and the needs served by the subsidiaries to the subsidiaries, and on down the line.

Reverse adaptation has a ratcheting effect, and brings a kind of irreversibility to the technological process. The original purpose, once altered to accommodate the technology adopted for its pursuit, becomes something different. We can't go back to simpler times in the past because the operative purposes of those times no longer exist. Technology has rendered them inert or irrelevant. This extends to far more than just the fact that the adoption of the automobile means that we no longer need blacksmiths and livery stables. Entire domains of potential meaning and purpose fall by the wayside and are replaced. The ratcheting effect of reverse adaptation serves only to feed the delusion of progress. Our present-day needs and purposes are fitted snuggly to the operation of present-day technology. Surely the fit is better now than it was with the inferior technology of the past. But, of course, the needs and purposes of the past were somewhat different, and aligned just as closely with the operation of the technology of the time. Take communication technology as an example. Modern communication technology provides us with instantaneous and continuous contact with anyone we choose, regardless of who they are or where they happen to be. As a result, many people of today's cellular generation don't give a second thought about the propriety of sending a casual acquaintance a poorly crafted text message about the most inane thought or minor detail of their momentary experience. The content of a message to a distant friend is considerably different when the only mode of contact is through a courier-delivered letter, perhaps taking weeks to arrive. And the motivation for communication is considerably different as well. The popularity of text messaging and internet sites like Twitter suggests that our ability to communicate instantaneously is generating a perceived need for instantaneous communication of trivial information. How was it even possible for the inhabitants of prior generations to make it through the tumultuous teenage years without cellphones and the internet as outlets for adolescent angst?

Human needs and activity are not the only things that are subject to reverse adaptation. The larger social and political institutions of technological society, Arthur's "purposive systems" are subject to reverse adaptation as well. What this means is that the ends that these systems were originally designed to facilitate become transient motives that fall into obscurity as new technology forces their realignment. The ends themselves, because they are constantly in flux, constantly being altered by the presence of new technological means, cease to be a focus at all: "There is, then, a twofold movement affecting all social practices and institutions: (1) the process of articulating and criticizing the matter of ends slips into oblivion, and (2) the business of discovering effective means and the ways of judging these means in their performance assumes paramount importance."[30] In other words, *what* and *why* take a back seat to *how*. What we are doing and, more importantly, why we are doing it, become irrelevant, completely overshadowed by the operation of the technology itself. All that matters is whether a new technology performs its designed function, or whether it performs its function faster, more efficiently, or with higher precision than a previous version. What the technology actually does—the ultimate purposes to which it is being directed and the ways in which the whole of society is being affected by pursuing these purposes—is rarely if ever considered.

As a result of the narrow focus on the "how" of technology, reverse adaptation can lead to a variety of unintended consequences. In discussing side-effects, the unintended consequences of technology, Winner points out two interesting features: first they are invariably negative. Positive unintended consequences are taken in stride as "expected" in terms of their eventual emergence if not in terms of their specific form. That a technological innovation should turn out to provide additional unforeseen advantages is included as part of the motivation for innovation in the first place. Winner asks us to imagine a world where any technological innovation solved only the specific problem for which it was designed, where additional functions or applications were never discovered. It would be a world far different from the one in which we currently live. In this vein, Winner talks about *function drift*, in which technology designed for one set of purposes becomes re-appropriated and applied toward others. In this way, an ax originally designed to chop wood becomes a weapon for use in battle. A certain amount of function drift can be expected with any new technology. The second interesting feature of unintended consequences, and for our purposes here the most important, is that they are not *not* intended. That is, there is nothing in the original planning, development, or application of the technology in the way of intentionally preventing them. Technologies are born into the world with little or no intentional forethought directed at potential unexpected consequences. It is in fact impossible to imagine specific consequences if they are unexpected. So, technological innovation involves intentionally creating new technology that is virtually guaranteed to have negative consequences, the specific form and scope of which we have no way to judge beforehand.

What could possibly go wrong?

Reverse adaptation is an inevitable part of the technological process. But the extent to which authentically human motives and desires are included in this process decreases with an increase in the complexity of the technological order. This can be seen in the historical changes associated with both the role and the nature of aesthetic considerations within the technological process. I doubt that anyone would argue that aesthetic motives are not authentically human. There are likely some who would argue, to the contrary, that the capacity to experience beauty is a defining feature of human nature, and I would be inclined to agree. But reverse adaptation to technology has steered our aesthetic sensibilities.

> Almost unconsciously, men kept abreast of techniques and controlled their influence. This resulted not from an adaptation of men to techniques (as in modern times), but rather from the subordination of techniques to men. Technique did not pose the problem of adaptation because it was firmly enmeshed in the framework of life and culture . . . . The modifications of a given type were not the outcome of an exclusively technological will. They resulted from aesthetic considerations. It is important to emphasize that technical operations, like the instru-

ments themselves, almost always depended on aesthetic pre-
occupations. It was impossible to conceive of a tool that was
not beautiful. As for the idea, frequently accepted since the
triumph of efficiency, that the beautiful is that which is well
adapted to use—assuredly no such notion guided the aesthetic
searchings of the past.[31]

Where once we would decorate our tools, weapons, and machines
with ornate but functionally irrelevant artistic flourishes, we now
speak of the elegance of a technical function or the beauty of a mechanical design. Consumer appliances, from automobiles to
touchscreens, are marketed in ways that highlight the aesthetic qualities of their appearance and operation. Note the sleek and attractive
contours of latest car model (designed primarily to produce enhanced
aerodynamics and improve fuel efficiency)—and, while you are at it,
those of the attractive (human) model perched seductively on the
hood. A refrigerator is not just a box to keep things cold; its mono-
chrome metallic surface is a beautiful addition to your kitchen. The
beauty of technology is more than skin deep, however, and extends
to efficiency of function, the "smoothness" of operation. The new
aesthetics of efficiency—and that this inversion of art and functionality is now a natural way of thinking about beauty—is echoed by Arthur as well: "Good design in fact is like good poetry. Not in any
sense of sublimity, but in sheer rightness of choice from the many
possible for each part. Each part must fit tightly, must work accurately, must conform to the interaction of the rest. The beauty in good
design is that of appropriateness, of least effort for what is achieved.
It derives from a feeling that all that is in place is properly in place,
that not a piece can be rearranged, that nothing is to excess."[32] Efficiency has become beauty. And, by contrast, inefficiency is ugliness.
There is, perhaps, nothing quite as inefficient—and thus nothing
quite as hideous—as a biological human being pursuing authentic
human purposes.

Taken together with the technological imperative, the process of
reverse adaptation suggests that "a significant deflection and restructuring of human motives occurs when individuals approach technol-

ogies for the solutions to their problems."[33] What emerges in our modern technology-saturated world, then, is humankind locked in the increasingly oppressive grip of its own technological systems. The modern era is one in which authentic human needs and purposes are swept aside in an uncontrollable and escalating build-out of technology, where, in the name of efficiency, varied and multidimensional human beings are wherever possible forced to function as standardized mechanical units operating in the two dimensions of production and consumption—with the distinction between these two modes of action becoming increasingly blurred. At this point, we are little more than servomechanisms.

Servomechanisms

The term servomechanism is used here in something more than a metaphorical sense. A servomechanism is a kind of mechanical control system that is itself actuated or controlled by something else. Servomechanisms are self-contained, independent technologies in their own right, but their functions are yoked to a larger system; they serve only the internal purposes of larger technological systems. The use of this term is meant to highlight the subordinate mechanical role that human activity plays within the power complex. The term is also meant to highlight the lack of anything resembling human autonomy in this system-directed activity. Human individuals are truly individual, conceptually separable entities. But our functional embedding with the technological order places severe restrictions on the degree to which we are allowed to express anything remotely close to true individuality.

Ever-expansive and increasingly sophisticated systems of authority have reduced the potential for individual autonomy to its lowest point in the history of the human species; and it will only be reduced further—potentially to the point of total annihilation—as these technologies of authority and control continue to evolve and become more subtle and effective, as they become more efficient at what they have been designed to do. Note that there is a distinction to be

made here between two sources of autonomy-reduction. The technological order reduces autonomy through two distinct, but intimately
related, processes. Human interaction with technology itself reduces
autonomy, regardless of the specific technology in question. Autonomy reduction is an intrinsic feature of the logic behind the technological process. Although technology is frequently billed as extending the capacity to pursue human ends, to use any technology is to
limit or restrict activity in ways that the technology's operation requires ("to command, it must first be obeyed"). As technology becomes more complex, more and more of our activity is directed at
maintaining its operation until, eventually, the continued operation of
the technology becomes its own purpose—the technological imperative—and human ends become technological ends. In addition to this
intrinsic source of autonomy reduction associated with the technological process, there is a more extrinsic source: the power complex
has developed specific technologies of authority and control, technologies whose explicit purpose is to restrain or reduce individual
autonomy in the name of maintaining and enhancing the efficiency
of the systems of the technological order. With these two sources of
autonomy reduction operating within the technological order, each
sufficient in itself, our role as servomechanism is over-determined.

At this point it might help to briefly reexamine the idea of autonomy as it applies to human activity. The definition of autonomy that
I am using is fairly simple and direct: if an action is generated by a
person engaged in the pursuit of a freely chosen goal, and the person's goal pursuit is free from the governing control of other persons, it is an autonomous action. Thus there are two critical elements
or conditions to consider when judging to what extent an act is autonomous: (1) whether and to what degree the ends to which it is
directed were freely chosen, and (2) whether and to what degree the
pursuit of those ends are controlled or directed by another person.
These two conditions often interdigitate in complex ways that can
make judgments of autonomy impossible in anything other than a
relative sense in specific concrete cases. For instance, if you are pursuing an end that was forced upon you in order to avoid the consequences of not pursuing it, complying with the boss's request in or-

der to avoid being fired, for example, you are clearly not acting autonomously. But what if you are working voluntary overtime in order to save up enough money to buy a new car for your commute to work? According to the view of autonomy I am supporting here, whether an individual possesses autonomy is not an either-or question, but a question of degree: goals can be more or less freely chosen, and an individual's actions can be more or less under the influence of other people. To the extent it is possible to make these determinations, a person's behavior can be judged more or less autonomous—and, although it should go without saying, the more, the better.

The technological order of modern civilization has negative ramifications for both critical conditions of autonomy. Many, or even most, of the goals we are pursuing at any given moment are not of our own design; they are provided for us, and in that sense they are not freely chosen. Our goal-pursuit is conditioned by the "purposeful systems" that comprise the technological order. In addition, our actions in pursuit of our goals are channeled and directed by other people acting in their roles within potent systems of authority and control. What is important to reiterate is that humans, even held firmly within the autonomy-destroying grip of the technological order of modern civilization, are active participants in our own circumstances. We make choices and set and pursue goals. To suggest that we have been reduced to little more than servomechanisms is to say that our capacity to act autonomously has been severely curtailed, and in many situations has been completely eliminated. Although we make choices and pursue ends, we are not free to pursue our own freely chosen ends, and we are coerced and goaded by persons in positions of authority into pursuing ends that are not our own. And I am not using the word coerced lightly. I mean to include all of its connotations and entailments of force, threat, and oppression. And although the proximal source of this coercion is other people (real or imagined) in positions of authority over us, the ultimate source is the aggregate of the technological systems that have ostensibly been designed to serve our own goals and purposes, and those in positions of authority have little choice but to exercise their authority as dictated by their own coerced role within systems designed to serve and protect the technological order.

We need to bear in mind that human behavior is necessary for the machine to function. Leaving aside for the moment those specific technologies of authority and control that operate directly on human behavior, human activity is an essential component of the technological order—and it always will be. The notion that humans are becoming less and less essential for the machines of civilization to operate, eventually to be replaced entirely by mechanical simulacra, makes for great science fiction, but reflects a serious misinterpretation of the actual situation. To say that humans have become servomechanisms is not the same thing as to say that humans have been replaced by machines—these are in fact directly opposite states of affair. Humans are becoming more highly metabolized into the mechanical order. "The crucial difficulty with the existing technological order is not so much that individuals are 'unemployed' by automatic processes (although, certainly, this is a source of grief for a significant minority) but that they are overemployed in ways destructive to their humanity."[34] Increased automation has in fact led to an increase in necessary human labor: more automation means more actual mechanism and a more densely articulated hierarchical structure, which means more need for planning and design and a variety of other essential human-mediated operations. People are required to work far longer hours today than they did a generation ago, before we had access to all of our high-tech "labor saving" devices. What has changed, and what the science fiction robotic revolution misinterprets as the eclipsing of biological humans by machines, is the level of mechanization of humanity itself. Maybe the zombie genre is more directly applicable to our present situation: humans converted into mindless walking corpses rather than humans being replaced by machines. It's not so much that the machines are replacing humans; it's that the humans are becoming machines themselves. Then again, maybe this is a distinction without a difference.

The crucial point with respect to autonomy is that the activity of human beings in forced interface with the technological order of modern civilization is externally controlled activity, activity that is effected and directed by the ubiquitous and multifarious control systems of the power complex, activity that serves the purposes of the technological order. My goal here is to direct the focus to critical features of our oppression, not by providing a detailed, high-resolution image of our situation, but by painting a rough sketch of the landscape; my goal is to provide a picture that captures to some degree the bleakness of life in technoculture from the perspective of authentic human needs and desires. Not only is the vast bulk of our lives spent serving the needs of the machines of civilization while our authentic human needs go unmet, but we have been convinced that the needs of the machine are in fact our own most urgent needs. We have been programmed through a reverse adapted attraction to efficiency to think of our authentic human needs—the need for deep, meaningful connection with other people, the need to bond and form lifetime attachments with specific physical places, the need for continual and intimate congress with the natural world, the need to create and recreate meaning through shared personal experience, the need to sit unencumbered by deadlines and commitments and contemplate the mysteries of the universe, and even the need for real food and clean air and water—as unimportant relics of a primitive pre-human state and that building and maintaining the powerful planet-devouring machines of civilization reflects the highest calling of humankind. And, should our humanity begin to surface despite our programming and threaten to interfere with the operation of the technological order, there are several highly-effective (and heavily armed) technologies of control to keep our negative impact on efficiency to a minimum.

As a brief aside, the use of the term "programming" evokes the computer metaphor in a way that is potentially illuminating, and entirely consistent with the notion of servomechanism. It suggests that humans are "hardware," physical components whose activity is manipulated and directed by instructions coded in the architectural design of specific "software." The software in this case includes the various systems of the technological order. The computer metaphor also provides an entire domain of euphemisms for talking about resistance. In addition to the mechanical malfunctions that can befall cybernetic servomechanisms, damaged connections and contacts, short-circuits, defunct relays, input-output and feedback errors, we can talk about installing patches, the potential susceptibility to viruses and malware, the possibility of hacking and spoofing the systems, or the possibility of simply overwriting existing code with less dehumanizing variations. In Part 4, I look at the specific nature of our programming in terms of the underlying source code: how is our evolved psychology being reconfigured as part of the technological process?

The historical traces of our gradual and cumulative dehumanization are easy enough to read, and are frequently presented as the natural unfolding of a stage-like process, starting with the conversion of people, individual "persons," into "subjects," literally *subject* to the whims of those in positions of power, then to "citizens," dependent participants in regimes not of their own choosing, and finally to "consumers," homogenized end users of the standardized products of technological civilization—although I would strongly caution against the interpretation of historical events as reflecting a strict stage-like progression. Even to call history a "process" evokes the notion of a natural progression and presumes a certain level of inevitability that is unwarranted given the nature of the facts at our disposal. And, of course, there is the ever-present threat of bias from the delusion of progress. Nevertheless, the increased restriction of autonomy through history has a cumulative quality to it that suggests a kind of developmental unfolding. As a subject—even the subject of a ruthless tyrant (or maybe especially then), individuality and autonomy are preserved to a large extent. A king can demand loyalty in overt action only. Citizenship takes a variety of forms, but always establishes a dependency relationship between what was once an entirely autonomous individual with individual needs and desires, and a reified public "community" where the needs of the abstract collective supersede those of the concrete individual. The idea of personal sacrifice emerges in conjunction with the idea of a reified collective, as a prerequisite to the full-blown notion of citizenship. But the role of citizenship cannot be allowed to gain a too-solid foothold—there is too much power in the collective to allow it free reign; uprising and revolution are inevitable when the masses discover they have collective power and can in fact act "en masse" to actuate that power. And so the primacy of concrete individual needs is surreptitiously reinstated by the technological order in the form of manufactured desires for manufactured consumer products and services. The notion of citizenship remains, but is morphed into something far more isolated and self-focused: "The technological order includes a notion of *citizenship,* which consists in serving one's own function well and not meddling with the mechanism."[35] The definition of community is inverted, as collective needs are equated with the needs of the technological systems providing consumer products and services. "The adaptation of men [sic] has been thorough. Each person simply obeys the performance criteria appropriate to his station and happily receives the promised rewards: security, leisure, and material goods. The technological society is one in which obvious social 'needs' are fully taken care of. Even the desire for freedom is preserved in the arena of consumer preference. Shopping centers become the public space for the exercise of human liberty. Through a wonderful coincidence . . . the free choices produce an aggregate 'demand,' which matches exactly what the system of production is best able to provide."[36] So while we are ostensibly pursuing our own self-interests, we are in reality feeding the needs of the machine. "A need becomes a need in substantial part because a megatechnical system external to the person needed that need to be needed."[37]

Anything that is not in the interests of the technological order is simply ignored. Human activity that is irrelevant for the machine simply finds no traction; we are too busy oiling the gears with our incessant material consumption to pursue other forms of activity. Anything that is counter to the interests of the technological order is eliminated with extreme prejudice. The power complex does not sit idly by; rather it actively and jealously guards its own efficient operation. The order has monitoring technology directed specifically at ferreting out human activity that has a potentially negative impact on efficiency. Such activity cannot be tolerated, of course, and will be eliminated whenever its presence is detected. But first, however, it is necessary to detect its presence. Detection requires surveillance. But surveillance has additional benefits beyond simple detection. These will be discussed in Part 4.

Most of us have little occasion to question our role in the technological order. We are too busy enacting our role to see that it is a role. And since everyone around us is similarly engaged, similarly enmeshed in ubiquitous hierarchical structures of power and authority, our activity is normalized; a fish living its entire life in water has little way of understanding what water is, let alone any reason to question water's presence—water is just the way things are. But even for those who do question the legitimacy of the technological order or the roles that we are being forced to play, the question itself is usually expressed in technological terms. Asking "What do we do to improve our situation?" is a technological question—a question originating in a mind that has been deformed by life-ways deeply immersed in the service of technology, a mind that has been groomed to see the world as a collection of technical problems to be solved.

Perhaps we need to be asking a distinctly different sort of question.

The functionality of a servomechanism is dependent on the structural integrity of its connections with the larger machine. In the next section, Part 4, I take a closer look at the nature of our individual connections with the power complex, connections that bind us to the technological order in ever more subtle and ever more global ways. As technologies of authority have become more sophisticated and more intrusive, we, paradoxically, have become more accepting of their tyrannical presence and their autonomy-destroying impact. The reason for this is because technologies of authority are designed specifically to exploit our preexisting social and psychological tendencies; they can operate only by piggybacking off of our genetic expectations for a social milieu far removed from that of modern civilization. The more sophisticated these technologies become, the more seamlessly they are able to insert themselves into our lives, and the less likely we are to question their legitimacy—or even notice their presence. Authority is becoming simply the air we breathe.

To the moon!

In this part, I have provided a rough overview of the technological order of civilization in terms of the relationship between authority and complex technology. We have seen how the incorporation of a new technology can change the web of goals and purposes that led to its creation in the first place, how our lives become organized around the "needs" of our technological systems, and how our dependency on these systems forces us to sacrifice our autonomy in order to accommodate the technological order's demand for efficiency. What emerges is an unsustainable and globally-expansive civilization built upon the accelerating accumulation of increasingly urgent technological demands. And we are helpless to do anything but continue to facilitate civilization's continued despoiling expansion.

"We" is an abstraction, of course, with no potential causal efficacy. There are only individual persons—seven billion and counting. Civilization is an aggregate of loosely interconnected and self-perpetuating technological systems (remember, government bureaucracies and corporations—to the extent that there is a distinction to be made between them—are technological systems). There is no one or no thing, no "us" or "we" or "them" running the show. Committed individuals working within a system do have some power to change the system. But that's not going to help any if the existence of "a system" is what's causing the whole problem to begin with. Civilization (of any kind) is unsustainable in the long term, and what we have now is likely to disintegrate in an extremely ugly fashion when it does—unless it is intentionally and rationally dismantled first. Pulling the plug on the technological order is a damned if we do and damned even more if we don't proposition. Given the nature of our circumstances, a reasonable response would be for us (meaning concrete committed individual human beings) to direct our energy at figuring out how to disengage in a way that causes the least amount of long-term pain and suffering. An incalculable amount of pain and suffering is unavoidable at this point. But the longer the festering sliver of civilization is allowed to persist, the deeper the infection and the more extensive the pain and suffering will be when it is eventually (forcefully or otherwise) withdrawn.

I will save discussion of ways we might encourage the de-civilizing process for Part 5. For now, I want to paint part of the background for the discussion of the psychological substrate of our acquiescence in the next section. And I will do this by briefly dis-secting a particular kind of response, frequently given by engineers and others who have become mesmerized by the sparkle and glitter of high-tech, to the charge that modern postindustrial civilization, with its linear consumptive and exponentially expansive operation, is ultimately unsustainable and will eventually render the planet unin-habitable: "No problem," the say, "we'll simply pack up and move somewhere else."

The future colonization of space is a really cool idea, and makes for great science fiction. It is, however, a complete fairytale. Humans are creatures adapted to and crucially dependent upon conditions on Earth, conditions not found anywhere else in our solar system or any place outside of our solar system close enough to be a genuine desti-nation. The thought that we could set up a self-sufficient colony on, say, Mars, and replace all of the things provided for free by the Earth and its biosphere—things such as breathable air, drinkable water, a diet with sufficient nutrients, and a gravity field within the range necessary for the healthy operation of basic cellular processes—with technologically-generated simulacra is pure fantasy. Despite that, there are several folks, some of them otherwise intelligent, who hon-estly think that extraterrestrial colonization is a viable trajectory for the human species. Be that as it may, let's set the question of possi-bility aside. In fact, let's assume that it is a real possibility. Let's as-sume that our technology will eventually allow humans to travel to and colonize planets throughout the galaxy. What I'm interested in exploring here is the premises and underlying assumptions latent within this idea when offered as a solution to the problems of our present unsustainable civilization. Space colonization is not a solu-tion, but rather a way of avoiding the problem, and at the same time rationalizing the perpetuation of expansive technology—the very thing that is causing the problem. When you look closely at this idea, you will find it has the technological imperative written all over it.

The delusion of progress is clearly a central feature of the space colony idea as well; and I hardly need to waste ink here to show how thoughts of a future Mars colony reflect belief in the natural drive toward progress. To conquer the universe is our new manifest destiny. The idea of space colonization results from an implicit recognition that the existence of any civilization requires continual territorial conquest. The space-colonization solution also underscores a fundamentally linear consumptive mindset. It fits quite well with the pattern of life in consumer society: we buy a product, extract whatever value it was purchased to accommodate, and then dispose of it when it is used up. The Earth as a whole is no different than any individual part of it, say, a coal-laced West Virginian mountain. When the Earth is used up, we will simply move on and find another planet to exploit into oblivion. Several important systems within the technological order depend on this unidirectional approach to resource consumption in order to function, and our ability to conceive of alternative approaches has been severely curtailed by reverse adaptation to their operative demands. We think like linear consumers because it is more efficient for us to think that way. Perhaps an even more interesting hidden facet of this idea is the fact that historical colonial expansion here on Earth typically involved small and categorically-distinct subsets of a larger society. The obvious question then becomes how do we choose the colonists? Who gets to move and start a new life somewhere else and who stays behind on the dying Earth? It seems that there are only three kinds of people who could possibly fit the bill: the pure (from a eugenics standpoint), the powerful (e.g. the extremely wealthy), and, most importantly, those who know how to operate the necessary technology.

I find it particularly interesting that advocates of space colonization emphasize technology as the solution to our problem in a way that ignores anything other than the expansion of technology itself. The fact that technology is also the cause of our problem, the reason our planet is becoming too crowded and increasingly uninhabitable, is either not understood or simply ignored as irrelevant. But, then, we have addressed this tendency in detail above. Also consider that the solution is that we direct our technological energies to developing the means to leave the Earth and spread our planet-destroying activities like some kind of interstellar parasite rather than taking those same technological energies and directing them to cleaning up our mess here.

The next section examines the psychological nature of our acquiescence to authority. The corpus of psychological science includes a sizeable number of studies on obedience and its social and psychological correlates. The ethically-questionable work of Stanley Milgram in the middle part of last century is still referenced widely.[38] Milgram's participants were led to believe that they were delivering painful electric shocks to other individuals, and continued to obey the directives of a lab-coat wearing "researcher" even when it became apparent that the individuals receiving the shocks were suffering immensely. Probably more relevant to our discussion of human servomechanisms above is the infamous prison role-play study by Phillip Zimbardo.[39] Zimbardo randomly assigned his participants to be either a prisoner or a guard, that is, to have authority or to have none, and then documented the ease with which they assumed their respective roles, with some of the guards becoming sadistic and brutal, drunk on their power, while some of the prisoners displayed symptoms of serious emotional disturbance. I will be looking at recent psychological research in these areas as well as relevant studies from some of the other social sciences.

Although not meant to be anything close to a comprehensive list, the chapters in Part 4 each take on a separate feature of our acquiescence to authority. I start with the way that the natural course of human psychological development has been stunted and deformed by civilization's artificial structuring of experience. The chronic immaturity that results from our arrested development provides the technological order with powerful carabiners of insecurity and dependency to latch into. Then I explore our symbolic capacity to organize experience hierarchically, a requisite feature for the conceptualization of power relations. In addition, our experience with the world and with each other is becoming increasingly mediated. Mediation provides a controlling interface for those providing the medium of mediation, enhancing their power and authority. Ubiquitous surveillance also serves as a potent mechanism of control. As does the latent threat of violence that sits just below the surface, channeling and restricting virtually all of our public social interactions. And, as if all that were not enough, the very act of questioning authority has become redefined as a kind of mental pathology to be drugged into submission. Part 4 ends with a brief discussion of civilization as a mode of traumatic entrapment, and the sense of helplessness and paralysis that result from the forced relinquishment of autonomy.

PART 4: THE TOPOGRAPHY OF ACQUIESCENCE

Arrested development

The question being addressed in this part of the book is "What is necessary, psychologically speaking, for hierarchical systems of power and authority to function?" This question implies that there are supporting contexts and previous events—circumstances that paved the way or served as prerequisite conditions. This implication is in some sense residue of modernity, with its delusional notions of progress. But when something suddenly appears on the scene, something unique that didn't previously exist, for example an oppressive way of life dominated by artificial hierarchies of power and authority, it makes some sense to ask where it came from or how it happened. For millions of years, humans and their proto-human relatives lived in social situations that involved hierarchical relations of authority in only a very limited sense. Note, again, that the dominance hierarchies seen in social animals are not the same kind of thing as the hierarchical social systems imposed by civilization: those that manufacture authority and its autonomy-annihilating coercive power relations. I have suggested that authority is able to get traction only by exploiting preexisting social-psychological mechanisms that evolved for a far more egalitarian existence. This is no simple trick, and requires more than making minor changes to modes of life that existed previously. It involves nothing short of rewiring our psychological development from the ground up.

Humans have been called the most adaptive animal. Although the claim is frequently motivated by anthropocentric hubris, it has some empirical support both in terms of the range of raw physical environments in which we can thrive and in terms of the myriad social conditions we are able to accommodate. But this flexibility comes at a cost. In order to be able to adapt to such a wide variety of circumstances, the time it takes for an individual to reach maturity—both physically and psychologically—is far longer in humans than it is in other creatures. In terms of physical changes relative to our ape cousins, the evolution of the human species over the last several million years appears largely to be a matter of extending infantile characteristics (e.g., large head, flat face, in-line big toe) into adulthood. Likewise, our dependence on adults continues for several years after we acquire the capacity for body control and self-direction. Extended youth and a protracted period of development allow for maximal adjustment to specific environmental conditions that our genes would be unable to predict accurately ahead of time. But it also means that our maturation is critically dependent on the quality and timing of specific kinds of environmental input over an extended period of time.

One of the earliest distinctions to emerge in the history of thought about human behavior is a distinction between two potential sources of an individual's behavioral tendencies: nature and nurture, the distinction between our inherited predispositions and our learned responses and acquired habits. Obviously, our biological nature as humans sets the parameters for behavior. We are bipedal, have a digestive system that supports an omnivorous diet, have opposable thumbs, have brain systems and a vocal apparatus that support language, etc. At a more fine-grained level of analysis, it is clear that physical differences among people are to large degree the result of inherited traits. What is not so clear is the degree to which our actual behavioral tendencies are a result of inherited predispositions and to what degree they reflect learning. Two humans with very similar biology can behave in very different ways as a function of their different life experiences. The nature-nurture issue has frequently emerged as a question of the relative contribution of these dichotomous sources of human behavior. Some more thoughtful persons have realized that it is not a dichotomy; instead, human behavior involves a complex and unimaginably elaborate ongoing dance between biology and experience. In fact, the distinction between nature and nurture, between the relative influence of genes and the environment, quickly dissolves into incoherence unless framed in terms of complex interactions. Asking what part of a person's behavior is due to genetics and what part is due to experience is a bit like asking what part of the music is due to the instrument and what part due to the musician.

Only very recently has the mindboggling complexity of the interaction between biology and the environment started to become apparent. Every decisive moment of an organism's development involves a circular, cybernetic dance in which genetic mechanisms are directed and recalibrated in response to very specific environmental feedback. From a developmental standpoint, it's not genes so much as the interactive progression itself that is important. This circular expansive unfolding process goes by the name, *epigenesis*. The organism, the infant human, for instance, comes into the world with a set of hardwired general expectations about what the environment will offer, and develops and matures as these expectations are more or less met. Although development is a continual, ongoing process, there are identifiable stages, sequential patterns of progression in which the successful development and healthy maturation of various systems is dependent on the prior successful development and healthy maturation of other systems. The timing and sequencing is important, and there are numerous critical periods of development in which specific systems are coming online that will be necessary for the healthy development of future developing systems. If during an early stage the appropriate environmental input is absent or sufficiently different from what is expected, the critical systems forming during that stage will fail to assemble properly and remain incomplete, immature, or malformed. And, because later developing systems depend on the healthy development of these earlier developing systems, this malformation and immaturity can snowball as later systems come online.

Perhaps an example is in order. Consider research on the development of the visual system in cats. If a kitten is blindfolded from birth, and the blindfold is not removed until after a critical window of time during which the developing visual system expects specific kinds of input from the environment, the cat will be blind its entire life. If, instead of blindfolding the kitten, you put it in a cylindrical enclosure in which the walls are painted with vertical stripes, and keep it in the enclosure for an extended period of time, the exposure to the limited stimuli (only vertical stripes) will leave the cat with a curiously deformed visual system such that if you subsequently place the cat in an environment containing surfaces painted with vertical stripes and others painted with horizontal stripes, the cat will be able to maneuver around the vertical striped surfaces but run straight into the horizontal striped ones as if it is completely blind to them. And analysis of the cat's brain will reveal a complete absence of neurons in the visual system capable of responding to horizontal stimuli.

There are, unfortunately, human examples of this kind of arrested development as well. The development of language in humans is marked by a number of critical periods in the developing brain. The existence of critical periods in language development is one of the reasons that young children find it easy to learn a second language whereas adults struggle. There is a period of time, for example, during which the ability to distinguish subtle differences among speech sounds develops. Once this window closes, starting perhaps within the first nine months, the person finds it difficult to hear differences among similar sounding phonemes in nonnative languages. There is also a period of time in brain development during which the child acquires syntax, or the rules of word order in his or her native language. There have been tragic cases of neglect and abuse in which a child has been isolated to the point of not being meaningfully exposed to spoken language of any sort until after the critical period for syntax development has passed. The most infamous case of this was a girl called Genie in the 1970s who was isolated until she was around 12 years old. Genie provided a crucial case study in a hotly contested debate over two competing theories of language learning at the time. According to one theory, language was learned through reinforcement. According the other, language was "acquired" as a function of the developmental progression of hardwired brain systems, and reinforcement was largely irrelevant. Genie provided evidence for the second theory. She was able to learn words, and she acquired an extensive vocabulary, but she was never able to learn the rules of syntax. The critical period of brain development had passed without the required input.

Genie's problems, as with those of the blindfolded cats, were a result of environmental deprivation. Brain systems were prevented from getting the input they needed in order to develop appropriately. Attachment theory provides a far more nuanced example of how development is dependent on the complex interaction between nature and nurture. In the 1940s, German ethologist Konrad Lorenz studied a phenomenon called imprinting. Newly hatched goslings are hardwired to notice and follow the first large moving objet they see. Normally, that's the mother goose, and the goslings will "imprint" on the mother goose and follow her everywhere she goes. Lorenz demonstrated that the imprinting process will occur in the absence of its normal target by having goslings imprint on him. In this case, the gosling's brain systems did what they were supposed to, but assembled themselves in an inappropriate and (potentially) deleterious manner because they were given the wrong environmental input at a critical point during development. Humans are not geese, but there is evidence that we form powerful bonds of attachment to our primary caregiver during the first few months of life. There is a large body of empirical research showing that the specific nature of the relationship between the infant and his or her primary attachment object (usually the mother) can have a pronounced influence on how the infant deals with his or her social world later in life. The infant forms an "insecure" attachment to a parent who is either neglectful or over-intrusive, and this insecurity can carry over into all of his or her future relationships.

The take-home message from attachment theory is that our ability to interact with others in the social world relies on the critically timed development of complex cognitive and emotional systems. These systems have been shaped and finely tuned over several million years to accommodate circumstances in small-group foraging society. We are hardwired to expect community conditions consistent with nomadic or semi-nomadic hunter-gatherer band society, and our developmental programs are designed to incorporate specific types of environmental and social input that are very different from what we experience today. For one thing, direct contact with the natural world is extremely limited by lifestyles dense with technology and immersed in manufactured enclosures and artificial outdoor spaces. Artificial environments, despite the glitter and sheen and mechanical ruckus, do not come close to the complexity and subtlety of natural spaces. The people in our lives are of a different sort as well. We grow up surrounded by a sea of strangers. People we will never know regularly appear, inhabit our experience briefly, and then permanently disappear. Someone living 10,000 years ago might very well live her entire life without ever meeting a stranger, that is, someone she would see only once in passing and whose name would remain unknown. Although young children can be leery of people they don't know, they don't really understand the idea of *stranger,* and many (especially those children who have formed a secure attachment) will wave and greet the other people in public places such as the grocery store without fear, as if each new person they see is an important part of their personal community whom they have yet to meet. "Strangers" is not a common feature of ancestral environments; as a feature of the modern world, it is something that has to be learned in the same way that we learn about electrical outlets and automatic doors.

We are all suffering from arrested development, cognitively, socially, and emotionally, because the demands of modern life interfere with the sequencing and evolutionary fine-tuning of hardwired developmental programs. Anthropologist Paul Shepard argued that this can be traced to changes in community life associated with domestication.[1] The social and environmental conditions that attend agricultural and pastoral life disrupt natural human development and generate chronic immaturity. And the social and environmental conditions that attend "community" life in post-industrial civilization are orders of magnitude removed from our evolved expectations. For all of our ostensive sophistication, we are, from an authentically human standpoint, psychological infants.

According to Benjamin Barber, in his 2007 book *Consumed,* not only are we infants, but our immaturity is being intentionally inculcated and extended in time in order to support corporate interests and to enhance our consumptive behavior: we are infantilized by consumer society.[2] Infantilization brings childish impulsiveness and narcissism to "adult" purchasing decisions, and increases both the rate of consumption and the degree to which we are malleable targets for the marketing of nonessential products. Marcel Danesi claims that the entire period of time known as adolescence is an artificial construction designed to accommodate the social changes that occurred during the industrial revolution.[3] Hunter-gatherer societies have nothing corresponding to adolescence: you are a child and then, perhaps after completing a traditional rite of passage or merely as a function of the physical changes of puberty, you become an adult with all of the rights of community participation that your adult status entitles. In recent years, the timeframe with which the period of adolescence is said to cover has been extended well into what was once clearly considered the adult range. Infantilization exploits and extends our arrested development for the purpose of corporate profit. But infantilization also increases our dependency.

No other primate species engages in parenting in the way that humans do. The parent-child attachment process that is necessary for early brain development appears to be largely complete by the time the child is three years old.[4] Parenting of human children for several years beyond weaning is entirely unnecessary from the standpoint of either physiological or psychological development, but it is thought to be necessary in order to sufficiently prepare children to participate in complex modern society. What extended parenting actually does, however, is instill a perpetual sense of dependency. Children are intrinsically motivated to learn—naturally and without any prompting from adults—how to handle the world around them. What parenting in modern society has to do is counteract the child's natural programming; children have to learn that that their own abilities are not sufficient. In a hunter-gatherer society, children learn very early to be able to provide for their own immediate needs (e.g., for food). In civilized society, children are taught to be dependent on others for satisfying all of their needs (and even as adults are entirely unable to provide their own food, relying instead on a massive corporate food system). They are trained through the routines of public school and participation in sports to be "good citizens" and "team players," all the while corporate marketing is presenting them with a materialistic world based on narcissistic hedonism. What should be conflicting messages, "You are insufficient in yourself and need to rely on others," and "You are an individual entitled to all of the material pleasures of the world that you can get your hands on," are resolved into: "You need to use others in order to get what you want." Our immaturity follows us into adulthood and leaves us in need of perpetual parenting. The state fulfills this role in many situations, for example by telling us what food is good for us (the food pyramid, and more recently, MyPlate)[5] and by regulating our access to substances deemed bad for us (tobacco, alcohol, marijuana, sexually-explicit media). Modern civilization is a society of dependent and self-centered children, and governments and corporate bureaucracies play the role of indulgent and protective parents.

Autonomy is a hallmark of maturity. But autonomous adults are a potential problem for authority. Autonomous adults tend to question authority and tend to rely on their own conscience when it comes to issues of compliance and obedience. Authority requires a person's natural tendencies toward autonomy be broken, as a wild horse needs to be broken before it can be saddled. The best time to do this breaking is during childhood, while the child's capacities for autonomy are still inchoate. It is informative to notice that the terms "rearing" and "raising" that we apply to children come straight from a domestication frame. Children's natural growth needs to be guided, pruned, and redirected. The ground has to be properly prepared and conditioned for the seeds of authority to take root. Left to their own devices, children would surely turn into feral beasts (or worse: anarchists).

Early developmental theorists (e.g. Piaget), thought that young children saw adults as "socially powerful and infallible." More recent research shows this is not the case. Research has shown that young children already have sophisticated understandings relating to adult authority, for example. "Studies have shown, first, that children do not judge authorities to have absolute power but make judgments about their legitimacy on the basis of the nature of the commands they give . . . . The fact that children reject authorities [such as parents] when they issue commands that would cause harm is an indication that in their reasoning children are not solely oriented toward obedience to authority but draw boundaries regarding what they consider to be acceptable."[6] Many features of children's authority reasoning are consistent with the conditions found in typical band society, where there is no overarching authority and leadership is context-limited and transient. Children use context-relevant information about an authority figure's knowledge within the domain of authority as well as the authority figure's social standing—and see these two things as highly overlapping categories—when making judgments of legitimacy; that is, judgments of legitimacy are linked to the situation and not to the context-independent attributes of the individual.[7] Even the legitimacy of traditional authority figures such as teachers is screened through the lens of the teacher's social position within the school.[8] Social position trumps adult status, and knowledge trumps both, although children see knowledge and social position as mutually implied.

For children, as for adults, obedience is not the same as acceptance of legitimacy. Obedience is linked directly to the ability to punish: "Justification responses show that children view obedience in light of punishment and problem-solving concerns more than they view legitimacy that way. These results suggest that children are aware of the techniques used to manage their behavior; they recommend obedience to those individuals who hold social position because they know that those individuals can punish them."[9] There is an interesting developmental trend in which young children have a difficult time conceiving that either an adult or a peer who has been assigned a position of authority can be incompetent within the domain of authority, but where older children recognize that a teacher, for example, can be incompetent in the classroom, but assume that, as an adult, they probably have the knowledge relevant to giving commands that should be followed on the playground or in a non-school context. "The findings indicate that social position is of great importance in children's authority judgments . . . . However, knowledge and social position together are given more weight than is social position alone . . . . Adult status is of little importance across a wide range, when put in opposition to knowledge or social position. Furthermore, the addition of adult status to an individual with any combination of attributes does not cause more subjects to view his or her command as legitimate . . . . Young children do not focus on adult status per se when assessing legitimacy; rather, they infer that those with adult status and social position must be in possession of problem-solving knowledge."[10] In sum, children conceptualize authority in ways that are consistent with the way authority operates in egalitarian hunter-gatherer society: authority is a function of context-dependent knowledge, and compliance is strictly a matter of pragmatic considerations with respect to the potential consequences. The pragmatic nature of compliance, of course, is why the technological order requires lethally armed systems of enforcement.

The human brain is "experience-expectant and experience-dependent." Its development is patterned on the complex and sequential unfolding of systems that emerge in interaction with very specific forms of environmental input and feedback. In the presence of unexpected input, or in the absence of appropriate forms of feedback, emerging systems can be damaged or deformed in ways that impact the future maturity of the organism. The fact that development follows sequential, stage-like processes, means that the damage caused by the mismatch between expectation and experience can be permanent, and result in chronic immaturity. The mismatch between our developmental expectation for hunter-gather life-ways and our experience in post-industrial consumer civilization leaves us immature and needy. Our immaturity, and the impulsiveness and dependency that it entails, provides traction for the technological order with its artificial systems of power and authority.

The psychology of hierarchy

Part 2 addressed our inborn affinity with dominance relations in the social world. Humans, as social primates, are sensitive to power differentials that are always present in group situations. The fact that all humans possess this natural sensitivity, the fact that human history since the agricultural revolution (that is, all of "history") has been a protracted tale of violence and conquest, and the fact that modern-day consumer capitalism follows an amoral "dog-eat-dog" prime directive, suggests to many only one possible conclusion: humans are driven by a will to power. We are power-hungry both as individuals and as a species.

I would like to suggest a slightly different perspective. The will to power, rather than reflecting an entrenched feature of human nature, reflects instead a response to the social architecture of the technological order and the direct threat to personal autonomy posed by its systems of authority and control. At least two million years of (largely) egalitarian and (mostly) peaceful society preceded the post-agricultural power-orgy with its chronic warfare and genocide, widespread slavery and oppression, and perpetual political intrigues. Lust for power can't exist in any meaningful sense until a power structure is in place. This is commonsense logic. Without the division of labor, the isolation of knowledge, and a hierarchical organization of authority, we are left with a severely limited notion of power. Power implies an operative system of authority. Sure, you might be bigger and stronger and have more friends, but in an egalitarian society, without the ability to permanently restrict my access to needed resources or my ability to provide for my own life needs (or my ability to sneak up and kill you with a poison arrow when nobody is looking), you might be able to temporarily affect my comfort, but you can have no real power over me. It is only with the emergence of artificial hierarchy, when I become dependent on the operation of technology that itself depends on the hierarchical ordering of social relations, that I can be subject to another's power. And the will to power itself, according to this view, is a reaction to the absence of egalitarianism, not a latent drive to control other people. It reflects a desire to maintain personal autonomy in the presence of those who would limit it. I want to be the boss, not so that I can enjoy some kind of pleasure in the power to boss other people around, but so that I can be free from having to obey the commands of others.

At least one set of studies on the psychological impact of power provides evidence in favor of the autonomy-preservation perspective of the will to power, suggesting that power serves as a prophylactic, protecting people from the influence of others even on a psychological level.[11] Specifically, the researchers found that powerful persons generate creative ideas that are less influenced by examples (i.e., ideas that are in fact truly more creative), express attitudes that conform less to the opinions of others, and are less influenced by the value orientation of an opponent during negotiations, among other results. The motivation for power, accordingly, is driven by the desire to maximize autonomy in circumstances where autonomy is under potential threat; and we would expect this motivation to be present in a given situation in direct proportion to which autonomy is threatened or absent. This also suggests that the sadistic tendency that expresses itself within steeply hierarchical systems of artificial power is an aberration caused by the systems themselves, a deformation caused by the erosion of autonomy.

Our evolved psychology is attuned to relatively simple patterns of dominance such as those seen in other primate social groups, where my submission to a more dominant member of the group does not entail any permanent reduction in my autonomy. In fact, at any point I have the choice as to whether I submit or refuse, or simply walk away. And in an egalitarian society, the latter option is almost always a viable one. The hierarchically ordered mechanisms for power dispersion in technological society follow a different sort of pattern than the dominance relations to which we have evolved. When presented with the commands of a person in authority, I still have the choice to submit or refuse, but noncompliance almost always represents a threat to my access to resources. And in the densely structured and ubiquitous technological order of modern civilization, the choice to walk away has been for all practical purposes entirely eliminated. From a psychological standpoint, I have no way of processing this situation other than in terms of my evolved sensitivities for primate dominance relations. That is, there is a mismatch between my actual situation, embedded in complex systems of impersonal power and authority, and my evolved capacities to interpret and accommodate my situation, based on (intimately personal) group dynamics in a small egalitarian foraging band.

There are several facets of our response to authority that derive directly from our evolved responses to social dominance relations. Consider for example the use of signaling to reflect our knowledge of, and acknowledgement of, relationships of dominance and submission (power differentials) that exist between individual people. In addition to a number of primate nonverbal signals (e.g., smiling), we employ a variety of formalized protocols and conventional linguistic signaling devices. Psychologically speaking, the dominance-signaling functions of these social navigation tools are transferred largely intact and applied to the navigation of artificial hierarchies of authority; but not without consequences. What's more, asocial, impersonal technologies of authority and control operate largely by exploiting our tendencies toward dominance and submission in response to these social navigation devices. For example, asymmetries in conventions of greeting or address such as those traditionally practiced in academia and in the factory workplace, where students and laborers are referred to by their first names and teachers and managers by their last preceded by an honorific (Dr., Professor, Mr., Ms.) help to maintain the artificial authority structure by mapping out relations of relative power. Also relevant here is the use of formalisms in the typical customer service situation, where the customer is called "sir" or "ma'am," promoting the illusion that the customer is somehow the one who has ultimate power in the situation.

Because power as it functions in artificial systems of authority is different from anything anticipated by our evolved social-psychological tendencies, it might be worthwhile to explore how we conceptualize social power, and how our thinking has been molded by the imposition of an artificial hierarchical template. One of the defining features of hierarchical systems is asymmetry: hierarchy entails a fundamental asymmetry. It is, in a sense, the intentional

structuring of asymmetry. The way this asymmetry is applied to authority-based social relations is perhaps easiest to see with simple
pyramidal power structures such as those found a stereotypical nuclear family, the command structure of a military unit, or the seniori-
ty and promotion structure of a small business. But it applies to the
more complex branching hierarchies of government bureaucracies
and international banking corporations as well. Authority assumes
real or imagined asymmetries of power: it assumes at the very least
an expected power differential. Another defining feature of hierarchy
as it applies to systems of authority is verticality. We conceptualize
power in terms of a "vertical space" metaphor. Power hierarchies are
arranged vertically with power and control increasing as you progress toward the top. Authorities exercise their power "over" those
"under" their command. The Occupy Wall Street movement is directed at the "top" 1 percent. People move "up" the corporate ladder.
This way of thinking about power and authority is so ingrained that
it's hard to see it as metaphor. And there are numerous concrete features of society that further enhance the applicability of the verticality metaphor: the powerful frequently occupy physically high places,
for example; they travel by helicopter or private jet, and they room in
the penthouse suite, which is usually on the very top floor. And, in
the other direction, the street gutter is the residence of "down and
out" persons who have hit "rock bottom." An interesting feature of
vertical space as we actually experience it is its asymmetry with respect to potential physical mobility. The ground places very solid
limits in the downward direction, but the sky is boundless. This
asymmetry in potential mobility is inherited by our vertical metaphor
for social power.

Psychological research has shown that the ways we tend to conceptualize power are more subtle and contextually-sensitive than the
mere metaphoric mapping of physical verticality to the social world,
however. For example, one group of researchers tested whether our
way of conceptualizing power was in terms of an absolute hierarchy
where up is powerful and down is powerless, or in terms of context-
dependent relationships where those in power are seen as above
those with less power.[12] They found empirical evidence in support of

the context-relational hypothesis. Note that our concrete experience of the vertical dimension, the ground versus the sky, incorporates asymmetrical limits. So if power is spatially anchored and based on an absolute vertical spatial dimension, there should be limits to how powerless a person could be but no limits to the "height" of one's potential power. If power is relational and contextual, however, then there are no absolute limits in either direction; and even amongst the most severely oppressed slaves you should find power differentials. Also, there appears to be an asymmetry in our thinking about the relative difference between the powerful and the powerless: the powerful are seen as above the powerless more so than the powerless are seen as below the powerful. Power is linked more to a spatial hierarchy, corresponding to the schematic design of typical systems of authority, but powerlessness is more spatially amorphous—so a powerful CEO at the upper-end of the power hierarchy in a corporation is also somewhat powerless in terms of her dealings with the chairman of the board of trustees. Two things result from this. First, there are no limits to the height of one's potential power. Second, verticality has more relevance when talking about power than when talking about powerlessness. Powerlessness is more situational, relational, contextually-bound, and transient. So you in fact *do* find substantive power differentials even among slaves. In contrast to powerlessness, power is seen as a more durable and absolute quality of the social world. The loss of power means that it now belongs to someone else—the power itself remains. This might help explain why mass protestations of unfairness and inequality such as that seen with Occupy Wall Street focus on calls for "sharing the wealth" while leaving the scaffolding of power largely intact.

Cross-cultural investigations have identified an additional dimension of orientation to power and authority called power distance.[13] Power distance essentially has to do with the steepness of verticality in hierarchical relations. Persons (or cultures) with high power distance tend to have autocratic expectations with respect to the relationship between subordinate and superordinate. They tend to expect the authority of the superordinate to be respected unquestionably. By contrast, persons (or cultures) low on this dimension expect a more consultative relationship, and value discussion and the opportunity for criticism of authorities' decisions. Although you find people at different points along the power distance dimension in every culture, the ideals of Western culture tend toward the low end of the continuum. A question we might ask is why? Given that Western ideals are rapidly supplanting traditional cultural practices globally, we might suspect that either there is something about high power distance that reduces efficiency or otherwise poses a threat to important systems of the technological order or, conversely, there is something about low power distance that facilitates their operation. Along these lines it is suggestive that people on the low end of the power distance continuum "have stronger personal connections to authorities, viewing them as more like themselves. In such personalized relationships, subordinates have a stronger bond with authority. In contrast to low power-distance people, people with high power-distance orientations are likely to have role-constrained interactions with authorities, as occur in cultures in which authority relations are more strongly regimented by the relative positions of the superior and the subordinate."[14] People in the latter category feel little personal connection or identification with authorities. Power distance "shapes people's social connection to authorities and the organizations they represent. Those low in power distance feel that they draw more of a sense of self from the organization, and feel more committed to that organization."[15] So low power distance helps to obscure our roles as powerless servomechanisms and at the same time provides us with a surrogate sense of connection to the purposes of the corporate machine. Low power distance also provides psychological space for the operation of subtle modes of propaganda and persuasion, whereas high power distance runs the risk that the person would blindly comply with an authority other than those sanctioned by the technological order (a family member, or church leader, for example). Perhaps low power distance neither helps nor hinders the technological order. Perhaps the increase in ideals reflecting low power distance is just a reflexive reaction to the global proliferation of powerlessness, an increasing awareness that nobody, even our bosses, really has any true power.

As a side note, much of the social scientific research on authority is directed, implicitly or explicitly, at questions concerning how to enhance authority. Consider the following, taken from the conclusion to an article describing a series of studies on power distance, as the authors underline the complexity of the task at hand:

> These findings suggest that the psychology of authority relations is unlikely to produce a single model describing the mechanisms for the effective exercise of legal authority. Instead, the basis of such evaluations is intertwined with the social values of those evaluating authorities. Without understanding the cultural values held by subordinates, it is not possible to understand the basis on which authorities can function effectively.[16]

It might be possible to publish a study demonstrating how authority can be resisted or undermined, but only because those in authority would find such information useful for developing counter strategies. Social science, for all of the subversive potential claimed by some of its left-leaning practitioners, is, after all, a technology. It really has no recourse but to promote the purposes of the technological order.

Authority is power that is linked to the roles and organizational structure of institutions.[17] Authority is a characteristic of artificial systems of human social control. It is not a feature of the natural world or an emergent property of natural human social evolution. It is a technological contrivance. A limiting factor of authority is that for it to perform its function it must operate within the parameters of human psychology, a psychology that evolved to navigate social power relationships far different from those within which we are presently embedded. The mismatch between our evolved social expectations and our coerced interactions with artificial systems of authority can have a profoundly negative impact on our psychological state. Our psychology is simply not designed to be organized by technology; the role of institutional servomechanism is foreign from the point of view of our authentic human nature; we can do it, but not without experiencing the friction of mismatch. Institutions, government agencies, small businesses, multinational corporations, colleges and universities, are organizational technologies. People employed by these institutions—the overwhelming majority of common working folk in the Western World—are forced to maintain a psychological state on the job that mirrors many of the pathological features of a condition psychiatrists call dissociative identity disorder, more colloquially known as split personality. It is not uncommon for there to be conflict between what a person believes or desires in a given situation and what their contrived role within the institutional framework demands that they do. This can be particularly true for those employed as administrators in middle management. Regardless of the institution in question, the administrator's prime purpose is to reduce and eliminate any threat to efficiency. Human nature is almost always a potential threat to efficiency. Whenever the goals and needs of people are in conflict with the "goals" and "needs" of the institution, it is the administrator's job to see that institutional "goals" and "needs" are met. Human needs are not merely relegated to secondary status, they are to be removed from the equation completely if at all possible. And when not possible, for example, people need to eat and attend to other biological functions, the satisfaction of human needs is systematized in a way that causes the least possible reduction in efficiency (e.g., scheduled and time-restricted lunch breaks).

Administrators are people too, however. But while they are playing their role as administrator, their authentic human motives are to be pushed aside. They are gears in the institutional machine. Their job is to see that the machine gets what it must. It's nothing personal—literally. This bifurcation of roles, human being versus institutional servomechanism, has the potential to create substantial cognitive dissonance. The military, of course, has had to deal with this situation from the very beginning. Historically, the military solution has been to simply eliminate the human component entirely. You are a soldier, not a person. You are a mindless unit in the fighting machine and you will do what you are told when you are told and without question. Cognitive dissonance nevertheless still occurs on occasion, for example, in situations where human suffering is extensive and unwarranted (e.g., the Mai Lai massacre), and the violence it is capable of doing to the psyche is evidenced in such mental conditions as post-traumatic stress disorder and an extremely high incidence of military suicide. Corporate functionaries such as college administrators do not usually face combat-scale moments of self-doubt. If there is some minor cognitive dissonance that emerges from a conflict between their humanity and their institutional role, it is quickly eliminated by simply reducing their humanity, by blurring their role as administrator and their place as a member of the human community. Being an administrator is a way of being human, they tell themselves. And so the line between corporate servomechanism and human being is faded into oblivion.

There is some empirical support for this. Studies have shown that persons in positions of authority are more likely than their subordinates to change their attitudes so that they are consistent with their institutional role.[18] Someone who is powerless to choose can dissipate any cognitive dissonance that occurs as a function of being forced to act in ways that are inconsistent with their attitudes by simply acknowledging their lack of power within the context of their job. Persons in positions of authority, however, ostensibly have more choice with respect to their actions. When forced to act for the benefit of the institution in ways that conflict with their attitudes, they are more likely to change their attitudes to match with institutional demands in order to reduce the ensuing cognitive dissonance. Where institutional "needs" are frequently in conflict with the authentic needs of real people, the attitudes of managers will quickly change in ways that promote the institution and disregard humanity. Authentic human needs are trumped by the corporate machine's "needs" for efficiency. In theory this applies to the a silicon valley software firm no less than it does an Indonesian sweatshop, although the subordinates in the latter are far less likely to experience cognitive dissonance because they have a far more salient context for rationalizing their counter-attitudinal actions in terms of a lack of power.

In discussing the relationship between artificial hierarchies of authority and our natural psychological design, there is one final issue that I want briefly to address: how these artificial hierarchies interact with our larger symbolic capacities. Two things are relevant here. First, although it probably goes without saying, hierarchy is in some sense a product of our cognitive representational capacities. Our ability to see the world in terms of hierarchical orderings is a function of our more general ability to categorize, our ability to organize our experience of the world into discrete entities. Second, because artificial systems of authority are so ubiquitous, because they are such a major feature of our lives—humming in the background, setting the tone, and providing the landscape for our daily social experience—we are seduced into invoking authority hierarchies in a metaphorical fashion outside of our social world where they don't perhaps belong.

Ultimately, hierarchy is tied to our symbolic capacities. A fundamental prerequisite is the capacity to partition the world into distinct (or distinguishable) component parts that can be placed in systematic relation to each other. Hierarchy requires the ability to adopt a systemic world view, a world view that includes individuated (symbolic) entities that can be organized into systems. Hierarchy is a particular kind of abstract organization, an organization not given directly in our experience of the world. The ability to abstract and to objectify, to perceive distinct objects as entities separable physically or conceptually from the surrounding context, is a capacity that is not limited to humans. Even the ability to perceive transitive relationships of power in the social world, a simple kind of hierarchical relationship of the kind "A is dominant over B and B is dominant over C, therefore A is dominant over C," as we have seen, is something we share with other species. The ability to impose hierarchical arrangements on the world follows a developmental sequence. It remains controversial as to whether this developmental sequence provides direct evidence that hierarchy reflects an innate property of our human cognitive design, however. Children learn to name objects with basic level categorical assignments that do not appear to reflect an awareness of hierarchy. They learn "dog" long before they learn "poodle or "animal," "tree" before they learn "oak" or "plant," and "car" before they learn "Chevy" or "vehicle." Also, different cultures partition the world into systemic arrangements that correspond to different sorts of hierarchies. The place that humans occupy in the grand scheme of the cosmos, for example, differs greatly from one culture to the next. Probably the most that can be said definitively about the relationship between hierarchy and human psychology is that we naturally partition the objects of experience in ways that are consistent with learning hierarchical arrangements, but that the specific details of these arrangements are largely a product of culture and tradition. This applies both to the relations among concrete objects of the natural world and to the relations among people in the social world.

Technologies of authority and control are mechanical systems. The hierarchical distribution of power is how they function. The hierarchical distribution of power is a unique feature of all mechanical systems. Because of our experience with these systems, because they permeate the tissues of our lives and carve out so many facets of our day to day activity, we have come to see the rest of the world in terms of power and hierarchy, and, more specifically in terms of authority and control. We frequently generalize our social experience with controlling authority to other domains. Hierarchy has become an essential organizational strategy and a primary means by which we conceptualize and understand the world, a primary metaphor for comprehension that is applied to processes and phenomena outside of our social world. Hierarchy has become for us a metaphorical template, and a way of reducing the incomprehensible complexity of the universe to something that can be made consistent with the limitations of human symbolic capacities. This is especially noticeable in scientific discourse, both professional and popular. Consider the following excerpt, a description of the role of the hormone leptin, taken from a popular book on nutrition:

> Leptin essentially controls mammalian metabolism. Most people think that is the job of the thyroid, but leptin actually controls the thyroid, which regulates the rate of metabolism. Leptin oversees all energy stores. Leptin decides whether to make us hungry and store more fat or to burn fat. Leptin orchestrates our inflammatory response and can even control sympathetic versus parasympathetic arousal in the nervous system. If any

part of your nervous system is awry, including the adrenals or sex hormones, you will never have a prayer of truly resolving those issues until you have brought your leptin under control.

This is a key thing to understand: the endocrine system is an exceedingly complex system of interrelationships that ultimately is regulated via an intricate hierarchical system of management.

At the top of the management pillar is leptin. Immediately below it is its subservient sidekick, insulin, which serves as somewhat of an antagonist to leptin. Beneath that are your adrenal hormones, adrenalin and cortisol. Then come the pituitary hormones, which regulate the thyroid and growth hormones (and others), then your thyroid hormones, then your sex hormones, and on down. It's a chain of command.[19]

As anything but metaphor, this passage is entirely incoherent. Hormones cannot "decide" or "orchestrate" or serve as an antagonizing sidekick. But we are explicitly told that this is not metaphor: the endocrine system is an actual hierarchical "chain of command" with a mysteriously disembodied "you" at the pinnacle.

In addition to, or perhaps because of, the ubiquitous metaphoric application of hierarchy, hierarchical organization can serve a powerful mnemonic function. We remember things better when they have been organized into larger systems of relationship. Hierarchy serves as a convenient template for mnemonic organization. The memory and comprehension enhancement features of hierarchical systems of organization make our acceptance of hierarchical arrangements in the social world all that more seductive. It also makes it easier for us to interface with mechanical technology and organize our activity in ways that conform to the hierarchical contours of the technological order.

Mediation and the illusion of participation

Technology serves as an intermediary separating human beings from direct contact with specific features of the world around them (and frequently separating different parts of the world from itself in the process). Mediation is a feature of all technology, from the simplest tools to the most complex corporate bureaucracy. There are countless forms and degrees of mediation possible: using a stick to mediate the distance to a high-hanging piece of fruit; looking through a glass window at the tree; inspecting a photograph of the fruit; gazing at a digital screen image; reading a narrative description; consuming a pill containing a synthetic compound meant to mimic one found naturally in the fruit. A given technical arrangement or apparatus can help us to connect with features of the world around us in ways that might be impossible otherwise. But the technology of modern mass society more often serves as a wedge separating us from meaningful parts of ourselves. Mediation is frequently the explicit purpose of a particular technology. But forms of mediation can occur as unintended consequences of the technological process as well.

There is an obvious difference between experiencing the world through direct physical or sensory contact and experiencing it with the aid or intervention of a technical apparatus. In many cases, a technical intervention is designed specifically to ameliorate a negative circumstance or some unwanted conditions associated with direct contact: a window provides for visual contact with the outside world while reducing exposure to unpleasant climate conditions; an oven mitt protects the hand from the heat of the pan; a telescope brings a distant image into clearer focus; an automobile reduces both the time and the discomfort associated with travelling. What is often not so obvious is how the technical apparatus structures the experience itself: a window allows us to see the outside world, but it also restricts and frames our perspective. We addressed this feature of technology in our discussion of reverse adaptation in Part 3, and I want to reexamine it here in terms of how technological mediation can deform our relationships with each other and with the world around us.

Technological mediation exists at several levels in the social world. Civilization's artificial systems of power and authority, bureaucratic systems that provide an artificial topography for structuring our social experience, lie at one end of the spectrum; at the other end are a variety of technical mechanisms for interpersonal interaction. As a species, we are equipped to send a variety of different kinds of signals, from gestures and facial expressions to the utterances of spoken language, to mediate the physical separation between individuals. But very recently, starting in the late Neolithic, we have also developed a variety of communication technologies: written language; semaphore; telegraph; radio; telephone; email; cellular text messaging. It is commonly thought that the development of complex communication technologies is what allowed for civilization (the delusion of progress again).[20] But it might just as easily be seen the other way around: civilization necessitated the development and use of complex forms of mediated communication. The need for technologically-facilitated communication cannot be separated from the larger purposes of the technological order.

From the intercom at the drive-up window to internet-based systems such as Skype, much of our daily communication with other people is dependent on machine mediation. What kind of impact might this intrusion of mechanical apparatus have on the communicative process? One obvious feature of mediated communication is that it allows for a separation in space. The capacity of modern communication technologies to mediate distance has led to an increase in actual physical separation between communicating parties. So along with an increase in the ability to communicate at a physical distance comes an increase in the potential for physical isolation. Just as the automobile allowed for an increase in physical distance from important people and places, present-day digital cellular communication networks have allowed for an increase in seclusion, with each of us sequestered in an electronic bubble, immersed in a shared digital monolog with the lonely inhabitants of other bubbles.

Much has been made in recent years about the democratizing potential of the Internet. "Considered in the abstract, enhanced interactivity, information access, and the ability to build community over long distances certainly sound like positive, if not necessarily revolutionary, additions to the media landscape. [However], an abstract consideration of such issues is both incoherent and misleading: incoherent because it makes claims diametrically opposed to the evidence supplied by concrete applications; misleading because it implies that actual applications are determined by the technical capabilities themselves—that, for example, the Internet, by its very nature, ought to be inherently threatening to centralized, hierarchical power relations."[21] The internet, like all technology, is a zero sum. And like any other broadly applied technological application (e.g. automobile, television), one of the first negative consequences to emerge is dependence. The internet has gone from a useful communication medium to an essential feature of the global economy in just a couple decades.

The negative consequences of mediated forms of communication have been studied for years.[22] Although our high-tech communication technology should make us feel more connected, its development has in fact coincided with an increase in the prevalence of loneliness. One study found that social isolation increased dramatically in the 19 years between 1985 and 2004—the time when both the internet and cellphone use became popular.[23] During this period, the average person's social network decreased by one-third while the number of people who reported having zero people with whom they can discuss important matters tripled. There was also a reduction in the number of connections with people in the neighborhood and fewer contacts with people through memberships in voluntary associations. A related study that focused specifically on internet use found that access to the internet reduced communication with family members living in the same household, led to an increase in loneliness and depression, and reduced the size of an individual's social circle.[24] The results of other studies include: a relationship between internet text messaging and depression and a positive correlation between compulsive internet use and both depression and loneliness in adolescents;[25] and a negative relationship between social wellbeing and media use, a negative relationship between social wellbeing and media multitasking, and a positive relationship between social wellbeing and face-to-face communication in preadolescent girls.[26]

Social media appear to lack any true ability to enhance real friendships. Research has found a predictable correlation between the amount of time spent using internet social media and the number of online "friends" a person has, but no relation between the size of a person's online and offline networks. In addition, online social net-working appears to have no effect on emotional closeness with off-line friends.[27] These findings make sense in light of the cognitive limitations on (offline) social network size, limitations that prevent us from establishing and maintaining meaningful relationships with more than about 150 people, sometimes called Dunbar's number af-ter the researcher who first reported the phenomenon. A recent study examining the limitations of Dunbar's number as it pertains to stable social relationships on Twitter found empirical support for this limit in the online world as well.[28] There is very little evidence to support the claim that recent innovations in mediated social networking have actually enhanced our social situation, and continually mounting evi-dence to the contrary.

The extent to which interpersonal communication is shaped by the media through which it is transmitted is seldom appreciated. A text message, for example, involves several layers of technological deformation, and much of the intended content of the message can be lost in the process. A study conducted in 2005 explored the limita-tions on people's self-assessment of their ability to communicate electronically, and found that people think that they communicate over email better than they actually do.[29] The researchers linked this overconfidence to the difficulty in taking the other person's perspec-tive in non-face-to-face interactions. Presumably there are perspec-tive-enhancing signals and circumstances operating in face-to-face communication that counter this tendency—e.g., facial expression and voice inflection, eye-gaze, shared context, real-time message disambiguation, etc.

Mediation and dependency go hand in hand. It is easy to find ways that our daily activity has been built around and upon modern communication technology, leaving us entirely dependent on access to the technology. Although hunter-gatherers would certainly be able to find a good use for cell phone communication during a group hunt, instantaneous electronic communication is hardly necessary to bring down an antelope. That is not the case for a commodities trader trying to bag a juicy profit; the trader would starve to death (figuratively, and, perhaps, literally), if suddenly stripped of the ability to make instant electronic transactions. Recall our discussion in Part 2 about immediate-return societies. Individuals in immediate-return societies have direct, unmediated access to physical and social resources. This unmediated access to resources serves as both the foundation and impetus for an egalitarian society. Egalitarianism begins to dissolve as soon as dependence emerges. Dependence serves as both the foundation and impetus for steeply hierarchical systems of power and authority. Although paradoxical, the sturdy connections of interpersonal dependency that are forged in hierarchical society cause an increase in personal isolation relative to the situation in immediate–return societies.

One of the ways that the power complex is able to maintain its hold is through the atomization of the individual. By seeing ourselves as singular, independent units within society, we are less likely to see our personal interests as being shared by others, and less likely to then act on those shared interests against the system. Freedom and autonomy—in an authentic sense, not in terms of the pseudo-freedom of consumer choice—are held firmly in check as long as people see themselves as individuals in competition with everyone else for a good position in the hierarchy. Note that increased isolation functions to the benefit of a consumer economy both by increasing the number of isolated consumer units, each of which needs their own array of personal consumer products, and by providing the drive to seek out relief from their entrenched loneliness by participating in corporate-mediated events and activities. Spectator sports, politics, mass entertainment, the 24-hour news cycle, consumer fashions (to the extent that there are discernible differences among these) provide an artificial sense of involvement, and support the illusion of meaningful participation. But, like artificial sweeteners, they provide only a transient distraction, empty of nutritive content. This can be seen most clearly, perhaps, with the spectacle of professional sports. As a modern-day form of bread and circuses, professional sports serves as an obvious distraction. But sports also provide a useful template upon which to map our thinking in the political realm. Feelings of affiliation, the desire to support the team, nationalism, and corporate loyalty all tap into the same psychological substrate.

Participation in popular culture creates a shared reality and an artificial sense of belonging. On some level, we realize we are participating in an ersatz reality, and cynical skepticism serves as a kind of self-protective emotional shell. This, of course, also serves to the machine's advantage. "In the face of generalized wholesale skepticism, participation runs the risk of merely reproducing the limits imposed by the scientific management of culture on the imagination of an animated yet benumbed populace. Yes, they can participate, but the cultural imaginary that underwrites this participation comes pre-packaged. Freedom will continue to mean deregulation of the market; choice will continue to refer to a forced choice from a fixed range of goods and goals."[30]

While we are immersed in mass spectacle, it is easy to forget that the camera lens points in two directions. And at any given moment, several may be trained on you and me, passively recording our movements, making note of our consumer and political behavior, and mining our communication for information that can be sold to advertisers and others with an interest in exploiting our preferences and peccadillos.

A world of eyes

It knows exactly where you are and exactly what you want.

You work the night shift, and you just got off work. It's 9:30 in the morning. You step out into the street and the screen of your phone lights up with an ad from a local business: a restaurant, literally across the street from where you are standing, is open early and has a special on Thai basil, one of your personal all-time favorite foods. Your friend who works with you is standing right next to you, but the screen of his phone is aglow with Margi-Rita, a particularly pneumatic redhead who is scheduled to appear on stage at strip club around the corner later this afternoon. It turns out your friend has a weakness—a fetish, really—for busty redheads.

Machines using algorithms continuously collect and collate data from your email, your text messages, your internet activity, your credit card and debit card purchases, your organizational memberships, and a potentially open-ended variety of other sources. What emerges is a profile of you that can be used to predict your future consumer desires better than you can. These algorithms can also be used to tailor commercial advertisements and political propaganda to your individual psychology, tapping into your weaknesses and idiosyncrasies for maximum effect. And by tracking your cell phone (something already done without your consent to monitor traffic flow patterns), the ads can be localized and continually updated to accommodate your every movement. Think of the futuristic Tom Cruise movie *Minority Report,* where the wall-mounted video billboards greeted people personally as they walked by—only you carry the billboard around in your pocket.

Knowledge is power, and the more a person knows about you, the more potential power they have over you (i.e., over your thoughts and actions); There are several facets of "you" in which the corporate machine has more information than you do about yourself. Can you remember all of the internet purchases you have made over the last 10 years? What about your clothing purchases, and your grocery purchases, and your entertainment choices, and all of the web sites you visited, and people you emailed, and phone calls you made, and the specific street route you took to a friend's party on October 8th last year? By applying complex statistical algorithms to all of these data, it is possible to predict with uncanny accuracy the odds with which you are likely to buy a product, or the likelihood you will vote for a candidate you are not even aware exists at this point. More importantly, these algorithms can be used to assemble a persuasive message designed specifically for you, one that can tap your personal fears and insecurities, one that has a much higher chance of succeeding than old-school advertisements meant for the general consumer.

The technology for this particular kind of direct micro-marketing, individualized to the point tracking your movements and delivering content relevant to your specific location (in addition to your personal habits, fears, and idiosyncratic preferences) is available as I write these words, and will be business as usual by the time you read them. A friend of mine, whose upper lip is deeply stained with a techno-Kool-Aid moustache, told me that there is really no downside to this. He happens in fact to like Thai basil, and the fact that the restaurant across the street has a special on it is something he wouldn't want to miss. What I didn't think to ask him was how he originally found out about Thai basil. How many of our most cherished things (and people) were a result of an unplanned encounter? Chances are that he stumbled across Thai basil by accident. Perhaps his car broke down in front of a restaurant that he would have never visited otherwise.

Our desires and preferences are already highly groomed by corporate marketing. Many of them are completely manufactured and would have no traction at all if our lives weren't so deeply embedded in consumer culture. The more complex mass society becomes, the more we need the corporate machine to sift our priorities. The more individualized this process becomes, the more that our preferences become canalized. A fundamental paradox of mass society: more options mean less real choice. In the case of micro-targeted advertising, each choice you make leads to a further restriction in the range of possibilities presented. Mint raita is at least as good as Thai basil, and the restaurant two blocks over has the best Indian food in town, but your phone will remain forever silent about that fact. And your friend may never have the opportunity to acquire a deep appreciation for the aesthetic qualities of waifish brunettes.

We have little or no ability to opt out. We are given a Hobson's choice of allowing our activities to be mined for data that can be used against us or simply not participating in mass culture. No one is forcing us at gunpoint to buy a cell phone or use email or drive a car or use a credit or debit card. But if we decide to use any of these things, the data we provide is for sale as part of the deal.

The ubiquitous surveillance that supports micro-marketing also serves a more direct, and, in many ways more insidious, purpose. Michel Foucault used Jeremy Bentham's Panopticon, a prison design that renders the behavior of inmates perpetually visible to unseen

guards, to explore the power potential of mere surveillance. The logic of the Panopticon is simple: if at any moment someone in power
might be watching me—and I have no way of knowing when or if—
then at any moment, to be safe, I need to assume that I am being
watched and adjust my behavior accordingly. The true beauty of
mere surveillance as a form of control is that it turns the target's own
psychology into a weapon, over time generating a docile personality
while greatly reducing the need to apply overt coercive force.

It seems to me that this has something nontrivial in common with
the logic of religions organized around a personal god, in terms of
their utility for controlling the behavior of the masses. God is unseen,
but sees all and punishes those who disobey his proscriptions. Since
he might be watching me right now, I need to adjust my behavior
accordingly. It is interesting to speculate about the functional significance of the emergence of monotheism in the late Neolithic in terms
of this panoptic form of behavior control over the masses. The savvy
and skeptical inhabitants of a sophisticated 21st century are far more
difficult to control with tales of a vengeful and all-seeing über-being.
His divine presence has had to be upgraded. God has had to become
digitized and sequestered somewhere behind a semi-opaque dome
projecting from the department store ceiling, a lens embedded in an
ATM machine or suspended from a traffic light, a seventh-grade student's school laptop computer, or a camera mounted in the grill of a
cop car or hidden in an innocuous trinket sitting atop the television to
spy on the babysitter.

Surveillance has been defined as "the focused, systematic and
routine attention to personal details for the purpose of influence,
management, protection, or direction."[31] One of the first places that
surveillance appeared was the workplace. "Many terms that refer to
work superiors actually contain the idea of surveillance within them:
'supervisor', 'overlooker', 'monitor'."[32] Surveillance, especially in
the workplace, but in other venues as well, promotes a theme of general distrust. "There is a sense in which such surveillance expresses
an ongoing theme, that those who establish some means of watching
over others are demonstrating that they do not trust those being
watched . . . ."[33] In our post-Patriot-Act world, surveillance has be-

come increasingly an overt activity of the state. "Although it often has protecting, entitling or caring components, surveillance expands primarily as a means of power in modern societies, due to military, geo-political and economic dynamics expressed through bureaucratic organizations."[34]

Surveillance keeps us passive while providing an illusion of safety and security. The idea of privacy had its time, and was actually a rather short lived concept. The idea no longer makes any sense. And the new generation, with the aid of Facebook and Twitter, and the chronic spewing of private thoughts into the public arena, the idea of privacy is becoming a quaint anachronism. "Part of the problem has been the tendency to think of privacy as a possession, something that can be acquired, surrendered, or exchanged, as implied by the question, 'Are you willing to give up some of your privacy in exchange for greater security or convenience . . . ? The question is not 'how much privacy has been surrendered,' but 'who benefits from and who is disempowered . . . and in what ways? Who is subjected to more sophisticated forms of management and control, and to what end? How does knowledge about individuals facilitate forms of control over them?"[35] And for those of us who are still concerned about privacy, we run again into the Hobson's choice of privacy versus participation. "Thus the ability of consumers to choose whether or not they enter into the digital enclosure increasingly comes to resemble the forced choice of the wage-labor agreement. Consumers are free not to interact, but they find themselves compelled to engage in interactive exchanges (and go online) by what [author of *Da Vinci's Ghost*, Toby Lester] describes as 'the tyranny of convenience.'"[36]

Being watched—or just thinking that you might be watched—serves a self-regulating function. Bentham's idea of the Panopticon as detailed by Foucault is paradigmatic. But there are countless other examples in modern society. "In the case of Homeland Security, the invitation to participate in defending the nation against terrorism doubles as an invitation to identify with the administration's policies and with its definition of the problem: terrorism is an inexplicable force in nature, born of irrational hatred and not amenable to shifts in foreign or domestic policy. Because there is no causal explanation for terrorism, according to this ideology, root causes cannot be addressed, and any attempt at understanding can be dismissed as appeasement."[37] Surveillance can thus serve to set the parameters of acceptable behavior—not through any consideration of moral appropriateness, but strictly as a means to establish normative patterns that best serve the efficient operation of consumer society. "If we don't have enough people to monitor the surveillance cameras, the work of watching can be delegated and automated. But this means equipping cameras with algorithms that define behaviors associated with 'normal'—nonthreatening or noncriminal—behavior and imposing these norms on individuals."[38]

The ubiquity and oppressive functions of surveillance serve as tremendous obstacles for those who call for making dramatic changes to the status quo. However, "[t]he fact that we cannot disappear 'under the radar' of the assemblage does not mean that counter measures are pointless. It means rather that the ensuing struggle is complex."[39]

Resistance as pathology

A teacher of mine once told a story about an old man who lived in a basement apartment in Brooklyn during the 1950s. Outside his window was a fire hydrant, and every day after school a group of local boys would use the hydrant as home-plate in a rowdy game of stickball. The old man hated the noise and would run outside to yell at the boys every time a missed pitch would bounce off his window. The boys would just laugh at the old man and continue to play their game. Then one day, the old man got an idea. He went to the bank and bought several rolls of change: quarters, dimes, and nickels. The next time the boys came around to play, the old man gave them each a quarter and told them that he so much liked to have them around that he was going to pay them money just for playing stickball in front of his window. The kids thought he had lost his mind, but they took his money. This went on for a few days, and then the old man came out and gave them all dimes, saying that he could no longer afford to give them quarters. The kids shrugged their shoulders and took his money. After giving the boys dimes for a few days, the old man switched to nickels, again claiming that he was too poor to keep giving them dimes. The boys started to complain openly at this point, calling the old man a cheapskate (and other choice epithets, I'm sure). Finally, the old man came out and told the boys that he could no longer afford to pay them any money, but he pleaded with them to continue playing in front of his window. The boys left with their stick and ball and never returned.

My teacher's story was fictional, a reworking of a Jewish folktale. It does, however, demonstrate a principle that lies at the heart of another story, one that is true and one that has been repeated countless times. A child is born with a strong innate motivation to learn. She actively explores her environment and she is fascinated by all that she sees. She wants to understand her world, and is constantly asking the adults in her life questions about how the world works. Her desire to know is insatiable. Then she starts school. At first, school provides a wondrous whole new world that she must explore, and her drive to learn is indefatigable. But slowly, almost imperceptibly, she begins to invest her energies toward rewards. The teacher puts a star on her paper when she gets all of the colors right. Then, in later years, the star is replaced with a letter. A's are better than B's. By the time she gets to high school, her inborn desire to learn about the world has been all but completely replaced by her desire to perform. In college, she wisely refuses to direct her energies to any academic activities that are not directly relevant for supporting her GPA. Exams and quizzes have to be employed to coerce her to read texts that she has no patience for. What happens after she graduates? What happens to her motivation to learn when there is no longer any external incentive? She leaves with her stick and ball and never returns.

Formal education is indoctrination, pure and simple. It serves no other purpose and never has. In order for the technological order to function efficiently, natural, in-born human inclinations need to be yoked to an external drive-train. This is accomplished primarily by replacing internal motivation with incentives, threats, and rewards. I spoke to my five-year-old granddaughter on the phone after her first day of school. She was excited and talked at length about her day and how much she liked her teacher and the other kids. She told me that her school had a huge playground and started to list all of the various slides and swings—then she paused and her voice changed dramatically, becoming stern and serious. "But before we could play, we had to learn the rules," she said. The real reason kids go to school is to learn the rules. Some kids respond better to this process than do others. Some, especially young boys, seem to have a hard time over-riding their developmental predispositions for autonomous play and exploration. In addition, humans are anti-authoritarian by design, and in order to accommodate the demands of an artificial, authority-embedded social system they have to learn to sequester their natural egalitarian inclinations. Those who have trouble with this process need special attention.

Attention-deficit/hyperactivity disorder (ADHD), according to the psychiatric party line, is a mental disorder involving a dysfunction in some as of yet unspecified brain systems involved in sensory and/or behavioral inhibition and control. In the classroom, ADHD children have difficulty following instructions, staying on task, standing in line, sitting in their chairs, keeping their hands and their thoughts to themselves, and are generally disruptive of the educational process and a nuisance to the teacher and the other students. The disorder is treated with the regular application of stimulant medication, which has a "paradoxical effect" on ADHD kids and calms them down. A few psychologists—a maligned minority—have begun to suspect that the ADHD label is really just a way of dealing with kids who are having an adverse reaction to the mindlessness of formal education and who resist the authoritarian strictures of the classroom environ-ment. Many ADHD kids who can't stay on task for more than 30 seconds in the classroom can concentrate for hours at a time on tasks they find personally interesting—and the stimulant drugs work pre-cisely because, like other recreational substances, they make things more interesting. From an authentic human standpoint, it is the non-ADHD kids, the ones who follow the rules without question, the ones who readily take on a posture of passive subservience to adult authority and group conformity, the ones who are able to acclimate to the captivity and the mindless routines of the classroom, who are truly dysfunctional.

Consider a recent study that looked at how the inclusion of an ADHD child impacts the social behavior of school children working in cooperative problem-solving groups.[40] The researchers compared the performance of groups that did and did not include a child labeled at-risk for ADHD. Although the at-risk children engaged in more negative, off-task, and "uncooperative" behavior, the groups that included an at-risk child were more than five times as likely to be successful at the problem solving task than groups that did not include an at-risk child.

The researchers called this simply an unexpected result.

And in fact the result makes no sense at all if ADHD reflects a dysfunctional condition. If ADHD reflects a psychological disorder that leads to social dysfunction, then it is, in fact, extremely unexpected. The inclusion of an ADHD child to the group should be a clear detriment to the group's problem solving potential. But if ADHD is simply a label given to kids who refuse to relinquish their freedom and autonomy, kids who can still think outside the box because their thought process has yet to be totally boxed in, then the result makes perfect sense: adding an at-risk-for-ADHD kid to the group should lead to better problem solving success relative to groups consisting entirely of children who are already firmly on the path to becoming full-fledged sheep.

There are numerous other reactions to the mismatch between our evolved expectations for relative egalitarianism and the demands of an authoritarian technological order that have been mislabeled. "Americans have been increasingly socialized to equate inattention, anger, anxiety, and immobilizing despair with a medical condition, and seek medical treatment rather than political remedies. What better way to maintain the status quo that to view inattention, anger, anxiety, and depression as biomedical problems of those who are mentally ill rather than normal reactions to an increasingly authoritarian society."[41] Psychologist Bruce Levine suggests that the keepers of the status quo have good reason to redefine anti-authoritarian behavior as mental illness: "In every generation there will be authoritarians and anti-authoritarians. While it is unusual in American history for anti-authoritarians to take the kind of effective action that inspires others to successfully revolt, every once in a while a Tom Paine, Crazy Horse, or Malcolm X come along. So authoritarians financially marginalize those who buck the system, they criminalize anti-authoritarianism, they psychopathologize anti-authoritarians, and they market drugs for their 'cure.'"[42]

The DSM, the official repository of psychiatric labels, has recently included a new category to apply to kids who have the audacity to question arbitrary authority: oppositional defiant disorder. This from the Mayo Clinic's Website:

> Even the best-behaved children can be difficult and challenging at times. But if your child or teen has a persistent pattern of tantrums, arguing, and angry or disruptive behavior toward you and other authority figures, he or she may have oppositional defiant disorder (ODD).
>
> As a parent, you don't have to go it alone in trying to manage a child with oppositional defiant disorder. Doctors, counselors and child development experts can help.
>
> Treatment of ODD involves therapy, training to help build positive family interactions, and possibly medications to treat related mental health conditions.

First off, notice that ODD is something you can "have," like the measles or a broken leg. Also notice that, unlike ADHD, ODD is entirely based on a failure to acquiesce to authority. Tantrums and angry outbursts are natural responses to restrictions of autonomy. Put a bull raccoon in a cage and see how it responds. Reactionary responses to externally-imposed power and control are to be expected, and fall on a continuum that reflects the degree of power differential involved. When the differential is relatively small, you get passive-aggressive behavior and social back-biting. A larger differential yields overt anger and physical violence. A massive differential gives you suicide bombers.

Stockholm syndrome is most often linked with hostage situations, but it can be applied to just about any abusive relationship. It is a non-diagnostic term for paradoxical situations in which victims not merely comply with their abuser(s), but actually idealize them and identify with them—frequently beyond the point of disengagement. When viewed as a natural mammalian defense reaction, as an evolved adaptive coping strategy, the paradox disappears. Mammalian responses to threat follow a predictable pattern depending on the nature and proximity of the threat. For distant or mild threats, the first defense is avoidance. If the threat is more proximal, the animal engages in attentive immobility where it freezes in order to better assess what to do about the situation. The next step is active withdrawal (running away). If withdrawal is not possible or unlikely to be successful in the situation, the animal engages in aggressive defense (fighting). If fighting is not possible (when the opponent has a clear and present advantage), the animal engages in appeasement behavior. Finally, as a last resort, the animal engages in tonic immobility, freezing in an attempt to confuse the predator (opossums are notorious for this). Stockholm syndrome happens in *traumatic entrapment* situations that are perceived to be well beyond the fleeing or fighting stage but not yet to a terminal stage that would call for tonic immobility, and so appeasement becomes the relevant choice. Appeasement behavior causes cognitive dissonance (treating an aggressor nicely does not make sense given the victim's true feelings about the aggressor), and in order to make sense of their own appeasement behavior, the victim comes to believe that they must really be on the side of the abuser.

Psychologists have identified four conditions that need to be present in order to produce Stockholm syndrome: perceived threat to one's physical or psychological survival at the hands of an abuser(s); perceived small kindnesses from the abuser to the victim; isolation from perspectives other than those of the abuser; the inescapability of the situation.[43] Notice how easily these conditions can be applied to life under the thumb of the global corporate machine:

- Perceived threat: it is not just our personal physical and psychological survival that is under direct threat, but the survival of the entire biosphere.
- Small kindness: the corporate world gives us polio vaccines, iPhones, and professional sports even as it enslaves us.
- Isolation of perspective: corporate media provides the only valid perspective.
- Inescapability: industrial civilization has become the air we breathe, and the corporate machine has the power and demonstrated will to use overwhelming lethal force against any and all who would resist.

We are all victims of traumatic entrapment. We are all corporate hostages. We should pity those civilization apologists who promote the status quo, those who want to appease their captors, those who argue that the corporate rapists really have our best interests at heart, those who believe that mass technology is our lifeline, those who claim that industrial civilization is our salvation. Their cheerleading is a symptom of Stockholm syndrome. Their pleading appeasement today will become silent immobility tomorrow.

Aboriginal people make fish traps by assembling structures that become progressively narrow. Once inside, fish are unable to return the way they came and their continued forward movement only leads to further restriction. A strategy for capturing monkeys that has apparently been used in a variety of places around the world involves placing a piece of fruit or a favorite kind of nut in a narrow hole carved into the ground or in a jar tied to a tree. The opening to the monkey trap is just wide enough for the monkey to reach its hand into but too narrow to take it out while simultaneously holding onto the food. The monkey instinctually grips the food more tightly when it realizes it is trapped, and is unable to remove its hand in time to keep from being captured—and not necessarily because the monkey is too stupid to realize that it can't have both food and freedom, but more likely because, as a tree dweller, its natural reflex when scared and confused is to grip more tightly. Both the monkey trap and the fish trap function by exploiting the animal's natural behavioral propensities and instincts. Technology is a trap that exploits our instinctual reflexes. Like the fish, we need to recognize that redoubling our effort and pushing forward is not a way out. Like the monkey, we need to find a way to override our instinctual reflexes and simply let go.

PART 5: HUMANARCHY

The path of most resistance

I have never seen quicksand in its natural habitat. All of my quicksand experience, like far too many of my other experiences with the natural world, has been vicarious, mediated by a printed page, television set, movie screen, or computer terminal. Quicksand nevertheless found frequent rotation with hot lava, piranha-infested water, bottomless pits, and similar dangerous obstacles that my childhood friends and I were forced to navigate daily in the vacant lot across the alley. As a potentially dangerous medium, quicksand is different from ravenous piranhas and lava and bottomless pits in that it is possible to survive a fall into quicksand—provided you understand how quicksand works. The first thing that you need to do when you find yourself in quicksand is override your natural inclination to move. The more that you thrash about, the deeper you go. To free yourself from quicksand—the real stuff, not the patch of mud in the vacant lot—I am told that you need to lie flat and actually immerse more of your body in the muck. With patience and a little luck, you can then gently "swim" or roll yourself to safety. Not only is this entirely counterintuitive, but it is directly counter to automatic reflexive reactions that in other situations might save your life.

Our problem is not quicksand. Our problem is far more pervasive and far more lethal than anything my childhood imagination could have conjured. Over the last several thousand years, we have stumbled into something from which it may be exceedingly difficult—perhaps impossible—to extract ourselves. We are already deeply embedded, and, as with quicksand, our natural inclinations work against us and seem only to be driving us deeper and deeper. I have chosen to call the substance in which we are ensnared *the technological order*, for lack of a better term. Although global civilization is its present material form, its historical emergence occurred millennia prior to the industrial revolution, its ultimate essence is the technological process itself, and its ultimate source is perhaps found in the conceptual bifurcation of nature that attends patterns of life based on domestication.

In some sense, the preceding four parts of this book have been prolog. They provide a foundation and a potentially useful way of framing our situation as we sink into the suffocating grip of our own technology. Perhaps more important is what I haven't said in the earlier parts of this book. I haven't said, for example, that our problems are due to a flawed human nature. Quite the contrary, our problems are a direct result of the restraint, constraint, and intentional deformation of authentic human nature. The world is going to hell in a hand basket, but not because of any moral failure on the part of human beings or any glitch in our genetic programming. The world is going to hell in a hand basket because of the hand basket. This final part is meant to address the question of what can be done about it; how do we shake ourselves loose?

I'm not sure whether that is a meaningful question to ask, and, if so, whether it has a meaningful answer. One thing that should be abundantly clear at this point, however, is that we should be highly suspicious of answers that are technical in nature; the technological process is the problem and business as usual is not an option. As William Koetke suggested, "The impulse of civilization in crisis is to do what it has been doing, but do it more energetically in order to extricate itself. If soaring population and starvation threaten, often the impulse is to put more pressure on the agricultural soils and cut the forests faster."[1] The impulse to thrash about ever more furiously with technical "solutions" needs to be subdued, or, perhaps, redirected.

I begin this final part first by providing a brief review of the discussion so far, highlighting the positive value of anarchism as both a conceptual frame and a social trajectory—as both a tool and an anti-tool for facilitating the disassembly of the technological order. Then I return once again to modernity's misguided and immensely destructive notions of progress. The idea of progress reflects reverse adaptation at the conceptual level: our habitual ways of thinking have been structured to conform to the ratcheting expansion of technology. And the problem with the idea of progress is not merely that it is false. The delusion that human society is on a journey toward some future perfection of the species, and that history is a travelogue of the trip so far, provides not just an illusory and highly deceptive perspective on our present situation, but it also serves to rationalize—and legitimize—the accelerating erosion of personal autonomy, the expansion of dehumanizing technology, and the degradation of what little there remains in us that is authentically human: the real problem with the idea of progress is that it generates progressive solutions that can't help but make things worse. The remainder of this final section deals with more practical considerations. Practically speaking, what can be done about our situation? Who is it that should be doing it? Where should efforts be directed? A focus on our evolved propensities toward anarchy and egalitarian social relations, and on the contrast between these evolved expectations and our present circumstances, suggests several targetable lynchpins. Although far from a novel idea, self-reliance, both as individuals and at the community level, might provide a path toward disengagement from the technical impulse and a way to redirect our aimless thrashing about toward more authentically human goals.

So let's recap, starting with the authentic human need for autonomy.

Autonomy as I have defined it here is the degree to which an individual is able to pursue goals of his or her own free choosing. More specifically, a person is autonomous to the extent that his or her goals and actions are not being directed, coerced, or otherwise controlled by other person(s) or by artificial systems that have been designed to direct, coerce, or otherwise control his or her goals and actions. Autonomy goes beyond the freedom to select from among a limited array of consumer options. It also goes beyond making a forced choice from among a limited set of "careers." Autonomy has to do with the degree to which the individual is free, from moment to moment, to assemble a set of potential goals, and to pursue purposes of his or her own—*without any other person controlling, directing, coercing, or otherwise manipulating the process.* Autonomy, as I have defined it here, does not mean to be free from external constraint. It means only to be free from governing control by other persons. An extremely high degree of personal autonomy has been the norm for over 99 percent of our species tenure, and in that sense, autonomy, along with the reciprocal tendency toward egalitarianism, can be considered part of our authentic human design as foraging hunter-gatherers. A return to more autonomous living means a return to social conditions consistent with those found in small egalitarian foraging bands.

Hierarchical systems of authority are social technologies designed specifically to constrain autonomy and direct human activity toward goals and purposes that have not been freely chosen. Systems of authority are artificial constructions and do not reflect a natural development of our social sensibilities or an evolutionary extension of more primitive primate dominance relations; it is possible that they first emerged in conjunction with the division of labor and the restriction of access to knowledge that are associated with large-scale domestication technology. Although not a product of human evolution, these systems have themselves evolved over time to become more effective, more powerful, and more efficient. The loose assemblage of hyper-complex, ultra-sophisticated, and massive-scale technologies of modern global civilization, the technological order, is possible only because of the penetrating operation of equally complex, equally sophisticated, and equally massive systems of authority and control underwritten by the power to employ overwhelming lethal force and designed to direct human activity away from authentic human needs and purposes and toward the needs and purposes of its various systems.

And, finally, these artificial systems of authority and control are able to achieve and maintain traction only by exploiting and deforming our natural evolutionary design for a substantially different kind of life. Our evolved human nature provides the teeth in the sprockets and gears that turn the machine's drivetrain. Arrested development provides a potent source of our enmeshment. By removing and replacing the social and environmental input essential for natural psychological development and healthy maturation, we are rendered chronically immature, acutely dependent, and in a perpetual state of emotional need—a state of need that is easily exploited by the superficial enticements of consumer culture with its technological trinkets and two-dimensional community affiliations. In addition, our immaturity leaves us vulnerable to the operation of hierarchical systems of power, systems designed to tap directly into our instinctual responses to social dominance relations. And as emotional infants, we find comfort wrapped in power's controlling embrace. Our lifelong childishness makes us averse to ambiguity even as adults. The technological order removes ambiguity, and soothes us by replacing the cluttered uncertainty of free choice with the ordered barrenness of a prison cell and the calm inevitability of an executioner's rifle.

Our immaturity and dependency are enhanced by substituting direct human-to-human contact with technologically mediated forms of communication. In addition to diluting the richness of authentic human interaction—a richness that would surely interfere with efficiency were it allowed to operate at full potency—our social experience is reduced to mediated social "connections," where our interpersonal, and, increasingly, also our intra-personal, interactions, are deformed in ways that serve the technological order. Add to that ubiquitous surveillance, internalizing our acquiescence: making us effectively into our own jailors, our own as well as our brother's (and sister's) keepers. And let's not forget the power of words. By relabeling opposition and rebellion as pathology, anyone who would refuse to relinquish residual crumbs of his or her latent humanity and resist the demands of artificial authority is pathologized and redefined into submission: those who refuse to accept the role of servomechanism are suffering from a mental disease and are in need of therapeutic recalibration (frequently of a chemical nature).

As a rebuttal to those who would insist that some form of government is necessary, that we *need* systems of authority and coercive control, I would ask two questions: first, what, exactly, do we need these systems of authority for? And second, who is "we"? To list all of the specific features of postindustrial global society that require coercive authority would be an impossible task. In general terms, systems of authority are necessary for any technology beyond simple tools and crafts. Authority is necessary for any technology that involves division of labor and specialized knowledge—at a bare (and rare) minimum to serve a coordinating function, and usually to impose "divisions" of labor that force some people into undesirable stations—somebody has to work in the mines. So without highly oppressive systems of authority underwritten by lethal coercion, we could never have computers or automobiles or professional sports. But, and here's the clincher, since most of our goals and purposes are, through reverse adaptation, being generated by technology itself, without authority and the technological order that it supports we as individuals would be left to our own devices (both literally and figuratively). Authentically human motives and goals would emerge as the only motives and goals possible. In other words, our perceived needs for the technological systems that require coercive authority and control are generated by the systems themselves; remove the systems and our needs for them evaporate. And in regards to the "who is we" rebuttal: when people say such things as "we need government" they are referring to an abstraction, an imagined collective humanity. This "we" does not exist. Instead, there are real concrete individuals who have real concrete needs as individuals. Many of our own individual needs are similar to those of other individuals. But, once again, the majority of needs that are in play at any given time are needs that have been generated as a function of life embedded in the technological order. Remove authority, and the technological order evaporates along with these needs. So it is true that we (the abstract human collective) "need" systems of authority as long as we (individual people) continue to pursue purposes generated by those same systems of authority. Which is to say that we (both collectively and as individuals) really don't need these systems of authority. If anything, the systems of authority need us to continue to act as if we need them. But the idea that technology can have actual needs is nonsensical. Corporations are *not* people, my friend (no apologies to Mitt Romney).

Anarchy is the only social condition that is consistent with our authentic human nature. Anarchy is not chaos. It is the absence of legitimate authority. Even stronger, it is a condition in which the word "legitimate" has no referent. Anarchy is also the absence of politics. Humans are social primates. We are not, fundamentally, political animals, as Aristotle so famously claimed. Aristotle called humans political animals because he believed that we could not be authentically human unless we were participants in civilization. It would be understatement to say that he had things backward. Politics is a feature of the artificial technological ordering of the social world. Yes, people in egalitarian society engage in a wide variety of social intrigues, back-stabbing, power maneuvers, etc. But it is a mistake to call this politics and equate it with how people act when social power is bureaucratically distributed. The first egalitarian societies to be processed by Western science, as with their animal-colony counterparts, were processed according to the framework of hierarchy. As a result, we have !Kung politics and chimp warfare. Just semantics, I suppose. Nevertheless, it is important to recognize that what happens within the structured machinations of the technological order is different in qualitative ways from what happens when no such order is present.

A reversion to the base-anarchy of our pre-domestication past seems to me to be the only option if the goal is to live an authentically human life. And any goal that is inconsistent with authentic human living is not an authentic human goal. Unfortunately, any attempt to promote authentic humanity, however modest, is sure to engage the protective defenses of the technological order.

So, at least at some level, the problem is well defined.

Anatomy of a delusion

The conceptual frame that encases our social institutions, schools, governments, media—our very language in terms of our base metaphors—is derived to a large extent from the goals of industrial mass production and the obligatory mass consumption that it entails. Qualitative features of human wellbeing are recoded into quantitative terms and measured according to standards of mechanical output and efficiency. Statistical indicators, proportions, averages—tools of Wall Street and corporate industry—have long replaced any reference to raw, qualitative human experience. This frame reinforces the delusion of technological progress and disguises the unrelenting and progressive dehumanization and the deterioration in the quality of human experience that the delusion of progress engenders.

Consider the case of infant mortality, a statistic that is frequently used as a quantitative indicator of the quality of life. Thanks to humanitarian international policy, modern medical technology, and the fruits of nutrition science—not to mention industrial agriculture—the global infant mortality rate is on the decline. What does that mean? From an industrial frame it represents a positive outcome: an increase in the overall quality of life. However, a positive quantitative outcome in this case does not mean a reduction in human suffering because a decline in the global rate of infant mortality does not mean that fewer babies are dying. In point of fact, more babies will die this year than died 10 years ago. Or 25 years ago. Or 100 years ago. In point of fact, more infants will succumb this one year than in any given 30 year period prior to the agricultural revolution.

"Lies, damn lies, and statistics."

Infant mortality is typically computed as the number of infant deaths per every 1000 live births. Infant mortality worldwide stands at just under 40 per 1000 live births according to the CIA World Factbook. With a yearly global birth rate of just over 19 babies per every 1000 people, and a global population of 7.1 billion, there are, in raw human terms, 6 million infants who die each year. Human global population estimates for the Paleolithic range from fewer than 2 million to not more than 20 million. Both birth rates and infant mortality were probably lower than they are now. Women who survived to childbearing age were likely far healthier and more robust than women living today in the third-world. And family planning takes on quite a different dimension when you are living in a small, interdependent, nomadic group. But, for the sake of argument, let's use the numbers found in Uganda and Niger, the countries with the highest birth rates—over 50 per 1000 for Niger, and let's take the country with the highest infant mortality rate, Afghanistan, at 122 per 1000. If we apply these numbers to the high Paleolithic population estimates, until the onset of large-scale domestication there were fewer than 125,000 babies who died in an average year (remember: the increase in global human population since the Paleolithic is a "byproduct" of "progress" in agricultural and industrial technology). To frame this in the quantitative terms of industrial production: there are somewhere between 48 and 480 times as many babies dying each year in our technologically advance modern civilization than died 10,000 years ago. Each of those babies dies an absolute death, not a statistical one. If you measure suffering from a human perspective, according to the actual experience of individual human beings, technological "progress" brings more suffering, not less—and not just a little more!

The technological order establishes the rules of engagement. All problems are essentially ones of implementation—literally a result of not having the right implements. If global warming is being caused by too much industrial CO_2, then we need to retool the industrial process in a way that leads to less CO_2 production. If factory agriculture leads to nutritionally deficient food, then we need to consume manufactured supplements or make modifications to the genetic structure of agricultural products. If honeybees die-off because of exposure to plants that have been genetically modified to produce their own pesticide, then we need to develop artificial means of pollination to replace the bees. And when the human psyche begins to buckle under the pressure of its industrialized burden, we have "emotional technologies" such as psychotherapy, 12-step programs, and selective serotonin reuptake inhibitors.

When a person contracts a cold virus, it is the symptoms that they are most concerned with. The coughing, sneezing, and physical discomfort are how we know we are infected. The symptoms are in some sense caused by the presence of the virus, but they are produced by the body; they represent the body's natural defenses. Increased mucus production is the body's way of transporting virus-infected tissues in the throat and nasal passages into the stomach where they can be destroyed by digestive acids. Fever is the body's attempt to overheat the temperature-sensitive virus. Commercial cold treatments target the symptoms and not the virus itself. Ironically, over the counter cold medications, by reducing the symptoms, actually work in favor of the virus by interfering with the body's natural defenses. Two things that we should take from this: first, that the true target might not be what we think it is, and in order to see this it is necessary to look below the surface; second, that if we don't look below the surface we run the risk that the most obvious "cure" might actually make things worse in the long run. There is an additional risk that the ability to alleviate a few of the surface symptoms can mislead us into thinking that we understand the true nature of the problem. The ability to devise a technological solution to a problem does not mean that the problem was caused by the lack of appropriate technology any more than headaches result from a lack of aspirin.

The delusion of progress is both a symptom and a problem.

Progress has two interleaved conceptual layers. The first harkens back to the conceptions of linear versus cyclical time that are reflected in Judeo-Christian religious tradition. History emerges with a linear conception of time. The notion of human history as a coherent (and potentially comprehensible) sequence of related events through time, when combined with modern realities involving industrial expansion and technological evolution, yields a powerful sense of directional progression. The Hebrew tale of exodus introduces the notion of historical past and its complement, the future—and the journey of humankind takes place, as all journeys do, between a beginning and end, a start and a finish, two distinct poles, with historical narrative recounting the footsteps of the past and directing our gaze into the future and the gleaming landmarks in the distance. That the "journey" is merely a productive (and deceptive) metaphor goes unnoticed. The second conceptual layer finds its clearest expressions in 19th century teleological survival-of-the-fittest interpretations of biological evolution as a ladder-like process of progressive species development, and in Lewis Morgan's well-received views of cultural evolution as a stage-like progression from savagery to barbarism to civilization—with the dramatic explosion in technological innovation resulting from industrialization providing substantial superficial confirmation of the latter. These two conceptual layers, progressive time and progressive technical improvement, serve to laminate each other, yielding a perspective that is highly resistant to the driving rain of reality. The construal of biological evolution as progress, combined with a failure to distinguish between biological and cultural evolution, makes our expansive global civilization into a natural and inevitable blooming of the human species.

The delusion of progress supports the continual expansion of the technological order in obvious ways. But it may also operate in more subtle ways. For example, delusion-prone persons are less cautious when it comes to decision making (they consider less information before making a choice), are more likely to jump to conclusions, and are more confident in their final decisions when under stress.[2] Delusions are demonstrably false beliefs. But they often serve to rationalize behavior that would otherwise be unacceptable. Without the notion of progress, without the belief that conditions are getting better, there would be no justification for the horrors of the status quo. The belief that things will be better tomorrow allows us to better tolerate the otherwise intolerable conditions of today. Medieval Christians had this figured out: this world was a veil of tears and the next would bring reward for those who behaved appropriately (read: obeyed the dictates of church authorities). In like manner, present-day promoters of the expansion of the technological order, corporate priests, tell us that the suffering we are experiencing today, clamped into the soul-crushing gears of mass technology, really isn't suffering at all, it's exactly what we need and want, and besides, things will be better when the newest version is released next month.

The most popular psychiatric approach to treating delusions is to chemically alter the brain. Antipsychotic drugs can reduce delusion, but they also tend to reduce non delusional mental activity as well—a somewhat pyrrhic solution. And I'm not sure that it would be possible to dispel the delusion of progress as long as the technological order continues to exist. The delusion of progress is self-perpetuating. Its source is the technological process itself, a process whereby innovation is focused on specific problems and assessed narrowly in ways that downplay negative and unintended consequences. The more enmeshed we are, the more dependent we become on sophisticated technologies, the more that the technological order is seen as simply part of the natural background conditions of human existence—that is, the less it is visible at all. So the question becomes not so much "how can false ideas of progress be dispelled," but rather, "how can their consequences be rendered inert?" False beliefs aren't a problem if they lead to benign or beneficial behavior. Maybe a useful model can be found in the Asian martial arts such as jujitsu or tai chi, where an opponent's force is redirected instead of being met head on. Perhaps we can take a cue from the technological order's use of relabeling. What if "progress" were to be redefined in terms of its direction? What if it was considered progress to become more autonomous, more egalitarian, less dependent on all forms of technological mediation, less civilized? What if "progress" meant becoming more authentically human?

Science is frequently employed as the poster child of progress. But the findings of empirical science, which are converted into corporate propaganda long before they enter general circulation, are always susceptible to reinterpretation, depending on the purposes to which they are being applied. And some findings, specifically those that are radically inconsistent with the idea of progress, are ignored into obscurity. Consider recent evidence that the human brain has been getting smaller over the last dozen millennia or so. To the extent that brain size is a marker of intelligence, this would seem to suggest that civilization emerged only after humans were dumbed down relative to their pre-Neolithic counterparts. Explanations for the shrinking human brain link reduced brain size to increased population density. Increased population density, according to the theory, put selective pressure on reducing aggression. With people living in closer quarters, aggressive behavior became increasingly maladaptive. Since aggression tends to increase with age, one way for nature to decrease aggressive behavior is to slow down maturation, a process called neoteny. The gradual juvenilization of the adult population was brought about by selective pressures that led to the retention of child-sized brains into adulthood. So, not only did we become dumber as a species, we became more childish as well. Unfortunately, the capacity for lethal aggression is not the only characteristic that increases with maturity. Where is the idea of progress in all of this? Easy, according to the scientists: our brains are smaller, but they are also more efficient! There is ample evidence to support the immaturity hypothesis, but, unfortunately, absolutely no evidence that a decrease in brain size was accompanied by an increase in efficiency. It is likely that an adult Paleolithic human transported to our time would consider our wisest elders to be emotionally immature children and look upon our "advanced" civilization as some kind of bizarre magical nursery for mentally retarded infants.

Consider another documented change, this one involving our tendencies toward obedience to authority, and this one occurring over a much briefer timespan. In 1963, Stanley Milgram conducted an infamous set of studies on obedience.[3] Milgram had people who thought they were participating in a learning experiment deliver what they thought were increasing levels of electrical shock to who they thought were fellow participants in the experiment. Milgram designed a simulated shock generator consisting of a large electronic device with 30 toggle switches labeled with voltage levels starting at 30 volts and increasing by 15-volt intervals up to 450 volts. The learning task involved the "learner" memorizing connections between lengthy lists of word pairs. The "teacher" would read the list, and then test the learner's memory for them. The learner was really a confederate, an actor wired up to the fake shock generator and instructed to fail to learn and pretend to experience shock. The basic procedure involved instructing the teacher to give an electric shock each time the learner responded incorrectly, and for each incorrect response, to move up one level of shock on the generator. An authority figure in the guise of an official looking "researcher" in a lab coat was positioned behind a desk in the same room as the teacher, and the learner was positioned out of sight in another room. The learner began to complain and then shout discomfort as the voltage increased, and eventually became completely silent after the 300 volt mark. Obedience was measured by how far the teacher would increase the level of shock before refusing to continue. Nobody refused to continue prior to the 300 volt mark (!) and 65% of the participants went the full distance to the 450 volt mark. In a variety of follow-up studies, Milgram found that the highest level of obedience occurred when the learner and teacher were isolated in different rooms and the learner could not be either seen or heard (93% went to the top of the voltage scale), and when the learner and teacher were in the same room and the teacher was required manually to force the learner's hand onto a shock plate, the rate of obedience dropped to a mere 30%. He also found that people were far more likely to refuse to obey if they witnessed someone else refuse.

Forty-five years later a psychologist at Santa Clara University conducted a partial replication of Milgram's study and found that there has been essentially no change in obedience since Milgram's time.[4] However—and this is the interesting part—obedience appears now to be unaffected by witnessing someone else refuse to obey. That is, people appear to be just as obedient to authority today as they were in the middle part of the 20th century, but they are less likely to take cues from others when deciding whether they should refuse to comply. This might simply reflect an increase in personal isolation, an increase in the tendency to view ourselves as independent consumer units. Whether it reflects progress, however, depends on whether you measure progress in human terms or in terms of the efficient operation of the technological order.

Next I want to turn to more concrete considerations: where can resistance have maximum long-term impact? Given our previous discussions, we know where not to look for answers. First, there is unlikely to be a technological solution to the problem of the technological order. More of what is killing us does not make for a cure. This fact suggests that part of the solution involves dealing with our technology-dependence. Second, there is unlikely to be a political solution to the problem of the technological order. The machinations of politics reflect the operation of gears that help drive the machine in the service of its own agendas. Third, the status quo is not an option. Even if we can adjust the bar of our expectations and learn to live with the status quo, accelerating change is part of the technolog-ical order, so what passes as acceptance of the status quo today will be quaint nostalgia tomorrow.

Linchpins

What does it mean to resist? The word itself, resistance, has numer-ous technical applications, most involving some kind of impedance or friction. Resistance, as a feature of the physical universe, is an essential component of all technological systems. In order for gears to transmit energy from one to the other, there has to be a minimum amount of friction. Resistance needs to be kept within a certain oper-ative range, however. Toward the upper end, too much resistance impacts efficiency, and toward the lower end, too little resistance reduces control. When it comes to direct acts of resistance against machines of authority, either by individuals or by coordinated groups of individuals, short-term positive results (for the individuals or groups) often yield a long-term negative outcome, as the machine either quickly assimilates the opposition into its own operative de-sign, becoming stronger as a result (consider the way that the rheto-ric of radical environmentalism has become commercialized to sell "green" products), or fortifies the areas of weakness that the re-sistance has been so kind as to uncover (consider how quickly osten-sibly free modes of expression on the internet have been legislatively channeled and, again, commercially re-appropriated). Thus when employing resistance in a piecemeal or gradual way, it is important to consider the ways in which the technological order is likely to re-spond as it attempts to accommodate. And, whether gradual or ab-rupt, resistance, to be at all effective, needs to be carefully targeted, directed at actual points of weakness.

Linchpins are devices for keeping rotating wheels or gears from flying off their axles. The term is also used to describe the securing mechanism of a hitching device. I am using the term linchpin here in something more than a merely metaphorical sense to refer to targeta-ble points of weakness, to features of the technological order that

play an essential role in the integrity of one or more of the connections among its various parts. The discussion of the technological
imperative in Part 3 suggests a rather fatalistic conclusion: the technological order creates our needs and dictates the purposes that we
pursue, and the compulsion to pursue these purposes expands along
with expanding technological order itself, rendering the possibility
for true autonomy and the pursuit of authentically human needs increasingly remote. There is, however, an important limitation to this
imperative that is tied to the fact that biological human agency is involved. The purposes that we are able to pursue are limited by our
nature as an evolved species. The technological order's existence is
dependent upon establishing and maintaining points of interface with
physical human beings. These points of interface—the active points
of contact between individual humans and the complex systems that
organize an individual's actions—must be configured in ways that
are on some level compatible with our evolved design. Further, because biological evolution functions by a distinctly different "logic"
than that of technological evolution, there is an inherent instability
involved in the mismatch that might be exploited to our advantage.
That is, each point of contact between an individual and the technological order is a potentially targetable linchpin.

Systems of authority are the primary way in which we are yoked
to the technological order. Authority, however, is not an inherent
characteristic of powerful individuals. Authority is part of a larger
technical social arrangement; its power is externally supplied by, and
relative to, a specific institutional schematic. Remove a person's
ability to draw from this external power, and his or her authority disappears. Although it sounds overly simplistic, the power of authority
is ultimately supplied by you and me. So the question becomes
"What is it about you and me that keeps us feeding the machine?"
We have already discussed several of the ways our authentic human
nature is deformed to facilitate our absorption into the technological
order. Each of these represents both one answer to the question and a
potential focus of resistance. Let's look first at what is perhaps the
most potent way in which we are entrained to the operation of the
machine: through arrested development, the stunting and redirection

of natural maturational processes. The adage "children are our fu-ture" has been warped into "the future is children," a future in which the hallmarks of adult maturity have been replaced with perennial childishness. The capacity for calm protracted deliberation is sup-planted by impulsiveness; tolerance for ambiguity is replaced by im-patience; the complexity of mature adult lifelong relationships is ex-changed for isolation and an endless series of temporary two-dimensional associations based on mutual exploitation. Our chronic immaturity makes us subservient, dependent, and easy to manipulate through material reinforcement.

Reversing or undoing this process involves removing those fea-tures of the technological order that prevent the natural expression of prewired developmental progressions. Children need to be allowed to experience childhood on their own terms, without the pressure of meeting predetermined benchmarks, without technologically-mediated forms of play, without behavior-control drugs, without the artificial regimentation of team sports, and without the forced com-pliance to arbitrary authority that comes with formal education. If you will recall from the discussion in Part 4, young children appear to have highly nuanced ways of assessing authority, and if left to their own devices (i.e., in the absence of the threat of punishment), they would be quite capable of determining for themselves when they should or should not comply with adult demands. Concrete ac-tions along these lines might include such things as reducing or re-moving state-enforced formal schooling in favor of a return to more mentor-based approaches, and allowing children to explore their world in more natural, unsystematic ways.

Another potential focus of resistance hinges on the fact that com-pliance to authority is ultimately a matter of self-interest on the part of the person who complies. One of the things that make our present situation different from situations in the past is that in the past, self-interest in compliance was generated to a large degree through the overt threat of severe punishment for those who opted for noncom-pliance. Although the threat of severe punishment remains, it has for the most part been pushed into the background. Instead, we have been trained to believe that when we comply with the demands of authority we are in fact doing it for our own positive benefit. The TSA agent, after all, has our best interests at heart as she tells us to step behind the curtain. The truth is that any act of compliance to artificial authority serves to validate its legitimacy and perpetuate the power of the technological order—and to that extent is not in anyone's long-term self-interests. The question here becomes how can the fact that compliance serves the interests of the machine be highlighted? Or, stated differently, how can the long-term self-interest inherent in noncompliance be brought to the forefront? Perhaps we should first find ways to expose exactly how self-interest is really being served by compliance; although counterintuitive, it might make sense to find ways to bring the threat of severe punishment out of the background—make a public spectacle of noncompliance and show the world what happens to those who refuse to relinquish their autonomy. Maybe we need a new kind of martyr.

A third potential focus lurks in the critical interdependency between power and knowledge. "Freely circulating information destabilizes existing power structures. As so strikingly exemplified by the phenomenon of blackmail, one's mere ability to spread potentially damaging information about one's superior can fundamentally subvert the existing power dynamics between them."[5] This suggests that a rather obvious mode of resistance is to make "public knowledge" of previously restricted information. The infamous wikileaks website serves as a paradigmatic example of this mode of resistance. But notice how fast those in power scramble to reconfigure the system to prevent future information leaks when leaks occur. Again, a problem with all acts of minor sabotage is that they highlight weaknesses that need to be reinforced, and thus ultimately benefit the technological order. Another, perhaps more subtle form of this mode of resistance involves making public previously restricted access to technological processes. Open source computer systems are billed by their supporters as liberation from the controlling grip of corporate software. However, the tools generated through open source are designed to accommodate ends generated by technological order itself. It is not unlike allowing indentured coal miners to design and manufacture their own pickaxes. Any liberation in this case is purely illusory. A similar illusion is produced by the open awareness and tacit acceptance of the fact that information is being purposely restricted and groomed in order to manipulate public opinion. I know that I am being lied to, and that very knowledge gives me an illusory sense of power in the situation. In addition, one way that individuals attempt to come to grips with their own ultimate powerlessness is to identify with the system and adopt a posture of jaded savviness. "The next best thing to having power, on this account, is identifying with those who do, rather than naively imagining that power might be redistributed or realigned."[6] I suspect that this was a common coping strategy employed by house slaves in the antebellum south.

What may turn out to be the most productive focus of resistance is our technological dependence. Jacques Ellul claimed that technical progress was generated historically by what he called "the technical state of mind." The technical state of mind is just one part of a larger perspective that views the world as a series of problems to be solved. Eventually, technical means become the only way to think about solutions. Life is a problem; technology is the solution. On some level, our ever-deepening dependence on technology is the whole of the problem to begin with. Dependence is both the purpose and cause of our arrested development. Dependence provides the corpus of needs that comprise our self-interests. Dependence is the glue that binds knowledge to power. Anything that reduces our dependence on technology increases our autonomy and reduces the power of the technological order. The challenge is to find ways of reducing our dependence without falling for the trap of creating yet another technical solution. Anarchism, with its requisite technical primitivism, offers a posture that may help avoid this trap.

Complex technology, technology that involves large scale division of labor, isolation of knowledge, and hierarchical authority, is not possible within a truly anarchistic social framework. Anarchy implies immediate-return, pre-domestication (or low-tech agricultural) modes of living that render complex technologies irrelevant. The elimination of technical mediation between individuals and their access to life's necessities (psychological, social, and biological) eliminates dependence. Whether you have access to the source code is irrelevant if you don't need the machine in the first place. And the connection between knowledge and power is severed if everyone has access to all the knowledge necessary for full community participation. In general, any form of resistance that works to decentralize knowledge, increase transparency, reduce mediation, encourage emotional maturation—anything that leads to a reversal in the tendencies associated with domestication-base life-ways—will lead to a flattening of hierarchy and a concomitant increase in personal autonomy.

Characteristic features of the technological process might be turned into weapons of resistance. Consider the feature of recursive modularity that Arthur maps out. Technologies are composed of component parts, each of which is a technology in its own right: self-contained subsystems that can be reconfigured and adapted to different purposes. Are there component systems of the global machine that can be disabled, altered in ways that prevent them from performing their designed function? Because technology involves a "highly disciplined process" in which modular components are orchestrated to perform harmoniously with one another, a small change in a seemingly inconsequential component could conceivably lead to a massive system failure, or what Winner called *apraxia*.

As nears as I can see, there are at least three problems with attempting to promote catastrophic system failure by targeting and disabling specific nodes within the technostructure. First, if the attempt is unsuccessful, the targeted nodes will be reinforced or equipped with back-ups or the network will be reconfigured in ways that prevent any similar attempts in the future. Second, knowing which specific nodes to target might be exceedingly difficult. "The technological society contains many parts and specialized activities with a myriad of interconnections. The totality of such interconnections—the relationships of the parts to each other and the parts to the whole—is something which is no longer comprehensible to anyone. In the complexity of this world, people are confronted with extraordinary events and functions that are literally unintelligible to them. They are unable to give an adequate explanation of man-made phenomena in their immediate experience. They are unable to form a coherent, rational picture of the whole."[7] Third, and probably the biggest problem, is that the network, the technostructure, is a complex dynamical system. A complex nonlinear system, rather than experiencing catastrophic failure, might instead spontaneously reconfigure, and in an entirely unpredictable way; even if a catastrophic failure is effected, something surprising is likely to emerge from the rubble, something unexpected, something unpredictable even with a thorough account of the structure of the relations among prior conditions, something even worse than what we have now.

Some anarchists claim that achieving a horizontal network structure is itself the goal. They believe that certain aspects of the technological order can be retained or reconfigured in a way that distributes power collectively. However, such a structure, as an alternative to strict power hierarchies, is a myth, at least in terms of the ideals of autonomy and independence.

> Care must be taken, however, not to draw absurd conclusions from this notion . . . that in an increasingly interdependent technological society or world system, all of the parts need each other equally. Seen as a characteristic of modern social relationships this is sometimes upheld as a wonderfully fortuitous bi-product of the rise of advanced technics, The necessary web of mutual dependency binds individuals and social groups closer together; lo, a new kind of community is forming before our very eyes. But this view involves distortion. It confuses interdependency with mere dependency. An individual may depend on [corporate providers] for services crucial to his way of living. But does it make sense to say that the companies depend on that particular individual?[8]

The technological order cannot be domesticated.

The first step in effective resistance is to determine exactly who or what it is you are resisting. Who is the enemy? It should be clear by now that the technology of authority and control is not a singular monolithic structure, and even less a person, but rather a diffuse array of coercive social phenomena and dependency relations that attend a technology-infused way of life—amplified, of course, by specific technologies designed to eliminate autonomy and thus keep human behavior within the tolerances necessary to achieve peak efficiency. Thus resistance has two very different targets, one more overt, concrete, and proximal, and one more hidden, nebulous and intangible. The first set of targets include military, police, and security forces that have been sanctioned to promote the needs of the technological order through the application of lethally violent means. Also included in this first category are the massive surveillance infrastructure and the grossly mislabeled correctional system. It would not be a mistake to include the legal system in this category as well, despite its less-than-concrete nature. There are innumerable specific foci to which acts of resistance might be directed within this first set of targets, many of which are physical or infrastructural (e.g., rail supply lines, communication networks, weapons manufacturing plants, banks). Unfortunately, any successful resistance leveled against this set of proximal targets will likely be short-lived.

Authority is the primary target. Not the external tools of manipulation and control used by authority, but authority itself. So the question simplifies to "How do we reduce or eliminate authority?" Authority is a feature of social hierarchy. The existence of hierarchical relations is a necessary condition for authority to exist. So the question can be restated as "How do we reduce or eliminate hierarchical relations?" Since anarchy, according to the etymological sense that I discussed in the introduction, means the absence of hierarchy, the question can be further restated as "How can we bring about or increase anarchy." Although each of these restatements refers logically to the same question, the last is different from a psychological standpoint. The proceeding ones are couched in negative terms, in terms of removing something (authority, hierarchy), whereas the last is in positive terms, in terms of adding something. Although this seems like a subtle difference, the distinction is profound. Anarchy is a positive state of affairs, not just the absence of oppressive hierarchy. Anarchy is the active and penetrating presence of individual autonomy, and a necessary condition for authentically human forms of life.

Technology is "a phenomenon captured and put to use. Or more usually, a set of phenomena captured and put to use."[9] The phenomena of primary concern for us here are those associated with human psychology. Technological systems require human behavioral input at some level in order to function. The specific nature of the human input is highly constrained by the requirements of the technology and relative to the purposes being pursued. The human role relative to any advanced technological system can be only as complex as that of servomechanism, and in many cases as simple as that of conduit, relay, or data recorder. None of the roles available are entirely commensurate with those to which our evolutionary preparation has prepared us. Because of this, and because of the risk that autonomous human behavior poses for technical efficiency, human activity must be continuously monitored and "corrected" to maintain the system's smooth operation. So, in addition to the constraints that naturally attend our service to the machine as a part of the mechanism itself, autonomous human activity is restricted by technological systems of authority and control designed specifically to keep human behavior within specific systemic tolerances. As technology evolves and becomes more complex, as technology "builds out" and becomes more efficient, the tolerance for autonomous thought and action becomes vanishingly narrow. Lurking within this process, and made increasingly invisible on the surface, is the extent to which the relations between technology and human behavior involve *mutual* dependency. Rather than thinking in terms of action to reverse, destabilize, or disable the supporting structures of the technological order, realize that the order would vanish overnight if it were not for our collective continual—and intentional—action to maintain it. Imagine an increasingly expanding balloon. As the balloon gets larger, more and more air is required to keep it growing, and a soon as the airflow stops, it begins to shrivel.

Letting go is different from resisting. Resistance is necessary for the gears to get traction. Protest, violent or otherwise, only serves to strengthen the machine. If you or I attempt to change the system from within, our very participation renders the changes beneficial to the system itself—participation in the system can only make the system stronger. The logical alternative is intentional nonparticipation. "As everyone knows (especially revolutionaries), hierarchy maintains formidable defenses against attack from the lower orders. It has none, however, against abandonment. This is in part because it can imagine revolution, but it can't imagine abandonment. But even if it could imagine abandonment, it couldn't defend against it, because abandonment isn't an attack, it's just a discontinuance of support. It's almost impossible to prevent people from doing nothing (which is what abandonment amounts to)."[10] What would "doing nothing" entail?

Tide pools of humanity

Daniel Quinn in his book, *Beyond Civilization,* sketches the faint outlines of an answer to that question. For Quinn, the answer to "doing nothing" is for like-minded folks to organize and coordinate their collective efforts around ways of making a living together in which each person provides a unique and integral community contribution, similar to what he imagines life in tribal society to be like. Quinn uses the tribal nature of social life in a traveling circus as a model for how we might realign our lives with our species' evolved hunter-gatherer expectations. A traditional traveling circus is a close-knit community of people involved in the pursuit of a related set of communal goals. Also, and the thing that makes the circus a good model, according to Quinn, is that the circus community exists to a large extent as an autonomous entity, and provides a more egalitarian alternative to the steeply hierarchical lifestyles found in the parent culture.

A traveling circus is different from a hunter-gatherer band in some fundamental ways, however. First, although everyone might participate in some aspects of community life, the circus involves a highly circumscribed division of labor. A small circus can use only so many acrobats and has no need for multiple lion tamers. In contrast, in a traditional hunter-gatherer band there might be individual people with specific abilities or disabilities, but, generally speaking,

everyone is their own lion tamer. Also, a circus, just like the larger
society in which it is embedded, is a delayed-return system in which
participating individuals have mediated access to life's necessities. A
circus is a kind of technology. And social life in a circus, no less than
social life in larger civilized society, is life organized and structured
according to a technological order. A circus is a human community
that is organized around a specific set of goals: a community designed to *do* something. Ancestral hunter-gatherer bands were (and
are) simply human communities, period, full stop. This latter difference is not a trivial one. Authentic human society is not organized
around a larger purpose or set of goals. It is not designed to do anything.[11] Its mere existence is its own justification for existing. Tribal
society is already society that is removed from a truly authentic human mode. Tribes in the way that Quinn envisions a tribe emerged
with domestication. Before domestication, there were groups of people living together and helping each other and quarreling with each
other and celebrating life with each other. After domestication, you
have society structured *systematically* by kinship affiliation and caste
and organized into specializations: slave, farmer, soldier, priest.

There are a couple of additional—and glaring—problems with
Quinn's sketch. First off, to abandon civilization doesn't mean to
abandon the physical spaces occupied by the civilized. At this point,
there are vanishingly few places that are not under the direct jurisdic-
tion of the machine—and most of those are in extreme environments
(mountains, the arctic, etc.). Quinn envisions his tribes of the non-
civilized living within the heart of civilization, inhabiting the same
physical places and navigating the same physical and legal infrastructure. Right away, this raises the question of how it is possible to
live with civilization without being part of it. Quinn points to the
homeless—many of whom in matter of objective fact have managed
to do just that—as an example of how it is already being done. The
homeless who are homeless by choice live *with* civilization in the
way one might live in a region with a less than hospitable climate.
The second problem is that civilization, along with its oppressive
systems of authority and control, will continue largely unabated even

as individuals abandon it. Quinn sails his boat off the edge of the map by claiming that this is in fact a *good* thing:

> Finally, we don't want the ruling class to disappear overnight. We're not ready to see the infrastructure of civilization disappear (and may never be). At least for the time being, we want our rulers and leaders to continue to supervise civilization's drudgery for us—keeping the potholes filled, the sewage and water treatment plants running, and so on.[12]

My question for Quinn is, once again, who is "we"? If "we" are the individuals who have abandoned civilization, then the rulers and leaders he speaks of are not our rulers and leaders. And, of course, the actual drudgery these powerful people are "supervising" is being performed by human beings who have been forced, coerced, threatened, cajoled, or brainwashed into subservience. In order for Quinn's "we" to live "beyond civilization" there needs to continue to be a substantial group of oppressed "them" to keep the machine running smoothly.

Nonetheless, I think that Quinn might be on to something. Going beyond civilization—whether we do so intentionally or as an unavoidable consequence of civilization's inevitable collapse—will involve a return to lifestyles fashioned around small, self-reliant cooperative groups. It's the transition that will be the truly hard part. Time heals all wounds, and in time many of the wounds caused by the global industrial nightmare will fade as natural systems are once again permitted to enact their homeostatic logic. In the transition, we will be forced to accommodate the toxic dross of the disintegrating technological order. Perhaps we can take our cue from coastal tide pools, fascinating and unique natural neighborhoods of interdependent organisms sharing limited space and resources. As civilization recedes it will leave isolated pockets of humanity scattered around the globe living—by necessity—in self-reliant cooperative communities. As centralized sources of control deteriorate, local communities will be left to their own recourse, each dependent critically upon cooperation among its individual members. Creatures that live in tide pools are different from their deeper water cousins in that they are far more flexible; they have developed unique strategies to weather dramatic periodic changes in local conditions. Likewise, it will be the adaptable among us who stand the greatest chance of weathering the transition as we disengage from civilization. But we will be aided in the transition by our evolutionary history and our genetic preparation for life in small hunter-gatherer bands. The primary difference between our future situation in the transition beyond civilization and the typical tide pool is that for tide pools, the sea eventually returns, bringing with it an infusion of water and nutrients. Once global industrial civilization recedes, it will not return—at least not in anything like its current form. And, with luck and in time, it will disappear completely, a brief and forgotten anomaly in the tenure of our species. And the tide pools themselves, the residual effluvia of the technological order, will evaporate leaving only people living authentic human lives for no other purpose than the expression of life itself.

Well, anyhow, that makes for a nice story. Meanwhile a young boy sleeps and dreams his very last dream as a bomb-laden predator drone hovers silently over a small mountain village in western Pakistan. . . .

The anarchism I have been promoting here is not merely a social or political posture. It is a call to embrace our deepest human nature. It is a perspective that views the conditions in immediate return societies as the only ones that promote true autonomy and support authentic human life-ways. The global technological order is about as far from immediate return as is humanly tolerable—check that, for a majority of the victims of the corporate machine, it is, in point of fact, intolerable. Anarchy is a social condition maximally conducive to human autonomy, and only possible within immediate return societies. Immediate-return society is only possible within small, local communities. The idea of a global immediate-return society is incoherent. To maintain society beyond the immediate physicality of a small territory or region, it is necessary to employ technological mediation. Technological mediation implies delayed-return, and with it, dependency, division of labor, and unequal access to knowledge and resources. If we are to have an authentically human future, it means we will be once again living is small self-reliant communities—not circus-like tribes bound to community-level purposes, but tide pools of autonomous individuals, each pursuing his or her own freely chosen ends in voluntary cooperative alliance with local others.

As a mode of resistance, a small self-reliant community works at several levels. First, in terms of combating arrested development, small self-reliant communities are more in line with developmental expectations, supporting epigenetic conditions maximally conducive to healthy maturity. Children are embedded in a multigenerational social group, each child an active participant in his or her own learning and maturation. Second, community self-reliance demands the free and open sharing of knowledge, and complete transparency with respect to the agendas of individual community members. This transparency is accomplished largely by the absence of mediated forms of communication. A move toward community self-reliance, by definition, means the reduction and eventual elimination of dependence relationships with large-scale technology.

Widespread disengagement from the global system would mean the eventual collapse of the global system itself. Because of this, and because of the extent to which the global system currently penetrates every facet of our lives, there are two practical considerations involved with the transition to community self-reliance: how to initiate and encourage the transition and how to weather the storm of civilization's collapse. With respect to the first of these, the technological order's self-preservation mechanisms will likely prove to be the most immediate obstacle. It is quite likely that self-reliance might be labeled as the threat to the system that it actually is, and that steps would be taken to undermine any attempts in that direction. In fact, several such steps have already been taken, for example with the widespread privatization of the commons, the legal declaration that corporate entities have the same rights as living human beings, local anti-squatting legislation, regulations concerning noncommercial food production, etc.

What about a return to an agrarian-based society? Is it really necessary to revert to the social circumstances of hunter-gatherer band society? Is it possible to have a farming society that nonetheless meets the anarchist egalitarian ideal? Some form or forms of agrarianism may be part of the transition from our present global industrial situation to local sustainable subsistence. And there are some nature-based approaches to agriculture, for example those being practiced within the permaculture movement, that involve shared governance and a meaningful level of community self-reliance. But the primary characteristics of modern civilization that make it unworkable as a long term alternative have their source in the division of labor and the asymmetrical distribution of resources that emerged during the agricultural revolution. "The point is plain: domestication is domestication, and embodies a qualitatively negative logic for the natural world. Agriculture per se brings a ruinous, unidirectional impact, despite the wishful thinking of those who envision a coexistence with domestication, consisting of benign, 'green' methods that would reverse the global destruction of the land."[13] A return to an agrarian or pastoral lifestyle is unlikely to be in the long term interests of our grandchildren and their grandchildren.

What will post-civilization society look like? I suspect that for many people, the thought of life in a post-civilized world conjures up post-apocalyptic images of humans living as wandering animalistic scavengers like those depicted in such classic science fiction movies as *Road Warrior* or *A Boy and His Dog*. Indeed, conditions very close to this already exist in our inner cities and in many parts of the third world—as a direct result, I must point out, of the technological order's approach to economic "development." But there are far more humane models of subsistence living, many of which have already been tried and have flourished for tens of thousands of years. And there are numerous possibilities that have yet to be explored. To say that the future of the human species will involve a return to subsistence living in small self-contained communities is only to say that it will necessitate living in a transactional state with nature in which neither party loses in the transaction. This precludes the generation of energy through fossil fuels, through nuclear power, through the use of hydroelectric power that involves the damming of rivers (and the *damning* of fish populations). This precludes a culture based on

mass-consumption and the unidirectional extraction of natural resources. This precludes an economic system in which the pleasures
and enrichment of a few are supported by the suffering and impover-
ishment of many. This precludes corporate capitalism. This precludes a system based on economic competition. This precludes a
society built upon a foundation of violence and estrangement, a society that actively promotes the isolation and alienation of individuals.

And it precludes any form of oppressive hierarchy. "The thing we
call civilization goes hand in hand with hierarchy—means hierarchy,
requires hierarchy. . . . You can have hierarchy without civilization,
but you can't have civilization without hierarchy; at least we never
have—not once, not anywhere, in ten thousand years of civilization
building. To have a civilization is to have a hierarchical society. . . .
To go beyond civilization therefore means going beyond hierarchal-
ism."[14]

Probably the only thing that can be said with any certainty about a
post-civilization world is that it will be far less populated with humans. Estimates of planetary human carrying capacity range widely,
with median estimates running from 7.7 to 12 billion.[15] However,
these estimates are frequently based on a single factor (usually food),
and assume the continuation of—or some minor technological additions to—the status quo. They also consider the human population in
relative isolation, and make no allowance for the number of other
species that will be "displaced" to make room for more humans.
With the cessation of industrial food production and distribution, it is
possible that post-civilization population will be not much larger
than 250 million, which corresponds roughly to the global human
population 2000 years ago, or less than 4% of the people alive today.
And it could eventually drop as low as the aforementioned pre-
agricultural revolution numbers of 2-20 million. I realize that the
thought of such a dramatic reduction in human population might
seem unpalatable, but it is going to happen whether we want to think
about it or not. How it happens, however, is at least to some extent
up to us. A strict moratorium on reproduction (a technological solution requiring recourse to coercive—and intrusive—authority) could
bring the population down in just a couple of generations. Or we

could simply let nature run its course and establish the proper balance through competition, disease, and starvation, as happens when any other organism reproduces beyond carrying capacity. How will people survive as civilization dries up and with it ready access to the necessities of living? The uncomfortable answer is that they won't. The cold and unavoidable reality is that many, perhaps most, will die. But those who manage to survive will do so by living the way humans have lived for most of our species' time on the planet: they will live in small communities of people working together.

In addition to being less populated, post-civilization society will involve a variety of living conditions and lifestyles. Without top-down multinational corporate interests to serve as a global homogenizing force, it is likely that human culture in a post-civilization world will again take on a distinctly localized flavor. The demands of living can differ dramatically from one location to another, and any community in a subsistence transaction with a specific local environment will by necessity reflect the idiosyncratic characteristics and demands of that locality. The patterns of life will mold themselves to the contours of local environments. Humans will once again be a species involved in a multiplicity of rich and distinct cultural traditions. And travel to distant lands, although likely infrequent, will once again involve a meaningful experiencing of otherness. But my purpose here is not to speculate about the many varied and rich future possibilities for humans living in authentic symbiosis with the natural world. I am much more interested in how we can get out from under the oppressive artificial state we are in right now. By the time this book is published, there may very well be a bomb-laden predator drone hovering silently over my own granddaughter's house in a small mountain village in western Oregon.

The end of words

In Part 2, I showed that the complex and oppressive hierarchical systems of authority that operate today are not modern extensions of natural primate social dominance relations. Rather, they likely emerged as labor-control technologies in early agricultural societies. In Part 3, I explored how systems of authority function as part of the larger technological order of modern civilization. In addition, I looked at the processes involved in technological change across time. All technological systems have a tendency to become more complex and expansive. In addition, through reverse adaptation, the needs, purposes, and goals that served as the original technological motivation are adapted to fit the operation of the technology. The migration and deformation of needs and purposes is part of the technological process. There is no sinister intent or occult force involved. Over time, the needs of our immense technological systems have gained precedence over authentic human needs, individual autonomy has been diminished or eliminated, and humans have been reduced to little more than biological servomechanisms embedded in a technological order too massive and too complex to comprehend. In Part 4, I examined a few of the consequences of the mismatch between our genetic and epigenetic expectations and the realities of life lived according to the dictates of autonomy-annihilating systems of authority. Throughout the book, I have attempted to attack and neutralize what I see as one of the most potent obstacles to clear thinking on these issues: the entrenched belief that things have gotten progressively better, something that I call *the delusion of progress*. My purpose throughout has been to identify complex technology, with its demands for the hierarchical restructuring of human relationships, as the ultimate source of our oppression. But, in the end, all I really have to offer is words—mediated through the technological distortion of a printed (or the electronic imitation of a printed) page.

Academics, educators, and other intellectuals who have spent much of their lives embroiled in ideas, notions, and theories, after a while start to think that ideas, notions, and theories have real substance to them. There is a tendency to invest ideas, notions, and theories with a degree of causal impact on history and the world that they do not in reality possess. In reality, ideas, notions, and theories are for the most part a product of historical circumstances rather than their cause; ideas emerge largely as a reaction to events. The causal fabric of the world is entirely uncommitted to any ideas we might form about it, and events in the past remain forever untouchable by even the most insightful interpretations. Nevertheless, the ability to paint causal pictures and frame them in terms of ideas, notions, and theories can, for those who spend a lot of time at it, lead people to assign more weight to the painting than to the actual landscape. Real problems are embedded in real causal circumstances, not theoretical ones. And the solution to any real problem is going to lie within the concrete causal fabric of circumstance, not with our ideas about it.

Ideas are important, of course, don't get me wrong—I consider myself to be a member of the "academics, educators, and other intellectuals" category. But real solutions involve more than just finding the right way to think about things. In a statement prior to the title page of the book, *Forever Young,* that I cited in the chapter on arrested development above, for example, we are told (it's not clear by whom) that the author of the book "provides concrete answers." Three of these "answers" are then listed. The first solution is to dispel the myth that "experts and professionals are the people best equipped to give advice on raising children." The second "concrete" solution "is to recognize the value of family . . . ." And the third solution is to "challenge the pervasive notion that teen culture is a sophisticated endeavor . . . ." Let's be perfectly clear about this, dispelling myths, recognizing values, and challenging ideas is not going to solve anything (with the possible exception of resolving cognitive dissonance on the part of a reader who has invested time an energy reading a book promising solutions). A similar kind of approach is found throughout the literature on environmentalism. We are frequently told that we need to "think" about our energy use differently. We need to change our consumerist values. We need to adopt a friendlier attitude with respect to the natural world. The problem is not an unsustainable industrial infrastructure that is draining the planet of all its life-essence as a function of its daily operation; rather the problem is that there is some abstract "we" out there who has a bad attitude and warped values, and all this "we" has to do is realize the error of its ways through some kind of magical insight. Somehow, simply thinking differently will make international corporations into benevolent caretakers of the biosphere. This is silly magical thinking. We aren't going to fix anything by changing our minds, even if we do so one mind at a time.

Perhaps I should come up with a name for this tendency. Maybe I'll call it "distraction by abstraction." It is a variant of the reification error, a kind of category mistake[16] or misplaced concreteness[17] applied to problems that are too big or too complex to comprehend in their entirety. That is probably part of the explanation for this tendency: the size and complexity of the problem forces us to couch its component parts in terms of abstractions. I have been forced to do this throughout my discussion, most notably with the notion of the technological order of civilization. That the technological order is an abstraction is clear. But in handling this abstraction, using it as a tool to aid in conceptually organizing the otherwise incomprehensible nature of our situation, it is important not to lose sight of the fact that, although an abstraction, it is meant as a conceptual placeholder for a very real aggregate of technological systems, systems of relationship among real concrete individuals and other real concrete individuals and real concrete physical objects and places. Hopefully by this point in our discussion it should be obvious why the solution to the problem of the technological order and its systems of authority is going to involve more than simply changing how we think about things. It is going to involved changing the way that relationships among humans are structured—specifically, it is going to involve an *un-structuring* or *de-structuring* or, perhaps better because it entails an active process of disassembly, the *deconstructing* of those relations.

Children learn early in their experience with building blocks that it is easier to destroy than to build. The exception to this rule is Lego blocks. Lego blocks are just as hard (and sometimes even more difficult) to take apart as they are to put together. The reason is because Legos, unlike simple smooth wooden blocks, are designed for specific attachment to other Legos. Notice the tradeoff involved. Legos can attach securely; but to do so, severe restrictions in their mutual orientation must be applied. Two smooth wooden blocks can be oriented in any manner allowable by gravity. This freedom of orientation is possible between Legos as well, but only if they have not been forcefully joined—and once joined, gravity is irrelevant and unnecessary for their continued association. The free association between two wooden blocks allows each block involved to move any way it wants, relatively unrestricted by the structure. This is of course why constructions built with plain wooden blocks are so vulnerable to the sweep of little sister's wrecking-ball arms. Structures built with Legos, on the other hand, are extremely durable. But this durability is purchased at the expense of freedom of movement for individual blocks.

Notice also that every projecting nib of every Lego block is emblazoned with the corporate logo.

Legos work through the homogenization of connections, through standardization. Small deviations in uniformity can be catastrophic. When I was a kid, I had a dog that would occasionally get ahold of a loose Lego and chew on it, the deformations caused by her bite marks rendering the block useless. Three things here: first, restriction of free association provides the means by which large and elaborate structures are built; second, this restriction is accomplished only by force; third, the possibility for ordered structure is orders of magnitude greater for Legos than for smooth wooden blocks, but this increase in order is accompanied by a reduction in the tendency toward novelty. If you want to build a novel structure with Legos that includes specialized shapes and objects not part of the generic block design, you are expected to purchase a "themed" Lego set that includes customized manufactured components. The potential for novelty is in some sense built in to the open-ended structures constructed with wooden blocks: plain wooden blocks can interface just as easily with a variety of household objects (e.g., dinner plates, beverage containers, etc.) as with each other.

The Lego block analogy shows why civilization and anarchism are incompatible. Without standardization, specialization, and forced (non-voluntary) association, there is no way that any of the major institutions of civilization could possibly be assembled in the first place, let alone stand for any length of time. What most anarchists want is the kind of open and unrestrictive associative possibilities found with plain wooden blocks. But how to achieve that in a world where interpersonal communication is increasingly mediated through standardized electronic conduits, where human beings are little more than servomechanisms, where our participation in the corporate orgy is obligatory, where we are groomed from infancy to be servile and dependent on the latest consumer pabulum to drip from the teats of power, where our connectivity is coerced, monitored, and enforced by subhuman servomechanisms in uniform licensed to use deadly force?

I keep coming back to the dog and her deforming bite marks. . . .

The lifestyles of our foraging ancestors and our still extant but rapidly disappearing hunter-gatherer relatives can serve as models. If we are to have any chance at a long-term future as a post-civilized species, it will involve an eventual return to lifestyles that are much more in tune with our Paleolithic heritage. But in the short term, because our corporate consumer wage-slave lifestyles are so dramatically different than the subsistence lifestyles of our Paleolithic expectations, we may need to adopt transitional ways of living—individually and collectively—that can serve as a bridge, ways of living that can be superimposed on the physical bones of an industrial civilization in the throes of disintegration; ideally, ways of living that might actually expedite its collapse. Lifestyles centered on the anarchist ideal of local egalitarian self-reliant communities might be just the kind of bridge that is needed. Anarchism is not a silver bullet or panacea or path to utopia. But neither is it merely a posture of rejection directed at the dehumanizing mechanization of human life; it is not merely a rejection of artificial and oppressive systems of control and the penetrating misery they impose on all but a lucky few. Anarchism is not in its essence a negative posture, it is not just a rejection of oppression and a denial of the legitimacy of artificial systems of authority; anarchism is the positive acknowledgement and open acceptance of humanity and all that that term implies. To stand as an anarchist is to demand your birthright as an autonomous self-directed being and to loudly rattle the shackles that bind you to a technological order that has stripped you of your human dignity. To stand as an anarchist is to embrace your own authentic human nature.

NOTES

Introduction

1. Sartwell, C. (2008). *Against the State: An Introduction to Anarchist Political Theory.* New York: SUNY Press.
2. Ironically, part of the reason that this is true has to do with our experience with artificial authority in the social world. More on this in Part 4.

Part 1: Against Authority

1. After Arthur, W. B. (2009). *The Nature of Technology.* New York: Free Press.
2. Winner, L. (1977). *Autonomous Technology.* Cambridge: MIT Press. pp. 2-3.
3. After Winner, ibid.
4. Seely, M. (2012). *Born Expecting the Pleistocene: Psychology and the Problem of Civilization.* OldDog Publishing.
5. Winner, p. 75.
6. Ibid, p. 184, italics mine.
7. Ibid, p. 185.
8. Ibid, p. 75.
9. Arthur.
10. Winner, p. 186.
11. Arthur, p. 65.
12. There is another, related way that authority is sometimes used with respect to knowledge. An expert is said to have "command" over her subject matter. This seems to be a clear case of authority used as metaphor, where information is something to be collected, controlled, manipulated—domesticated.
13. See Buchler, J. (1939). *Charles Peirce's Empiricism.* New York: Harcourt.
14. Hume, D. (1975). An enquiry concerning human understanding. In L. A. Selby-Bigge (Ed.), *Enquiries Concerning Human Understanding and Concerning Principles of Morals.* Oxford: Clarendon Press. (Original published 1748)
15. Wolff, R. P., (1970), *In Defense of Anarchism*, New York: Harper & Row, p. 4.
16. Ibid, p. 5.
17. Ibid, p. 9.
18. Weber, M. (1978). *Economy and Society.* G. Roth & Claus Wittich (Eds). Berkeley: University of California Press, p. 212.
19. Ibid, p. 213.
20. Ibid.
21. Wolff, p. 16.
22. Ibid, p. 15.
23. Ibid, p. 17.

24. Ibid, p. 18, italics in original.
25. Foucault, M. (1980) *Power/Knowledge: Selected Interviews and other Writings.* C. Gordon, Ed. New York: Pantheon Books, p. 39.
26. Ibid, pp. 151-152.
27. Ibid, p. 156.
28. Ibid, pp. 158-159.
29. Ibid, p. 38.
30. Ibid, p. 155.
31. Eidelman, S., Crandall, C. S., & Pattershall, J. (2009). The existence bias. *Journal of Personality and Social Psychology,* 97, 765-775.
32. Boehm, quoted in Kiernan, V. (1999). How Egalitarian Societies Rein In Potential Despots. *Chronicle Of Higher Education, 46*(17), A22.
33. Diamond, J. (1992). *The Third Chimpanzee.* New York: HarperCollins.

Part 2: Domestication and the Power Complex

1. There have been a variety of genetic-level adaptations in human subpopulations as a function of domestication-based changes in diet. For example, as an adaptation to a dairy-based diet, production of the digestive enzyme, lactase, continues in most adult Europeans, but discontinues after infancy in most Asians and Africans. But this sort of genetic adaptation reflects a geographic variation in a subpopulation, and not an evolutionary change in the human species. To claim otherwise is simple racism.
2. Paz-y-Miño C, G., Bond, A. B., Kamil, A. C., & Balda, R. P. (2004). Pinyon jays use transitive inference to predict social dominance. *Nature, 430*(7001), 778-781.
3. Mumford, L. (1966). *Technics and Human Development: The Myth of the Machine Volume One.* New York: Harcourt, p. 216.
4. Some have referred to conflict between insect colonies as examples of war. But here again this is a gross overextension of metaphor.
5. de Wall, F. (2005). *Our Inner Ape.* New York: Riverhead Books, p. 86.
6. Ibid, p. 64.
7. Ibid, p. 87.
8. Ibid, p. 78.
9. Woodburn, J. (1998). Egalitarian societies. In *Limited Wants, Unlimited Means: A Reader on Hunter-Gatherer Economics and the Environment.* John Gowdy, Ed. Washington D.C.: Island Press.
10. Rekers, Y., Haun, D. M., & Tomasello, M. (2011). Children, but Not Chimpanzees, Prefer to Collaborate. *Current Biology, 21*(20), 1756-1758. doi:10.1016/j.cub.2011.08.066
11. Hamann, K., Warneken, F., Greenberg, J. R., & Tomasello, M. (2011). Collaboration encourages equal sharing in children but not in chimpanzees. *Nature, 476*(7360), 328-331. doi:10.1038/nature10278
12. Olson, K. R., & Spelke, E. S. (2008). Foundations of cooperation in young children. *Cognition, 108*(1), 222-231. doi:10.1016/j.cognition.2007.12.003

13. Warneken, F., & Tomasello, M. (2007). Helping and Cooperation at 14 Months of Age. *Infancy, 11*(3), 271-294. doi:10.1080/15250000701310389
14. Woodburn.
15. Ibid.
16. Ibid, p. 91.
17. Ibid, p. 92.
18. Ibid, p. 93.
19. Ibid.
20. Adams, W.W. (2005). Ecopsychology and phenomenology, toward a collaborative engagement. *Existential Analysis, 16,* 269-283.
21. Rowlands, M. (2009). *The Philosopher and the Wolf.* New York: Pegasus.
22. Ellul, J. (1964). *The Technological Society*, p. 79.
23. Zeder, M. A. (2008). The Neolithic macro-(R)evolution: Macroevolutionary theory and the study of culture. *Journal of Archaeological Research, 17,* 1-63.
24. Skoglund, P., Malmström, H., Raghavan, M., Storå, J., Hall, P., Willerslev, E., & ... Jakobsson, M. (2012). Origins and Genetic Legacy of Neolithic Farmers and Hunter-Gatherers in Europe. *Science, 336*(6080), 466-469. doi:10.1126/science.1216304
25. Ellul, p. 65.
26. O'Sullivan, P. (2008). The 'collapse of civilizations: what paleoenvironmental reconstruction cannot tell us, but anthropology can. *The Holocene, 18,* 45 – 55, p. 46.
27. Ibid.
28. Ibid, p. 48.
29. Ibid.
30. Frangipane, M. (2007). Different types of egalitarian societies and the development of inequality in early Mesopotamia. *World Archaeology, 39*(2), 151-176; Yet another simple dichotomous distinction. I am reminded of the old joke: there are only two kinds of people in the world, those who believe there are only two kinds of people and those who don't.
31. Ibid, p. 153.
32. Ibid, p. 155.
33. Ibid, p. 164.
34. Ibid, p. 169.
35. Ibid, pp. 171-172.
36. Wells, S. (2010). *Pandora's Seed: Why the Hunter-Gatherer Holds the Key to Our Survival.* New York: Random House, p. 59, italics mine.
37. I borrowed this analogy from Nassim Nicholas Taleb's book, *The Black Swan*: Taleb, N. N. (2007). *The Black Swan: The Impact of the Highly Improbable.* New York: Random House.
38. Mumford, p. 127; Zeder.
39. Ibid, p.164.

40. Zeder.
41. Mumford, p. 188.
42. Ibid, p. 182.
43. Ibid, p. 183.
44. Ibid, p. 188.
45. Ibid, p. 179.
46. Ibid, p. 166.
47. Ibid, p. 212.
48. Ibid, p. 3.
49. Mumford, L. (1970). *The Pentagon of Power.* New York: Harcourt. p. 166.
50. Galbraith, J.K. (1968). *The New Industrial State.* New York: New American Library.
51. Arthur, W. B. (2009). *The Nature of Technology.* New York: Free Press.
52. Ellul (1964).
53. Mumford (1970). p. 183.
54. Winner, p. 181.
55. Ibid.
56. Mumford (1966). Illustration 16.
57. Mumford (1970). p. 165.

Part 3: The Ghost in the Machine

1. Arthur, p. 36.
2. Ibid, p. 43.
3. Ibid, p. 106.
4. Ibid, p. 88.
5. Ellul, p. 92.
6. Arthur, p. 170.
7. Winner, p. 100; italics in original.
8. Ibid, p. 101.
9. Ibid, p. 89.
10. Ibid, pp. 263-264.
11. Ibid, p. 41.
12. Ibid, p. 173.
13. Ibid, p. 191.
14. Ellul, p. 80.
15. Ibid, p. 84.
16. Winner, p. 29.
17. Arthur, p. 202.
18. Arthur, p. 204; italics mine.
19. Ibid, p. 216.
20. Winner, p. 200.
21. Ibid, p. 139.
22. Ellul, p. 84.
23. Winner, p. 262.

24. Arthur, p. 176.
25. Winner, p. 229.
26. Ibid, p. 205.
27. Ibid, p. 203.
28. Ibid, p. 227.
29. Arthur, p. 174.
30. Winner, p. 233.
31. Ellul, p. 72.
32. Arthur, p. 78.
33. Winner, p. 263.
34. Ibid, p. 203.
35. Ibid, p. 207.
36. Ibid, p. 221.
37. Ibid, p. 248.
38. Milgram, S. (1963). Behavioral study of obedience. *Journal of Abnormal and Social Psychology, 67,* 371 – 378.
39. Zimbardo, P. G. (1973). The psychological power and pathology of imprisonment. In E. Aronson & R. Helmreich (Eds.). *Social Psychology.* New York: Van Nostrand.

Part 4: The Topography of Acquiescence

1. Shepard, P. (1982). *Nature and Madness.* Athens Georgia: University of Georgia Press; (1998). *Coming Home to the Pleistocene.* Washington, D.C.: Island Press.
2. Barber, B. R. (2007). *Consumed.* New York: Norton.
3. Danesi, M. (2003). *Forever Young: The 'Teen-Aging' of Modern Culture.* London: University of Toronto Press.
4. For further discussion of the role age plays in early brain development, see: Nelson, C. A., Bos, K., Gunnar, M. R., & Sonuga-Barke, E. S. (2011). V. THE NEUROBIOLOGICAL TOLL OF EARLY HUMAN DEPRIVATION. *Monographs Of The Society For Research In Child Development, 76*(4), 127-146. doi:10.1111/j.1540-5834.2011.00630.x
5. The USDA has always recommended that we eat a balanced diet that includes options from each of their arbitrarily designated food groups, including dairy and grains. Recent evidence suggests that including dairy, grains, and legumes—all foods absent from the diet prior to the Neolithic—leads to a variety of serious health conditions, including diabetes, heart disease, and cancer.
6. Laupa, M. (1991). Children's reasoning about three authority attributes: Adult status, knowledge, and social position. *Developmental Psychology, 27*(2), 321-329. doi:10.1037/0012-1649.27.2.321
7. Ibid.
8. Ibid.
9. Ibid, p. 328.
10. Ibid.

11. Galinsky, A. D., Magee, J. C., Gruenfeld, D., Whitson, J. A., & Liljenquist, K. A. (2008). Power reduces the press of the situation: Implications for creativity, conformity, and dissonance. *Journal Of Personality And Social Psychology*, *95*(6), 1450-1466. doi:10.1037/a0012633

12. Lakens, D., Semin, G. R., & Foroni, F. (2011). Why your highness needs the people: Comparing the absolute and relative representation of power in vertical space. *Social Psychology*, *42*(3), 205-213. doi:10.1027/1864-9335/a000064

13. Tyler, T. R., Lind, E., & Huo, Y. J. (2000). Cultural values and authority relations: The psychology of conflict resolution across cultures. *Psychology, Public Policy, And Law*, *6*(4), 1138-1163. doi:10.1037/1076-8971.6.4.1138

14. Ibid, p. 1141.

15. Ibid, p. 1152.

16. Ibid, p. 1153.

17. Keltner, D., Gruenfeld, D. H., & Anderson, C. (2003). Power, approach, and inhibition. *Psychological Review*, *110*(2), 265-284. doi:10.1037/0033-295X.110.2.265; Weber, M. (1947). *The theory of social and economic organization* (A.M. Henderson & T. Parsons, Trans). New York: Oxford University Press.

18. E.g., Galinsky, A. D., Magee, J. C., Gruenfeld, D., Whitson, J. A., & Liljenquist, K. A. (2008). Power reduces the press of the situation: Implications for creativity, conformity, and dissonance. *Journal Of Personality And Social Psychology*, *95*(6), 1450-1466. doi:10.1037/a0012633, Experiment 5.

19. Gedgaudas, N.T (2009). *Primal Body, Primal Mind.* Rochester, VT: Healing Arts Press, pp 134-135.

20. Just as it is frequently assumed that the development of spoken language was a prerequisite for culture.

21. Andrejevic, M. (2007). *iSpy: Surveillance and Power in the Interactive Era.* Lawrence, Kansas: The University Press of Kansas, p. 191.

22. Williams, E. (1977). Experimental comparisons of face-to-face and mediated communication: A review. *Psychological Bulletin*, *84*(5), 963-976. doi:10.1037/0033-2909.84.5.963

23. McPherson, M. Smith-Lovin, L., & Brashears. M. E. (2006). Social isolation in America: Changes in core discussion networks over two decades. *American Sociological Review,* 71, 353-375.

24. Kraut, R., Patterson, M., Lundmark, V., Kiesler, S., Mukophadhyay, T., & Scherlis, W. (1998). Internet paradox: A social technology that reduces social involvement and psychological well-being?. *American Psychologist*, *53*(9), 1017-1031. doi:10.1037/0003-066X.53.9.1017

25. van den Eijnden, R. M., Meerkerk, G., Vermulst, A. A., Spijkerman, R., & Engels, R. E. (2008). Online communication, compulsive internet use, and psychosocial well-being among adolescents: A longitudinal

study. *Developmental Psychology*, *44*(3), 655-665. doi:10.1037/0012-1649.44.3.655

26. Pea, R., Nass, C., Meheula, L., Rance, M., Kumar, A., Bamford, H., & ... Zhou, M. (2012). Media use, face-to-face communication, media multitasking, and social well-being among 8- to 12-year-old girls. *Developmental Psychology*, *48*(2), 327-336. doi:10.1037/a0027030

27. Pollet, T. V., Roberts, S. B., & Dunbar, R. M. (2011). Use of Social Network Sites and Instant Messaging Does Not Lead to Increased Offline Social Network Size, or to Emotionally Closer Relationships with Offline Network Members. *Cyberpsychology, Behavior & Social Networking*, *14*(4), 253-258. doi:10.1089/cyber.2010.0161

28. Gonçalves, B., Perra, N., & Vespignani, A. (2011). Modeling Users' Activity on Twitter Networks: Validation of Dunbar's Number. *Plos ONE*, *6*(8), 1-5. doi:10.1371/journal.pone.0022656

29. Kruger, J., Epley, N., Parker, J., & Ng, Z. (2005). Egocentrism over e-mail: Can we communicate as well as we think?. *Journal Of Personality And Social Psychology*, *89*(6), 925-936. doi:10.1037/0022-3514.89.6.925

30. Andrejevic, p. 254.

31. Lyon, D. (2007). *Surveillance Studies: An Overview.* Malden, MA: Polity Press, p. 14.

32. Ibid, p. 34.

33. Ibid, p. 48.

34. Ibid, p. 47.

35. Andrejevic, p. 256.

36. Ibid, pp. 105-106.

37. Ibid, p. 45.

38. Ibid, p. 126.

39. Lyon, p.115.

40. Zentall, S. S., Kuester, D. A., & Craig, B. A. (2011). Social Behavior in Cooperative Groups: Students at Risk for ADHD and Their Peers. *Journal Of Educational Research*, *104*(1), 28-41. doi:10.1080/00220670903567356

41. Levine, B. (2012). Why anti-authoritarians are diagnosed as mentally ill. Slingshot, 110. http://slingshot.tao.ca/displaybi.php?0110002

42. Ibid.

43. Cantor, C., & Price, J. (2007). Traumatic entrapment, appeasement and complex post-traumatic stress disorder: evolutionary perspectives of hostage reactions, domestic abuse and the Stockholm syndrome. *Australian & New Zealand Journal Of Psychiatry*, *41*(5), 377-384. doi:10.1080/00048670701261178, p. 379; See also: Graham, D.L., Rawlings, E.I, & Ihms, K. (1995). A scale for identifying Stockholm syndrome reactions in young dating women: factor structure, reliability and validity. *Violence Vict* (10) 3–22.

Part 5: HumAnarchy
1. Koetke, W. H. (1993). The final empire: The collapse of civilization and the seed of the future. Reprinted in J. Zerzan (Ed.) *Against Civilization*. Feral house, p. 155.
2. Keefe, K. M., & Warman, D. M. (2011). Reasoning, delusion proneness and stress: an experimental investigation. *Clinical Psychology & Psychotherapy*, *18*(2), 138-147. doi:10.1002/cpp.683
3. Milgram, S. (1963). Behavioral study of obedience. *Journal of Abnormal and Social Psychology, 67,* 371-378.
4. Burger, J. M. (2009). Replicating Milgram: Would people still obey today?. *American Psychologist*, *64*(1), 1-11. doi:10.1037/a0010932
5. Zerubavel, E. (2006). The Elephant in the Room: Silence and Denial in Everyday Life. New York; Oxford University Press.
6. Andrejevic, p. 155.
7. Winner, p. 284.
8. Ibid, p. 184.
9. Arthur, p. 51.
10. Quinn, D. (1999). *Beyond Civilization.* New York: Three Rivers Press, p. 95.
11. That's not to say that life in primal society wasn't organized around certain community goals. The reindeer herds moved with a periodicity that would have "structured" the daily activity of the Northern European groups who hunted them, for example. But if the reindeer herds became scarce, the community didn't disband, with individual members seeking employment elsewhere, it merely adjusted its activities to accommodate alternative sources food.
12. Quinn, p. 96.
13. Zerzan, J. (2002). Running on Emptiness: The Pathology of Civilization. Los Angeles: Feral House, p. 156.
14. Quinn, p. 55.
15. Cohen, J.E., (1997). Population, economics, environment and culture: An introduction to human carrying capacity. *Journal of Applied Ecology, 34,* 1325-1333.
16. Ryle, G. (1949). *The Concept of Mind.* New York: Harper & Row.
17. Whitehead, A. N. (1929). *Process and Reality.* New York: The Free Press.

Index

abstraction, 5, 48–49, 76–77, 130, 133, 158, 162, 163,184, 212. *See also* reification error
ADHD. See attention deficit/hyperactivity disorder
adolescence, 145
advertising, 6, 166–168
aesthetics, 123–124
aggression and population density, 190
agrarian-based society, 144, 206–207
agriculture, 61, 70, 72, 75–79, 81, 83, 85, 186–187, 207, 210. *See also* domestication
anarchism, 1–9, 25, 40–51; defined, 1–8; the case for, 40–51, 180, 197, 205, 213–214
anarcho-primitivism, 7–8
appeasement behavior, 176
apraxia, 198
arrested development, 139–149, 184, 194, 197, 206. *See also* infantilization; neoteny
Arthur, W.B., 26–29, 92, 103–114, 116, 120, 124, 201, 215
asymmetry in hierarchical relations, 151–153
attachment theory, 143–145
attention deficit/hyperactivity disorder, 12, 173–173
authentic human habitat, 56–57
authority: and attitude change, 157; and knowledge, 25–32, 36–37, 41, 215; as a feature of technology, 114–115, 125–128, 132–133, 136, 163–166, 182–184, 200–201, 212, 215; children's conceptualization of, 146–147
autonomy, 2–14, 21–52, 60–61, 66, 88, 90, 125–128, 132, 133, 137, 146, 149, 150, 165, 174–175, 181–182, 194–200,

205, 210; defined, 126, 181–182
Barber, Benjamin, 145, 219
Bentham, Jeremy, 168, 170
birth rate, 186–187
brain size, 190–191, 219
carrying capacity, estimates of, 208
catastrophic system failure, 104, 198
category mistake, 212
circus, traveling, 202–203
cities, modern, 94, 120
citizenship, 130–131
civilization, 4, 5, 7, 9, 11, 12, 14, 15–16, 22–23, 44, 46, 51, 53, 70, 72, 74–79, 82–84, 87–90, 95, 162, 177, 180, 182, 185–191, 202–210, 212–214. *See also* technological order; as inevitable, 82, 85. *See also* delusion of progress, the; collapse of, 204, 206, 214
coercion, 21, 28, 38, 46, 51, 67–68, 78, 84, 87, 94–95, 98, 127, 128, 155, 169, 172, 181–184, 199, 204, 208, 214
cognitive dissonance 156–157, 176, 211
communication: electronic versus face to face, 96, 164; mediated, 87, 96, 162–165, 183, 206, 214
communication technology, 87, 96, 121, 162–164, 183, 206, 214
computer metaphor, 119, 129
critical periods of development, 141–143
culture as a mode of progress. *See* delusion of progress, the
cultural evolution, 74, 188–189
culture, definition of, 76
Danesi, Marcel, 145, 219